Shakespeare Alive!

TWO-MINUTE SPEECHES AND MONOLOGUES FOR STUDY, AUDITION, AND PERFORMANCE

written and edited by
Fredi Olster and Rick Hamilton

MONOLOGUE AUDITION SERIES

A Smith and Kraus Book

A Smith and Kraus Book
Published by Smith and Kraus, Inc.
177 Lyme Road, Hanover, NH 03755
www.smithkraus.com

First Edition: January 2005
Manufactured in the United States of America
10 9 8 7 6 5 4 3 2 1

Cover and text design by Julia Gignoux, Freedom Hill Design

Library of Congress Cataloging-in-Publication Data

Shakespeare, William, 1564-1616.
Shakespeare alive : two minute speeches and monologues for students and actors /
edited by Fredi Olster and Rick Hamilton.-- 1st ed.
p. cm. -- (Monologue audition series)
ISBN 1-57525-418-2
1. Shakespeare, William, 1564-1616--Quotations. 2. Acting--Auditions. 3.
Monologues. I. Olster, Fredi. II. Title. III. Series.

PR2771.O47 2004
822.3'3--dc22
2004052479

CONTENTS

THE MONOLOGUES

All's Well That Ends Well

As You Like It

Cymbeline

Hamlet

Henry IV, Part 1

Henry IV, Part 2

Henry VI, Part 1

Henry VI, Part 2

Julius Caesar

King John

King Lear

Love's Labour's Lost

Macbeth

The Merchant of Venice

A Midsummer Night's Dream

Much Ado About Nothing

Othello

Richard II

Richard III

Romeo and Juliet

The Taming of the Shrew

The Tempest

Twelfth Night

The Two Gentlemen of Verona

The Two Noble Kinsmen

INTRODUCTION

In most cases, before we get hired to act, we have to go through the *dreaded* audition process! We've both been in this business for over thirty years, and trust us, auditioning is not something that many actors look forward to. But, with good preparation and some idea of what's going on in the auditioner's mind, it can become a much more pleasant experience.

In this book, we offer 155 monologues with side-by-side vernacular translations — all under two minutes. Some are offered in their entirety; some have been strategically cut; others have been pieced together out of shorter speeches creating new monologues.

When selecting a monologue, find a speech that strikes a chord with you, something you can personally relate to, a piece that you will love to do. This piece will be your introduction to the various directors and casting people who will be meeting you for the first time and making judgments about you — about your artistic abilities and about you as a person. Be sure that you select a piece that represents the qualities you want those people to see in you.

Try to select a piece that is age-appropriate. Most of the speeches in this book have been chosen because they work for younger actors. We have included some speeches — the Macbeths for example — for those of you who will be considered for more mature roles. Casting is usually done relative to the ages of the available actors in a particular company. So, depending on your age range and type, you might find yourself being considered for more mature roles.

Remember, too, that a monologue is not a *poem* — it is not a set piece to be recited — but rather the words that a character uses to express him- or herself in a given situation. Therefore you must always discover a point of view from which to express these thoughts and not merely give a generalized recitation of the material. To this end — *read the play!* This is a critical and often overlooked element in preparing a monologue. Without determining first what's driving that character to speak, it's awfully hard to make truly good sense of the language. So read the entire play and make sure you totally investigate and invest in your piece. Remember, too, that the auditioner may ask you questions about the play, and it will serve you well to know what he or she is talking about.

Some general hints for doing Shakespeare:

- With Shakespeare, for the most part, we act *on the word*; with other playwrights, it could be through business, or in the silences between the words.

- Each line starts with a capital letter, but this does not mean that it is the start of a new sentence; it's merely part of the poetic form Shakespeare used, so don't let that distract you. Play through till you come to the end of the thought.

- Shakespeare often wrote long, involved sentences. To help shape and clarify speeches of this type, first highlight the major points by cutting out all the subordinate clauses. For example, examine the Captain's speech from act 1 scene 2 of *Macbeth*:

> Doubtful it stood,
> As two spent swimmers, that do cling together
> And choke their art. The merciless Macdonwald
> (Worthy to be a rebel, for to that
> The multiplying villainies of nature
> Do swarm upon him) from the Western Isles
> Of kerns and gallowglasses is supplied;
> And Fortune, on his damned quarrel smiling,
> Show'd like a rebel's whore. But all's too weak;
> For brave Macbeth — well he deserves that name —
> Disdaining Fortune, with his brandished steel,
> Which smoked with bloody execution,
> Like Valor's minion carved out his passage
> Till he faced the slave;
> Which ne'er shook hands, nor bade farewell to him,
> Till he unseamed him from the nave to th' chops,
> And fixed his head upon our battlements.

The major points of this speech are:

Doubtful it stood,
Macdonwald from the western isles is supplied.
But all's too weak.
Macbeth carved out his passage till he faced the slave, unseamed
him, and fixed his head upon our battlements.

Or look at the first part of Clarence's speech from act 1 scene 4 of
Richard III:

O, I have passed a miserable night,
So full of fearful dreams, of ugly sights,
That, as I am a Christian faithful man,
I would not spend another such a night
Though 'twere to buy a world of happy days,
So full of dismal terror was the time.
Methought that I had broken from the Tower,
And was embarked to cross to Burgundy,
And in my company my brother Gloucester,
Who from my cabin tempted me to walk
Upon the hatches. As we paced along
Methought that Gloucester stumbled, and in falling
Struck me — that thought to stay him — overboard
Into the tumbling billows of the main.

The major points here are:

I have passed a miserable night,
I would not spend another such a night.
Methought that I was embarked to cross to Burgundy,
and in my company my brother Gloucester,
who tempted me to walk
upon the hatches. As we paced along
methought that Gloucester stumbled and
struck me overboard.

Once you've established the through-line of the thoughts, verbally highlight them using the subordinate phrases to color and drive the speech. (Note
that often the character's own emotional and intellectual point of view is revealed through these subordinate clauses.)

- Explore all the possible colorations till the speech makes emotional and logical sense for you

- Most of the punctuation in the various editions was put there by an editor in subsequent centuries — not by Shakespeare. Quite frankly, Shakespeare was more concerned with meaning than with grammatically correct punctuation! He was writing for actors, and his primary objective was to clarify how an actor should interpret a line. (In fact, some believe that many of the actors in Shakespeare's company could not read and learning a script was a verbal process.) When working on your monologue, go to your library and compare the punctuation in the various editions and select what works best for you. The closest thing to Shakespeare's punctuation is in the First Folio (again, check your library).

- We have included some very short monologues that might be used as second, backup, or contrasting pieces. If you've chosen to do a long, dramatic piece, you might want to have a short, comic piece in your repertoire just in case the auditioner asks you to do something else.

- Note for women: Since the number of roles for men in Shakespeare's plays far outnumber those for women, there are fewer monologues for women to choose from. Some of the monologues listed here could be done by an actor of either sex: Ariel in *The Tempest*, Puck in *A Midsummer Night's Dream*, the Chorus or the Friar in *Romeo and Juliet*, Arthur in *King John*, the Messenger in *Julius Caesar*, York's speech in *Richard II*, and the Gentleman in *Hamlet*.

And finally, none of us were born knowing how to do Shakespeare. His works require particular skills. Acting is a craft passed down through generations. Although we all want to eventually develop our own distinctive style, when it comes to learning how to act in Shakespeare's works, much can be said for jump-starting our technical training by observing good actors and exploring what they do and how they do it. Therefore, we suggest you see plays, listen to recordings, watch videos — and then *steal!* Just as young painters learn their technique by copying the masters, so young actors develop their skills by watching the greats in our field and then learning to do what they do through stealing.

Stealing is one of the great traditions of theater, and anyone who tells you otherwise is short-changing you. This is not cheating. This is how the techniques and traditions of theater have been passed down through generations of actors. Mind you, we don't want to be *mimics* — we don't want to do impersonations of other actors — but we do want to observe their rhythms, pacing, phrasing, and timing. How do they structure a speech? Where do they pause? What words do they stress? Are they using upward inflections? Where do they breathe? We observe all this, and then we try to recreate it using our own instrument. Once we master these techniques, we can then determine what works for us and incorporate those elements into our own work.

What Is the Auditioner Looking For?

To help find the answer to this, we sent the following questionnaire to directors and casting people around the country.

Before the audition
- What, if any, time limitations do you set for a Shakespeare monologue, and why do you set them?
- Do you give any guidelines to the actor for selecting material?

At the audition
- What makes you sit up and take notice?
- What turns you off immediately?

Generally speaking
- What advice would you pass on to young actors auditioning for a Shakespeare play?
- Any other suggestions or comments?

After the fact
- Name pieces you never wish to hear attempted again.
- Name pieces you never tire of hearing.

Their answers follow. The most interesting aspect of these answers for us are the contradictions! What pleases one director, might turn another off. The speech you do may be one person's favorite, while another never wants to hear it again. You may look like the kid one director hated in third grade, or like another's favorite cousin. In other words — let's face it — this is a very subjective art form! In a sense, this is terrifically freeing for you, the actor, because it makes you realize that it is nearly impossible to please everyone you're auditioning for at all times. Some will love you; some will hate you. So, although you do have to prepare as conscientiously as you possibly can and give it your very best shot at the audition, the rest is really in the hands of the theatrical fates.

Before the Audition

What, if any, time limitations do you set for a Shakespeare monologue and why do you set them?

Edward Hastings (*former artistic director of the American Conservatory Theater, San Francisco; freelance director*): None, but more than one minute is usually redundant. If the best part of the speech is the second minute, I'd suggest finding a way to start halfway through.

Penny Metropolis (*associate artistic director of the Oregon Shakespeare Festival*): Normally two minutes. There's a good chance you will know in the first twenty to thirty seconds if the actor can handle the language — or has potential.

Sabin Epstein (*resident director at A Noise Within theater*): I prefer seeing pieces about two minutes in length. I can usually tell within the first fifteen seconds whether or not the actor knows what he or she is doing, and I can also evaluate training and experience in that amount of time. The rest of the time is spent wondering whether or not the actor will surprise me in interpretation or approach, and if I have a spot for him or her in the production I'm working on.

Also, keep the speeches brief unless you are extraordinary. In general, most young actors tend to emote rather than play action, and they tend to stay on the same action throughout the course of the speech. Therefore, there is no arc to the playing, and it all feels like one note. Better to be brief and have the auditor ask to see more, than go on and on and on, which is a definite mental turnoff. N.B.: Have more than one speech ready for any audition, something different, but something you also connect with and to.

Kent Thompson (*artistic director of the Alabama Shakespeare Festival*): Three minutes. (1) It is a rare Shakespeare monologue that is longer than three minutes; (2) three minutes allows an actor ample opportunity to use language to demonstrate their skills with verse, imagery, flow of thought, and rhetoric, which I define as the construction of Shakespeare's or the character's ideas — always developed in an active way; (3) three minutes gives the actor an opportunity to connect emotionally — "to have a moment."

Meryl Shaw (*casting director at the American Conservatory Theatre, San Francisco*): I give a three-minute limit, usually for two pieces: one classical, one contemporary. So the exact length of each piece is up to them.

Howard Jensen (*professor of acting and directing at Indiana University; director of productions at the Utah Shakespearean Festival*): Two minutes or less. The longer the monologue, the harder it is to impress. Two minutes is plenty of time to tell if an actor has the necessary skills for Shakespeare.

David Hammond (*artistic director of the PlayMakers Repertory Company*): I don't set limits, but I prefer monologues between two and three minutes long each. It's generally a good idea to show two pieces within five or six minutes, leaving a few minutes to talk. I can usually tell if I'm interested in the first thirty seconds; if that is then sustained and the actor continues to keep me involved, that's terrific. The worst situation occurs when the actor keeps going after my interest has run out. Then I just see the problems, and that can be irritating if the actor goes on too long. Then I just want the next person to come in soon.

Elizabeth Huddle (*freelance director, former artistic director of Intiman Theatre, Seattle and Portland Center Stage, Portland, OR*): Two minutes is great. If I want more, I ask for another monologue.

Ken Albers (*resident actor and director of the Oregon Shakespeare Festival*): I set a time limit of four minutes for three pieces. Operating from the basic principle that an auditor can usually tell within fifteen seconds whether an actor is appropriate or not, I think four minutes is more than sufficient to make the impression. I also think that such brevity requires the actor to be very selective with his material, picking the best part of a long monologue rather than the whole thing. The finest Shakespeare audition that I ever saw was a collage of nine pieces in less than four minutes, which began with *Macbeth* and included a song, a selection from Dogberry, a sonnet, and a combo of *Romeo and Juliet* and *Troilus and Cressida*. It was stunning, quick, and "hit and run" effective.

Nagle Jackson (*director of new plays, Denver Center Theatre Company, former artistic director, Milwaukee Repertory Theatre and the McCarter Theatre Center for the Performing Arts*): Two and a half minutes for each piece. One must be in verse.

Andrew Traister (*freelance director*): Maximum two minutes — can see all I need to know.

Peggy Shannon (*artistic director of the Sacramento Theatre Company*): My preference is sixty to ninety seconds. I simply want to hear if the actor understands how to score the text, speak the text, and if he or she makes interesting vocal choices.

Risa Brainin (*freelance director who serves on the acting and directing faculty of The University of California, Santa Barbara***):** One and a half to two minutes for an initial audition. This amount of time is sufficient to assess the actor's language skills and acting ability.

Sandy Ernst (*associate artistic director of the Milwaukee Repertory Theater***):** One and a half to two minutes is long enough for any audition piece. Most producers request two pieces not to exceed four minutes total. Choosing a piece that's three or four minutes — you have less chance of holding interest and focus.

Deborah Hecht (*Head of text, voice, and speech, graduate acting program at NYU's Tisch School of the Arts***):** At NYU (and when I did auditions at Yale and ACT) there is, I believe, a five-minute time limit, which includes two pieces: one classical (or heightened language) and one contemporary. Time limits are set because we see so many people (800 to 900 for eighteen slots) and because we really can usually tell *something* about the actor's abilities (is there an imagination, ability to personalize, etc.) in a short time.

John Shepard (*actor, writer, and chair of the department of theater arts, Point Park University, Pittsburgh***):** Two minutes or less. Because the first thirty seconds usually gives me a good idea of what you can do, it's best to keep the monologue short.

Mark Torres (*producing artistic director at Penobscot Theatre***):** We ask for one to two minutes. This time frame is to encourage an artist to keep the piece long enough to show us how he or she moves from moment to moment in playing a monologue but short enough for us to have some time for conversation to get to know the actor as a person as well. We usually allot five minutes for each auditioner, so this system works pretty well.

Robert Fass (*managing director, Georgia Shakespeare Festival, former executive director, Shakespeare in the Park, Fort Worth***):** Many producers and directors will see upwards of 500 to 1,000 actors during the course of casting a season. This immense task creates time limitations for two primary reasons: (1) Time must be budgeted to see the maximum number of actors in a constricted amount of time; (2) it does not take a long time for a producer or director to see what he or she needs to see in an initial audition. Greater detail can always be explored in a callback situation. Directors want to see that an actor can handle the language. They want to see that the actor can be animated or possess physicality inherent to the character. They want to see that mystical chemistry that makes you fixate on a person's words, actions, and intentions. In short, they want the actor to build their confidence in his or her potential. There is an old cliché that a director knows within twenty seconds whether or not to call back an actor during an audition. While this can be somewhat exaggerated, the principle is correct. Don't offer a full performance. Instead, offer a glimpse of your talent and ability to work well for the proposed job. Another cliché comes to mind: Leave them wanting more.

Donovan Marley (*artistic director of the Denver Center Theatre Company***):** Three minutes. This is enough time to tell if the auditioner understands scansion, knows the purpose of the speech, has any vocal techniques, is at home in his or her body, loves images, and has fire and passion.

Geoff Elliot and Julia Rodriguez Elliot (*artistic directors at A Noise Within theater***):** Two minutes — that's plenty of time to give us an idea as to whether the actor can handle language, act on the word, and work with an objective. Also, it is plenty of material to give direction to see if the actor can adjust.

Hal Cropp (*artistic and executive director of the Commonweal Theatre Company, Minnesota***):** Two minutes tops. If you can't demonstrate your skills in two minutes, four more won't help. It's not about the text, per se, but showing me you know how to handle the language.

Katy Brown (*artistic director of the Barter Players, Abingdon, VA***):** I usually prefer to see a monologue less than two minutes long. You can really see a person's potential for Shakespeare in less than one minute, amazingly enough. You can tell where they are with their skills and use of the words. Also, keeping it shorter forces them to make the emotional leaps needed to perform Shakespeare.

Jared Sakren (*artistic director at Shakespeare Sedona***):** One and a half minutes. Everything you need to learn about the actor can be (and probably *should* be) communicated to me in that amount of time or less. As an audience member (down the road), one and a half minutes is an eternity onstage, and I want to see if the actor is using his or her time well.

Henson Keys (*chair of acting programs, Department of Theatre at the University of Illinois at Urbana-Champaign***):** Two minutes is recommended. This gives plenty of time for the actor to make his or her point and play the action.

Jim Rambo (*director of the Department of Theatre at McLennan Community College, Waco, Texas***):** I usually request a two-minute monologue. I believe that you can package acting choices more concisely in a two-minute time period.

Do you give any guidelines to the actor for selecting material?

Sabin Epstein: I generally tell actors to do pieces they feel very close to and that they love. Never try to prepare a speech for a specific role unless you have a great deal of prep time. Auditions are performances, and they need to gestate and grow and mature with repeated exposure. You can't be giving it your all if you're thinking about what word comes next, or are still in the "teleprompter" phase — seeing the words of the text on the page while trying to speak them. The actor has to be way beyond that by the time he or she comes in to audition.

I hate actors doing material that is not age-appropriate. Don't attempt *Lear* if you are under fifty, I'd be wary of *Hamlet* unless you've had some experience and can handle the text, and just because you're young and pretty, don't audition with Juliet unless you thoroughly know and understand the text.

I like actors to audition with familiar pieces; it spares me from having to focus exclusively on the content of the speech and allows me to focus on the actor and what he or she brings to the material and how the actor can surprise me with his or her interpretation and point of view. If the material is unfamiliar to me, chances are I'll forget about the actor and focus on the writer — not a good idea for people trying to create an interesting impression.

In general I don't like people who shout and think they are emoting; restraint and withholding something so that I'll lean forward in my chair is always appealing and almost always works for me. I respond to people who are genuinely engaged in the material and who appear to be spontaneously thinking the thoughts as they are moving through the speech.

Edward Hastings: Choose a role you might play in a company made up of all ages. If it's a young company doing *Lear*, explain to the auditors you know that and want to show your "age" skills.

Nagle Jackson: An audition is a calling card — nothing more. One is rarely hired as a result; it leads to a callback. Pick something *active* (e.g., Julia's torn letter speech in *Two Gents*) *not* descriptive (e.g., Gertrude's "There is a willow").

Kent Thompson: I suggest that they *always* select age-appropriate material with which they have a strong emotional and intellectual connection. Less important but still wise is to avoid the extremely well known or popular pieces. If you *must* use one of these pieces, have another less well known piece prepared.

Meryl Shaw: None other than the above. Although, my definition of classical material is pretty liberal. What I'm looking for is elevated, or complex, nonnaturalistic language. But I don't insist on verse.

Howard Jensen: Always audition with a character who you think you could actually be cast as and play well. Do not use a piece that you enjoy working on as a challenge only. Use a piece that is active. Avoid narrative pieces. Do not choose a piece that requires extreme emotion.

Elizabeth Huddle: Have it be appropriate for their age range. Aim themselves at the roles they want. Usually best if they have already performed the full role.

David Frank (*artistic director of the American Players Theatre*): Two contrasting pieces, at least one of which should be in verse.

David Hammond: Choose something with which you feel a personal connection. Remember that the action of the speech is not simply making clear what you are saying — you're supposed to be able to make it clear as a starting point for the acting: that's a given. Remember, too, that the really crucial personalization work has more to do with the circumstances from which you are speaking than with the things you are speaking about. I don't care what Viola feels about Olivia's ring, for example, and I certainly don't need to hear it in her voice. Instead, I want to see and hear Viola working through the mess she's made of her life, taking a personal emotional journey. So understand the play and the circumstances before you decide what a speech is about, and pick the speech based on the character and the complete play — not just on the beauty or seeming tone of the speech by itself.

Sandy Ernst: (1) Choose pieces *you* love! I can always tell if someone has had a piece chosen for him or her that he or she is not really in love with. (2) Know the whole play. (3) For professional theater, choose characters you could and would aspire to play within the next five years. (4) Don't ignore unnamed or minor characters; some of the best speeches in Shakespeare are Choruses, Messengers, etc.

Geoff Elliot and Julia Rodriguez Elliot: Women should not feel inhibited about choosing men's roles to audition with. Stay away from sonnets unless you can really make them active.

Deborah Hecht: I recommend a piece that you feel personally and passionately connected to, whether or not it is particularly age- or gender-appropriate. I can see six of the same Hamlets (even the same speech) in a row, and the one who is *living in the moment*, from the personal humanity and passion of the actor, is the one I'm likely to connect with.

Ken Albers: Rule 1: Pick something you really like to do. You will probably be living with the material a long time, so be sure you really like doing it. Rule 2: Try to pick something appropriate to you an as actor. A fifteen-year-old should not essay Lear or Falstaff, but is more appropriate as Romeo or Juliet, Troilus or Hero. Rule 3: Since it's Shakespeare, try to pick poetry, not prose. Rule 4: Try to find something that is not outside your own emotional range.

Mark Torres: We ask for material that is similar to the project we are casting. For a comedy, we ask for comic pieces, etc.

Katy Brown: Choose something you feel comfortable and excited about doing.

John Shepard: Make sure it's appropriate for you — agewise. It makes no sense for younger people to play someone who is much older. I'd even suggest that cross-gender choices are OK as long as they are age-appropriate.

Hal Cropp: I encourage actors to pick material that speaks directly to the actor.

Robert Fass: I generally request that the actor perform two contrasting classical monologues with at least one written by Shakespeare and at least one written in verse. The total time limit for these two monologues is three minutes.

Jared Sakren: Pick material you understand, that is accessible to you, that you have a doorway into — that is technically within reach. In addition, pick material that allows me to see who you are and how that relates/applies to the roles I need to cast. Try to pick pieces that are heard less often, although that's hard.

Henson Keys: Always select material that you fully understand both intellectually and emotionally and is appropriate to your age and temperament and experience. What can you bring to the piece that is personal and unique to you?

Jim Rambo: An actor needs to choose material that is age-relevant. I also suggest that actors take an inventory of their strengths and attempt to market those strengths in the material they perform. For Shakespeare, a young actor needs to be able to command the text specifically and precisely.

At the Audition

What makes you sit up and take notice?

Penny Metropolis: Someone who is interested in the pieces he or she is doing. I also think there is a quality of "listening" — maybe it is just actor attentiveness — that gives an actor permission to pause or change rhythms. I also *love* to see someone genuinely smile or laugh. It basically comes down to breath. When the actor is breathing and present, you are more likely to get a good idea of what he or she has to offer — no matter what the piece.

Elizabeth Huddle: Ability to handle the language, simple honesty, nonmelodramatic passion, noncute comedic ability.

Kent Thompson: An actor who connects totally with a moment, e.g. emotionally connects to a moment or is absolutely engaged/engaging for even a moment; an actor with strong language skills (voice, diction, inflection and phrasing); an actor who is present in the moment, that is, an actor thinking/experiencing/speaking/feeling in the moment, as Michael Langham taught. Acting is the text unfolding — spontaneously discovering the next beat/idea/reaction as the speech unfolds: real-time acting.

Meryl Shaw: An actor with a zest and enthusiasm for performing his or her audition. A clear and dynamic take on a character. Strong, active choices. Real connection to both the language and the moment-to-moment emotional truth.

Howard Jensen: An actor who walks into the room with confidence, begins and finishes the audition with confidence, and exits the room with confidence. An actor who *loves* to act. An actor who can speak a line naturally and excitingly. An actor about whom I can immediately say, "I'd like to be around this person."

Sabin Epstein: Like most people I tend to be very visual, so I like a crisp, neat appearance, one appropriate to the tone and feel of the character. I like a strong, professional handshake upon introduction with eye contact, and I like to feel the actor is confident.

In some instances, the audition is the first chance to meet and establish a relationship. The actor may not be right for that particular production, but those who make a favorable impression might be right for something else, or right for a production someone I know might be preparing or casting. Ergo, I don't think actors should try and mind-read the director or the casting agent or make snap judgments about a future relationship.

I also respond well to people who take their time in the audition without being indulgent; actors who "own the space" and are comfortable within themselves and who like doing their material and who aren't looking for approval afterwards. I will go out of my way to keep a blank face if I sense an actor is working just for approval.

I prefer to see people in solid colors rather than print and patterns, which pull attention and focus away from the actor's face, and hair should always be pulled back so I can see the actor's eyes. I'm not wild about actors using props, but sometimes they are unavoidable. How do you do Launce from *Merchant* and not use a shoe, for instance, or Julia from *Two Gents* and not use a real letter? If actors don't use common sense, I'm automatically suspicious; if they go overboard, I get suspicious.

I'm a big fan of actors and root for them: I hope the person walking into the room will be perfect so I won't have to audition anyone else. It's important for actors to remember that the director is on your side — it's just as trying to sit still all day listening to people as it is to be in the waiting room wondering what's going to happen once you're in the room.

I really appreciate an actor with a sense of humor — not just in the work but in demeanor and sensibility. Gives me a big clue as the whether or not we'll be able to work together — if the actor gets my corny jokes, if she has some intelligence to get the witty banter, if he can toss the verbal ball back again.

I also like actors who aren't afraid to be intelligent in making choices and in asking questions when we talk after the audition piece. It's a fine balance between people who are intelligent and those trying to demonstrate intelligence. Again, if the actor is genuinely comfortable, I can get a pretty good read as to who he or she is — enough to make me think about calling him or her back. The first audition is, in my mind, an introduction. The point is to narrow the field and find actors to bring back for a second reading when we can be more focused on the work at hand. I think the young actor's goal should be to get to the callback and then have the opportunity to really focus on the role being cast and to establish a rapport with the director.

I also like a firm handshake at the end of the audition. Most often, actors are most interesting to me as they leave the room; after they feel a letup in tension, I can begin to see who they really are. I always wish an actor would enter the room as if he or she has just auditioned in the waiting room and this part of the process is just a piece of cake now.

Whenever possible, when entering or exiting the room, *smile*. It helps reduce stress, and if you can really do it, there's no better way to make a good impression. Also, try and have your photo look like you — you are who you are, not some concept of who you think they want you to be. After seeing tons of actors in the course of the day, the photo is the only reference in the days to come, and if you don't look like the photo, chances are I won't remember you accurately. And don't lie about credits. That is a definite turnoff. I might know the director or producer of the theater or have worked on a production of a play listed, and it's very embarrassing all around if references aren't truthful.

Edward Hastings: When vocal life, physical life, and emotional life all connect, you hear it. Wide vocal range. Especially women with low notes. Strong consonants.

Nagle Jackson: Simplicity.

Martin Benson (*artistic director of the South Coast Repertory Theatre*): Talent first, then training — voice, movement, etc.

David Hammond: The ability to live within the text with personal truth and the use of the text in pursuit of action; the ability to find and realize the rhythmic action patterns of the verse; a sensibility to the sound patterns and the actions they imply; an original spirit filling the text and the situation and carrying through a progression in a way I haven't seen or imagined before.

Risa Brainin: Good language skills. Passion. Bringing all of yourself to your pieces.

Peggy Shannon: Well-spoken, clearly focused text work.

Geoff Elliot and Julia Rodriguez Elliot: A résumé with Shakespeare credits at respectable venues; positive, relaxed energy; and openness to direction.

Sandy Ernst: An actor who can stand still and handle the language! An actor who arrives on time and ready to go (not to warm up!), dressed comfortably and casually, but also neatly and modestly. An actor who's professional and courteous to *all,* including the monitor, who states his or her name and pieces without explaining to me *what* it's about and what it means and where I can find it in the play! At the end of the audition, I like a smile and a thank you and an exit with grace and confidence.

Mark Torres: If we are seeing lots of actors at a common audition, then, invariably, something amusing makes us sit up and take notice. A truly funny monologue, well done, is a breath of fresh air during a long day of seeing actors. I would add that an unusual piece that is new to us can be noticeable.

Deborah Hecht: Someone who makes me literally *see* what the text is conveying — both images and situation — that ability to live fully the imaginative existence. Also, someone who let's him- or herself be affected by the character's experience while also seeming to reveal him- or herself. The techniques of language, structure, speech/diction can be taught.

Andrew Traister: Making sense of the language and proper scansion; developing some character.

Ken Albers: Command of the stage; confidence not cockiness; attention to the business at hand; a quick start and a strong closing.

David Frank: Work that I can both understand and believe.

Katy Brown: Honesty, someone who is actually communicating rather than performing. Sadly, at most auditions, you don't see much acting — and not because the auditionees can't act. Somewhere along the way, someone told them to show off their skills in an audition rather than to do what they do in a play — act, communicate.

John Shepard: *Confidence* — both in yourself and in the material. Someone who has a firm grasp of the verse, figures of speech, and the ability to deal with the vowels and consonants.

Hal Cropp: Text that's "dropped in" to the actor. Bold physical choices that emerge from or are justified by the text. Self-confidence.

Robert Fass: To be honest, I know of only three ways to grab a director's attention if you have never met him or her before. The first is to impress the director with your incredible résumé. Even if you do not have a large amount of experience, a well-organized and readable résumé is a must because it sells your professionalism immediately. Also, it's a must to get a headshot that actually resembles what you will look like in the audition. Directors find it very frustrating if the person in front of them is not the person on paper.

Second, do some research in advance to see if you and the director might have something in common. This could include fellow colleagues, theaters, geographical origin, etc. The point is to find some common ground that could spark a friendly conversation and give assurance to you both that you would work well together.

This leads me to the third and possibly most important technique: Remember that directors are people, too. They are often nervous about finding the right actors, and many of them have been in your shoes as actors in an audition. The way you present yourself before and after the performance of your monologue is as important as the performance itself. Directors want to work with people they will get along with. Without taking up too much time, try to engage the director in friendly conversation. This is your chance to sell yourself as well, and it is a highly effective way to get the director's attention during your audition.

Jared Sakren: A strong, well-supported voice — most important. Good use of language dynamics — variety, sense of play, a good understanding of thought, meaning. Bold, committed connection, especially in the body. The language should be "in the body" — breathing is not cut off but full and not "in the throat."

Henson Keys: Actors who personalize the text — who play *intention*, not mood, character behavior, or emotion. Actors capable of passion equal to the size of the language and dramatic situation.

Jim Rambo: I will tend to notice young actors who are in their bodies and comfortable with their physical presence. I will also notice an actor who chooses a Shakespearean monologue that is rarely performed. I will certainly notice a young actor's ability to interpret the text clearly and to articulate the sounds within the text fully and completely. I look for a spark, perhaps a personal signature with the performance, that shows his or her ability to make concrete choices and to show them in action, both in body and voice.

What turns you off immediately?

Meryl Shaw: Bad attitude. Some actors come in seeming to resent the process. Sloppy appearance. Lack of preparation. Not taking a moment to greet those in the room, to be available.

Edward Hastings: Poor speech, particularly sloppy *s* sounds. Also being addressed directly during the monologue.

Kent Thompson: Paraphrasing. Lack of preparation (which is very different from "drying," which happens to everyone). Poor verbal skills and/or inattention to the verbal demands of Shakespeare. Obvious bad attitude. Canned performance, not real work. No emotional connection, no spontaneous connection.

Penny Metropolis: The actor who stands and delivers with no investment. Material that is unsuitable to age or type. Not that this choice can't be interesting combined with something else, but we need to see the actor: The choice of material reflects greatly on the actor's personality. You can tell if someone has chosen something arbitrarily, thoughtlessly, or arrogantly. Sincere interest and involvement is compelling.

Sabin Epstein: I *hate* actors who come in apologizing through body language for themselves and their choice of material or who feel they haven't a chance in hell of being cast in the role. If you feel that way — don't waste my time.

I also don't like to be used as a scene partner in the audition. Ask if you can make eye contact or use me as a focus, and I will tell you truthfully no. I'd rather devote my attention to your work rather than feeling obligated to have to respond and feed you emotional cues.

Howard Jensen: An actor who uses a fake voice because it's Shakespeare. An actor who takes forever to get into character. An actor who is timid or withdrawn or defensive. I don't have time in rehearsals to deal with personal problems.

David Hammond: External work, illustrating the speech with artificial physicalization or vocal tricks — bending over languidly when saying "inclining," for example, or putting a fake laugh in the voice to demonstrate general merriment. Those things really repel me. I want to see people talking to people, not actors demonstrating the meaning of the text. Other peeves: a lack of objective and action, a lack of circumstances, poor or imposed speech sounds, vocal tension, and the imposition of inappropriate character choices due to inadequate knowledge of the play. The ultimate sin: an inaccurately memorized text. That shows laziness and disrespect.

Elizabeth Huddle: People playing to me — so look past me.

Martin Benson: When someone asks what I'd like to see (as if he or she had memorized *all* of Shakespeare). Lack of fluency with the text.

Nagle Jackson: Being looked at! Pompous versification. Props.

Peggy Shannon: Yelling. Crying. Screaming. Profanity. Also — too much cologne, perfume, and inappropriately attired actors.

Sandy Ernst: Being late! English accents for Shakespeare. Props and costumes! Any attempt to shock me with phallic props, obscene gestures, disrobing, etc. An apologetic manner upon entering the room. Invading my personal space.

Donovan Marley: Phony voices — a Shakespearian voice.

Risa Brainin: If the auditionee seems unhappy to be at the audition.

Mark Torres: Turnoffs include insensitive actors who use too much time, are late, or ill-prepared. We love prepared, professional, courteous people. The people who make the impression that they will be good to work with are more likely to be the ones we are interested in working with.

Ken Albers: Anything artsy. The long silent pause to prepare, for instance, drives me screaming from the room. Strange dress or grooming: spiked hair, dirty, unkempt clothes, bad shoes. Overlong introductions. Lack of preparation, difficulty with lines. Résumés that lie: listing a production at Skidmore College under Regional Theaters or The Theater of Second Hand Smoke in New York as a New York credit.

Andrew Traister: Pauses, bad scansion.

Geoff Elliot and Julia Rodriguez Elliot: Pushing, both in the work and during conversation.

Katy Brown: An actor treating auditioners or auditionees poorly. This is hugely telling about how this actor will be to work with. Also, showiness with no honest underpinnings.

John Shepard: Poor preparation and lack of discipline. This includes not knowing lines and poor choice of material.

Hal Cropp: Gimmicks, sing-song, a sense of no understanding of the lines, and fake English accents.

Robert Fass: Nothing is more frustrating than an actor who enters the audition unprepared and full of excuses. Directors do not want to waste time with an actor who has not as least given some forethought to the process. Also, never enter an audition with the attitude that you are better than the potential job. If you are too cocky, you will likely be unemployed. You must have confidence in your abilities, but present yourself in a positive manner at the same time. Treat the director as you would like to be treated yourself when acting for him or her in a rehearsal, and try to enjoy the experience if at all possible. Auditions do not have to be painful experiences.

Deborah Hecht: Someone who abuses the time limit, who goes far beyond the allotted time; it makes me think the actor is either unable to follow directions or is self-centered enough not to care — neither of which is appropriate for our ensemble-oriented training program. Also, I prefer that the actor not look at or use me directly, only because I feel obligated to participate when I also need to be writing notes, so it splits my focus and makes my auditioner's job harder. I do not penalize for this, however.

Jared Sakren: Reading the speech off a paper (it's happened!). Sitting in a chair and staying in it. Using audition time to warm up. Explaining each piece to me and the play it came from, as if I'd never heard of it. No vocal connection! Sloppiness, lack of focus, a disengaged body, no preparation on a piece, a TV-style acting approach (talking head.)

Henson Keys: Recitation or shouting too much (anger is cheap and easy!). *Any* paraphrasing. Sloppy diction, lack of understanding of verse, trying to play Shakespeare as if he were Mamet. Actors who try to make it real or true, rather than opening themselves to a larger truth.

Jim Rambo: Pushing emotions will turn me off almost immediately. Young actors tend to overact and underreact in a performance, and that tends to shut me down.

Generally Speaking

What advice would you pass on to young actors auditioning for a Shakespeare play?

Sabin Epstein: What works for contemporary material in methodology and approach for work doesn't always work for Shakespeare. Shakespeare involves high language skills, and you aren't going to be able to fake that by crying at the drop of a hat. It's nice if you have emotional resources, but if you can't communicate the language (or at least convince me that you are interested in learning how to), chances are I won't cast you. Simple as that. Language is everything in Shakespeare, and you have to be willing to act on the line rather than commit to only playing subtext.

I would be happy if I never see a young actress do Constance again, or a young actor doing "To be or not to be" without understanding the depth of what he's saying. But show me *you* in your speech, and chances are I'll be engaged and intrigued.

Penny Metropolis: It is not enough to just understand the words or the content or have a feel for the character. We are looking for people who have the mental and vocal muscle to grapple with complicated language. Clear, strong use of range combined with good character work will probably result in a callback. At the very least, that actor will remain on file for future calls. It is also good if we can get a gauge of the actor's physical expressiveness.

Elizabeth Huddle: Keep it simple. Keep it honest.

David Hammond: Know what you're doing and be properly trained to do it. If you have no experience and are auditioning for a school or class, have read and explored enough Shakespeare that you have some idea of what is required to bring it to life. Then go for it.

Kent Thompson: Perform a careful analysis of the text, using all the same techniques of acting in any genre, for example: given circumstances, intention, obstacles, but also the verbal/poetic demands (scansion, phrasing, operatives). And find specific meaning of *every* word and phrase. The biggest single error young actors make is not knowing specific meanings and then not making specific choices.

Edward Hastings: Build a strong context — emotional, scenic, physical. It's OK to explain conditions if they are unusual or not obvious.

Meryl Shaw: Read the whole play and understand who your character is and where he or she is at the moment the monologue takes place. Choose a character in your castable range. Break the speech down and really understand it. Pay attention to the scansion and the punctuation. Think about whether this character's status, tone, and age are right for you. Seek out someone to provide coaching.

Howard Jensen: Shakespeare wrote great roles for actors, but more important, he wrote very playable roles. Do not treat the material as something precious or elevated. Approach it naturally. Enjoy it. Relish it.

Sandy Ernst: Remember that Shakespeare is *English!* Our language! We've just gotten lazy and don't turn a phrase the same way. How you handle the words and thought is *always* more important to me than if you can move all over the room, dance, do cartwheels, etc. I can tell if you can walk and talk by the time you enter, greet me, and start your piece.

Nagle Jackson: Do what you do well. Remember T. S. Eliot's line in "Prufrock": "I am not Prince Hamlet, nor was meant to be." Don't do comedy if you're not funny; don't do tragedy if you are.

Ken Albers: Prepare yourself as best you can, understand clearly what you are saying, keep it simple, and say it clearly. Pick a single, clear objective and commit to it completely. Don't worry about it being right or wrong.

Andrew Traister: Work to get sense in the language, keep movement simple, and wear comfortable, quiet clothing.

Donovan Marley: Who are you talking to? What do you want from him/her/them?

David Frank: Play the idea (image) not the emotion; let the emotion happen as a result of the idea.

Risa Brainin: Choose material you can connect to and that you are passionate about.

Mark Torres: Know your material. Be clear and communicate the character's needs. Project a professional, friendly image. Be someone I would like to work with and who I can trust to do the hard work of playing a role.

Katy Brown: Commit 100 percent to your choices. Go for it bravely and honestly. Know what you want, and go for it rather than trying to give the auditioner what he or she wants. What we want is to see where you honestly go when you use these words. This will also keep you from overperforming the piece.

Robert Fass: Choose a monologue that will highlight your personal strengths. Avoid anything that is beyond your age range whenever possible. Keep in mind the cliché about impressing a director within the first twenty seconds. Don't choose audition material that is overloaded with exposition. Get right to the meat of a piece. Most likely, the director for whom you are auditioning already knows the storyline and needs no explanation. Simply introduce the character and play title. Then get right to the performance of your selection. Don't be afraid to let your selection breathe. Utilize the space physically and vocally. As a final note, never deliver your monologue directly into the eyes of the director. It forces the director to become part of the scene and creates a situation in which he or she must give back to you as a performer. A director's role is to observe your performance, not to be a part of it. It is always wise to play the scene over the head of the director so he or she can feel comfortable and still gain insight of your vocal and facial expression.

Martin Benson: Study it thoroughly; preparation is so important.

Peggy Shannon: Do a monologue from a similar play to the one you are auditioning for. Choose simple, direct speeches.

Geoff Elliot and Julia Rodriguez Elliot: *Be prepared.* Know the play you are auditioning for and know the play you are auditioning with. Know *exactly* what you are saying; use the words as tools to achieve the character's desire.

Hal Cropp: Be simple, clear, and real.

Deborah Hecht: Read the *whole* play. If it's too hard, rent the film or, better yet, find a recording and *listen!* Find all the facts about the character from the text. Audition as if you were already hard at work in rehearsal on the play. Love what you're doing; give the character a chance to live. When you think you've explored enough, do more — *before* the audition, of course. You can rediscover in the moment only based on the amount of preparation/exploration you've done before.

John Shepard: Don't be afraid of taking risks, as long as you don't compromise Shakespeare's intention. Use your energy and play the words.

Jared Sakren: Get some training first. Then apply that training. Choose three things you would like to demonstrate about your vocal skills. Choose three things you'd like to share about your movement skills.

The same with language: Don't be vague, general; be specific. Think about what you would like the auditioner to think/realize about you. The auditioner is scoring you, measuring your skills. Other qualities, such as likability and charm, are beyond your control. How realistic you are is a trap — avoid it.

Henson Keys: Use yourself; *choose* to speak in verse or heightened language in order to express your personal passions. And *do your homework* — illuminate the text, don't force your concept on these characters.

Jim Rambo: First of all, a young actor needs to read, read, read. The more the student reads, and reads Shakespeare often aloud, the better off that actor is to evoke the text.

Any other suggestions or comments?

Penny Metropolis: I suppose I feel, especially for young actors, that monologues that deal with discovery — "hammering out" — are great, because you watch the actor growing through the audition. How the actor discovers can be personal. I think too many young people do over-the-top emotional pieces, and that is simply too much to ask of that two minutes. Stay true and direct, and relish the time you get to do your pieces.

Sabin Epstein: I think the audition begins the moment the actor steps into the room. I'm busy reading nonverbal signals the actor is putting out about confidence, nervousness, desperation in getting the job. The moment the actor says hello, I'm also busy reading and evaluating his or her voice. In general, I'm also looking for "the vibe": Is this a person I want to spend five to eight hours a day with during the next month? Sorry, but it's the truth; the actor's energy, personality, and sense of humor are factors in the audition. And if an actor is smart, the actor is evaluating me and seeing if he or she wants to spend that much time with me!

More than showing technical skill, auditions help the director discover something about the actor. Therefore, the actor wants to do a piece that has real meaning and that he or she feels says something about who the actor is just through the choice of material. Comedy is terribly difficult but so much more challenging for an audition — to genuinely find the humor within the human character and not just do schtick.

I also think actors should stay true to the context of the speech and not select something that they feel will show them off to best advantage by making odd choices that have nothing to do with context and character. Stay true to the action and play it truthfully. If the auditor doesn't respond to that, than you don't want to be working with him or her in the first place.

Kent Thompson: Avoid British accents unless specifically requested to use one.

Edward Hastings: I like two or three short speeches connected by listening moments. Tricky, but often leads to good concentration.

Nagle Jackson: Don't do mad scenes — they tell us nothing. Look for hidden treasures: stuff from *All's Well* or the Gaoler's Daughter in *The Two Noble Kinsmen*.*

Mark Torres: More than anything, be yourself. We want you to succeed.

Robert Fass: Actors should be encouraged to take risks. And for God's sake, threaten the life of each reader if he or she does not read the whole play before the audition.

Katy Brown: Make sure the actors know what is occurring with the characters in the play. I've seen many auditions in which it was clear the actor had chosen the monologue without knowing its context.

After the Fact

Name pieces you never wish to hear attempted again.

Meryl Shaw: No rules. If a piece is really appropriate and well done, I hear it anew.

Howard Jensen: I think I am not typical on this point. I actually like to hear the well-known pieces. If I have seen the same Rosalind monologue ten

---

*Fletcher and Shakespeare, *The Two Noble Kinsmen*: This play is currently assumed to be coauthored by John Fletcher and Shakespeare. It was first performed in 1612 or 1613.

times and am then really impressed with the eleventh one, I will give that actor a lot of credit. I think it is, however, in the actor's best interest to avoid overworked pieces.

I will be happy if I never again hear Edmund's bastard speech from *King Lear* because almost all young actors scan it incorrectly (i.e., *Thou* nature, are *my* goddess; to *thy* laws *my* services are bound, etc.), and it drives me up the wall. Also, in the thirty years of observing young actors audition, I have seen hundreds of Phebes from *As You Like It,* and only once has an actor been able to pull it off. I'm willing to see more; however, I would advise anyone to avoid it. Because there are fewer women's roles, women have a harder time finding good audition pieces.

Edward Hastings: None.

Martin Benson: If the actor is good and the material chosen is right for him or her, the piece will be enjoyable.

Penny Metropolis: Lady Percy! Benedick, Prince Hal, Gloucester, Constance (just because we can see at least twenty to thirty of these out of 150 auditions).

Deborah Hecht: Really, it has to do with the hunger and connection of the individual actor. However, I do feel some pieces are difficult out of context: *Richard II,* "Come let us sit upon the ground," and Julia's letter speech from *Two Gents* usually aren't my fare.

Ken Albers: Julia's letter speech from *Two Gents;* Viola's ring speech; Portia's speech to Brutus; anything from the Nurse; anything from *Hamlet;* the Seven Ages; comic monologues that have long since lost their topical punch. Launcelot Gobbo, Dromio, Trinculo, Stephano, the Fool, Touchstone.

David Hammond: From *Two Gentlemen of Verona:* Julia's letter scene; Launce and his dog Crab; Launce with his shoes. From *The Two Noble Kinsmen:* the Gaoler's Daughter.

Sandy Ernst: I never want to hear Queen Mab again as long as I live. It is not a good piece when pulled from the play. I'm totally sick of Puck. Nobody under twenty-five should do Benedict or Hermione. I think too many people are telling students that "contrasting" means comic and tragic. That is so hard to find! I tell my interns that *light* and *serious* are better words. Trying to find a stand-up comic piece from Shakespeare has led many a young actor to bad choices.

Donovan Marley: If he wrote it, I will listen to it.

David Frank: Viola's ring speech; Sebastian's "This is the air."

Mark Torres: Well done, just about anything is enjoyable.

Nagle Jackson: The *Hamlet* soliloquies (except "How all occasions"),

Hermione in *Winter's Tale,* Constance in *King John,* Launce or Lancelot Gobbo.

Kent Thompson: "Too, too solid/sullied flesh," "What a rogue and peasant slave," "Friends, Romans countrymen," Macbeth/Lady Macbeth by twenty-year-olds, Oberon/Titania.

Hal Cropp: The truth is any piece well done is worth hearing, and any piece poorly done I never want to hear again.

John Shepard: None, as long as they are well done.

Katy Brown: Juliet's death speech. Almost anything from *Romeo and Juliet* is done too much.

Jared Sakren: Paulina's speech from *Winter's Tale* ("What studied torments"). The ring speech from *Twelfth Night.*

Robert Fass: Men: "To be or not to be . . . ," "Now is the winter of our discontent," "All the world's a stage," "I do much wonder that one man," "O for a muse of fire," "Is this a dagger which I see before me," "But soft, what light through yonder window breaks." Women: I hate to list anything here because the list of choices for women is so short.

Henson Keys: Unless you are brilliant at them: Edmund's "Thou, nature, art my goddess" (*Lear*), Margaret's handkerchief/Rutland speech (*Henry VI, Part 3*), Phebe's "Think not I love him" (*As You Like It*), Constance's "This hair I tear is mine" (*King John*). Duse could not work up this level of passion in a monologue!

Name pieces you never tire of hearing.

Penny Metropolis: That's tougher. Basically if there's a strong take and skills are good, it's a pleasure to hear anything.

David Hammond: Just about anything else is fine.

Howard Jensen: I have no favorites. I would like to see more comedy monologues *if* the actor can truly make them funny. If an actor can do comedy well, I know he or she can act and can probably do a wide range of roles.

Edward Hastings: All.

Elizabeth Huddle: I'll listen to anything that's done well.

Nagle Jackson: Anything from *Henry VIII* or *Richard II,* the *Henry V* choruses, *Merchant of Venice* (because no one does them).

Deborah Hecht: Or ones I'd like to hear more often! Cloten's two little speeches, even though not in verse; he's such a fun character. Anything by Lady Percy (very active, in the moment, good clear objectives). Young Queen Margaret — great stuff and again clear "wants." There are many secondary characters in the histories who have good pieces, for example Bishop of Carlisle in *Richard II.*

Donovan Marley: Anything wonderfully acted.

Ken Albers: Constance from *King John,* Lewis from the same, Hal and Hotspur, Lady Percy, Julia's monologue to Sylvia's picture, Orlando's speech when he encounters Duke Senior, Shylock's major speeches, Caliban, Miranda.

John Shepard: Anything, as long as it is well done.

Sandy Ernst: I never tire of hearing beautiful speeches done well. Don't shy away from *Hamlet.* He has *true* soliloquies for one thing, and some of the most beautiful speeches ever written. (I even learned one myself, years ago when I auditioned.) I also urge young women who are not going to be considered ingénues by most producers to look at Choruses and those "boy" parts.

Risa Brainin: Any piece if it is done well!

Katy Brown: If done well, Edmund from *Lear.* It's done a lot, but it usually proves a good vehicle for young actors.

Robert Fass: I think I've seen them all, and I eventually tire of them all for a brief period during the casting process unless a performer gives a reading that I am unfamiliar with or a performance sparks something intriguing in my imagination. The piece comes to life through the actor not because the actor chose a monologue that I favor. Actors give life to the words and to my interest as well.

Henson Keys: Any *Hamlet* monologues (Hamlet or Ophelia). Any Shakespeare juvenile/ingénue played with freshness, innocence, and a sense of wonder (Desdemona, Juliet, Sebastian, Orlando, Rosalind, Hal, Viola). We see too much easy cynicism.

Jim Rambo: Prospero, *Tempest,* act 4 scene 1; any Hamlet monologue; and Malvolio, *Twelfth Night,* act 2 scene 5.

Some Things to Note

- Although the act, scene, and line numbers are printed before each speech, different editions may number the lines very differently, so don't be surprised if you have to search around for a particular speech.

- Some of the monologues start midway into a speech, so again, look around.

- You occasionally find textual variations in different editions. This is not uncommon since some of the original texts are open to interpretation. When you come across a variation, choose the word you prefer.

- The vernacular versions of the speeches are not word-for-word translations; they are only intended to give you the gist of the speech.

- A grave accent (as in *amazèd*) indicates that the final syllable is accented. So *amazèd* is pronounced ah-*may*-zed (note that the stress is on the second syllable).

- An apostrophe within a word or joining two words indicates that a letter has been dropped and the word or words should be pronounced with one less syllable for the sake of the meter. Therefore *is't* (is it) and *show'rs* (showers) are both pronounced as one-syllable words, while *t'inherit* (to inherit) has three syllables.

- Sometimes we've added something to a speech, usually from another character's speech, to help a monologue stand on its own. Whenever we have done this, the added material is put into brackets ([ ]).

- A *cut* speech has been shortened, usually to accommodate time considerations.

- A *combined* speech has connected two or more speeches to form a longer speech.

- At the bottom of the page (except when the original speech is already in prose), you will find the speech reprinted in prose form. This is to show the flow of thoughts in the speech in a more recognizable way and is one of the many tools actors use to help shape a speech to determine a speech's vocal architecture. (Please note that the paragraphs or thought groupings indicated are only one way in which a particular speech may be broken up; it is by no means the only way. Each actor must find the shaping that works for him- or herself. Remember, this is merely a demonstration of a technique that some actors choose to employ; it may or may not work for you.)

THE MONOLOGUES

Act 1 scene 1, lines 76–96 (cut)

HELENA:
It's not my father I'm thinking of. What was he like?
I have forgotten him; my mind's eye
is filled with no other image but Bertram's.
I'm lost; there is nothing to live for, nothing,
if Bertram is not here; it's the same
as if my heart were set on some bright special star
and thought to marry it, he is that far above me.
I must be content to merely feel his radiance
and to exist in the periphery of his being, not in his circle.
The overreaching of my love is its own downfall:
the doe that wishes to mate with the lion
is bound to die for love. It was wonderful, even though it was a torment,
to see him constantly, to sit and sketch
his arched brows, his keen eyes, his curly hair,
and to imprint them in my heart — a heart too susceptible
to every characteristic of his perfect face.
But now he's gone, and all that's left for my adoration
is to worship my mementos of him.

Act 1 scene 1, lines 76–96 (cut)

HELENA:
I think not on my father. What was he like?
I have forgot him; my imagination
Carries no favour in't but Bertram's.
I am undone; there is no living, none,
If Bertram be away; 'twere all one
That I should love a bright particular star
And think to wed it, he is so above me.
In his bright radiance and collateral light
Must I be comforted, not in his sphere.
Th'ambition in my love thus plagues itself:
The hind that would be mated by the lion
Must die for love. 'Twas pretty, though a plague,
To see him every hour; to sit and draw
His archèd brows, his hawking eye, his curls,
In our heart's table — heart too capable
Of every line and trick of his sweet favour.
But now he's gone, and my idolatrous fancy
Must sanctify his relics.

I think not on my father. What was he like? I have forgot him; my imagination carries no favour in't but Bertram's. I am undone; there is no living, none, if Bertram be away; 'twere all one that I should love a bright particular star and think to wed it, he is so above me. In his bright radiance and collateral light must I be comforted, not in his sphere.

Th'ambition in my love thus plagues itself: the hind that would be mated by the lion must die for love. 'Twas pretty, though a plague, to see him every hour; to sit and draw his archèd brows, his hawking eye, his curls, in our heart's table — heart too capable of every line and trick of his sweet favour. But now he's gone, and my idolatrous fancy must sanctify his relics.

Act 1 scene 1, lines 106–160 (cut)

PAROLLES:

Are you contemplating virginity? It is not prudent in the natural universe to maintain virginity. Losing one's virginity is a profitable investment because no virgin can be born until another's virginity is first lost. The very stuff you are made of is the stuff needed to make other virgins. Once virginity is lost — it can make ten new virgins; but if it's kept forever it produces nothing. It is a frosty companion. Get rid of it! There's not much to be said for it; it's unnatural. If you speak on its behalf, you're insulting your own mothers, which is unquestionable disobedience. Virginity breeds mites. Besides, virginity is silly, selfish, wasteful, blatantly egotistical — which is the most forbidden sin of all. Don't hold on to it; you'll only be the worse for it. Kiss it good-bye! Within the year it will multiply — that's a reasonable return — and the original principal won't be much worse for wear. Dump it! Unload it while it's still desirable; sell while the market's hot. Because your virginity, your old virginity, is like a withered French pear: it looks bad, tastes dried out; come on, indeed, it's a withered pear; it used to be better; but face it, it's nothing but a withered pear. Would you want it?

Act 1 scene 1, lines 106–160 (cut)

PAROLLES:

Are you meditating on virginity? It is not politic in the commonwealth of nature to preserve virginity. Loss of virginity is rational increase, and there was never virgin got till virginity was first lost. That you were made of is metal to make virgins. Virginity, by being once lost, may be ten times found; by being ever kept it is ever lost. 'Tis too cold a companion. Away with't! There's little can be said in't; 'tis against the rule of nature. To speak on the part of virginity is to accuse your mothers, which is most infallible disobedience. Virginity breeds mites. Besides, virginity is peevish, proud, idle, made of self-love which is the most inhibited sin in the canon. Keep it not; you cannot choose but lose by't. Out with't! Within ten year it will make itself ten, which is a goodly increase, and the principal itself not much the worse. Away with't! Off with't while 'tis vendible; answer the time of request. Your virginity, your old virginity, is like one of our French wither'd pears: it looks ill, it eats drily; marry, 'tis a wither'd pear; it was formerly better; marry, yet 'tis a wither'd pear. Will you anything with it?

Act 1 scene 3, lines 187–212 (cut)

HELENA:
               I confess,
here on my knee, before high heaven and you,
that before you, but not as much as heaven,
I love your son.
My family was poor, but honest; so is my love.
Don't be offended, no harm comes to him
because he is loved by me. I'm not pursuing him
with the presumption of being a suitor,
nor would I want to have him till I deserve him;
and yet don't know how that desert might ever come to be.
             My dear madam,
don't hate the fact that my love
is directed in the same place as yours; but if you yourself —
whose revered maturity can trace itself back to a virtuous youth —
ever did, with such a true and burning passion,
desire as chastely and love as dearly as I do, oh then, have pity
on one who is in such a state that she has no choice
but to offer and give her love to one who will reject her;
who seeks never to be rewarded in her search,
but enigmatically will live where her heart pines!

Act 1 scene 3, lines 187–212 (cut)

HELENA:
                    I confess,
Here on my knee, before high heaven and you,
That before you, and next unto high heaven,
I love your son.
My friends were poor, but honest; so's my love.
Be not offended, for it hurts not him
That he is loved of me. I follow him not
By any token of presumptuous suit,
Nor would I have him till I do deserve him;
Yet never know how that desert should be.
                    My dearest madam,
Let not your hate encounter with my love,
For loving where you do; but if yourself,
Whose agèd honor cites a virtuous youth,
Did ever, in so true a flame of liking,
Wish chastely and love dearly, O then, give pity
To her whose state is such that cannot choose
But lend and give where she is sure to lose;
That seeks not to find that her search implies,
But riddle-like lives sweetly where she dies!

I confess, here on my knee, before high heaven and you, that before you, and next unto high heaven, I love your son.

My friends were poor, but honest; so's my love. Be not offended, for it hurts not him that he is loved of me. I follow him not by any token of presumptuous suit, nor would I have him till I do deserve him; yet never know how that desert should be.

My dearest madam, let not your hate encounter with my love, for loving where you do; but if yourself, whose agèd honor cites a virtuous youth, did ever, in so true a flame of liking, wish chastely and love dearly, O then, give pity to her whose state is such that cannot choose but lend and give where she is sure to lose; that seeks not to find that her search implies, but riddle-like lives sweetly where she dies!

Act 3 scene 2, lines 97–127 (cut)

HELENA: *(reading from a letter)*
'Till I am rid of my wife, I will not return to France.'
No returning to France till he is rid of his wife!
You shall have no wife, Roussillon, none in France;
then you can come home again. Poor lord, is it I
that keeps you from your country, and exposes
those youthful limbs of yours to the hazards
of war that spare no one? And is it I
that drives you from the pleasures of the court, where you
would be shot at with fair glances, instead of being the target
of smoking muskets? Oh you leaden bullets
that fly through the air with the speed of fire,
do not hit your mark; do not touch my lord!
Whoever may shoot at him, it is I who put him there.
And though I didn't kill him myself, I would be the cause.
Come home, Roussillon, I will be gone;
my presence here is what is keeping you away.
Shall I stay here and do that? No. Come night, end the day;
for in the dark, like a thief, I'll steal away.

Act 3 scene 2, lines 97–127 (cut)

HELENA: *(reading from a letter)*
'Till I have no wife I have nothing in France.'
Nothing in France until he has no wife!
Thou shalt have none, Roussillon, none in France;
Then hast thou all again. Poor lord, is't I
That chase thee from thy country, and expose
Those tender limbs of thine to the event
Of the none-sparing war? And is it I
That drive thee from the sportive court, where thou
Wast shot at with fair eyes, to be the mark
Of smoky muskets? O you leaden messengers,
That ride upon the violent speed of fire,
Fly with false aim; do not touch my lord!
Whoever shoots at him, I set him there.
And though I kill him not, I am the cause.
Come thou home, Roussillon, I will be gone;
My being here it is that holds thee hence.
Shall I stay here to do't? No. Come night, end day;
For with the dark, poor thief, I'll steal away.

'Till I have no wife I have nothing in France.'
Nothing in France until he has no wife! Thou shalt have none, Roussillon, none in France;
then hast thou all again. Poor lord, is't I that chase thee from thy country, and expose those tender limbs of thine to the event of the none-sparing war? And is it that drive thee from the sportive court, where thou wast shot at with fair eyes, to be the mark of smoky muskets? O you leaden messengers, that ride upon the violent speed of fire, fly with false aim; do not touch my lord! Whoever shoots at him, I set him there. And though I kill him not, I am the cause.

Come thou home, Roussillon, I will be gone; my being here it is that holds thee hence. Shall I stay here to do't? No. Come night, end day; for with the dark, poor thief, I'll steal away.

Act 4 scene 1, lines 24–60 (cut)

PAROLLES:
Ten o'clock. After about another three hours I'll be able to go home. What shall I say I have done? It will have to be a very believable story if I'm to convince them. They're beginning to suspect me, and there's been too much negative said about me recently. I know I have a big mouth. What the devil made me say I'd get back this drum, being well aware how impossible it would be, and knowing I wouldn't do it? I must inflict some wounds on myself, and say I got them while attempting it; yet minor injuries won't do. They'll say, 'How'd you get away with so little?' And I wouldn't dare inflict major ones. So then, what kind of evidence do I offer? Tongue, I'm going to have to trade you in and get myself a new one if you keep getting me into such trouble. I wish tearing up my clothes would be enough, or breaking my Spanish sword. Or maybe I could just shave off my beard and say it was part of my strategy. Or bury my clothing and say that I was stripped naked? I wish I had any old drum of the enemy's; I would swear that I had recovered it.

Act 4 scene 1, lines 24–60 (cut)

PAROLLES:

Ten o'clock. Within these three hours 'twill be time enough to go home. What shall I say I have done? It must be a very plausive invention that carries it. They begin to smoke me, and disgraces have of late knocked too often at my door. I find my tongue is too foolhardy. What the devil should move me to undertake the recovery of this drum, being not ignorant of the impossibility, and knowing I had no such purpose? I must give myself some hurts, and say I got them in exploit; yet slight ones will not carry it. They will say, 'Came you off with so little?' And great ones I dare not give. Wherefore, what's the instance? Tongue, I must put you into a butter-woman's mouth and buy myself another if you prattle me into these perils. I would the cutting of my garments would serve the turn, or the breaking of my Spanish sword. Or the baring of my beard, and to say it was in stratagem. Or to drown my clothes and say I was stripped? I would I had any drum of the enemy's; I would swear I recovered it.

Act 4 scene 2, lines 17–31 (combined)

DIANA:

Oh sure, you'll be of service to us
until we serve you; but once you've plucked our roses,
you'll barely leave us our thorns for us to prick ourselves with,
and then you'll taunt us for having lost our bloom.
It's not the number of times one swears that makes a thing true,
but a single straightforward statement of an honest truth.
What is not holy, we would never swear by,
we only swear by the most important things; then, I beg you,
    tell me:
just because I swore by Jove's great attributes
that I loved you deeply, would you believe my oaths
if I treated you badly? It just doesn't make sense
to swear by a god — whom I swore I loved —
that I would act against his teachings. Therefore your oaths
are nothing but words, only empty promises —
at least that's my opinion.

Act 4 scene 2, lines 17–31 (combined)

DIANA:

                      Ay, so you serve us
Till we serve you; but when you have our roses,
You barely leave our thorns to prick ourselves,
And mock us with our bareness.
'Tis not the many oaths that makes the truth,
But the plain single vow that is vowed true.
What is not holy, that we swear not by,
But take the high'st to witness; then, pray you, tell me:
If I should swear by Jove's great attributes
I loved you dearly, would you believe my oaths
When I did love you ill? This has no holding,
To swear by Him whom I protest to love
That I will work against Him. Therefore your oaths
Are words, and poor conditions but unsealed —
At least in my opinion.

    Ay, so you serve us till we serve you; but when you have our roses, you barely leave our thorns to prick ourselves, and mock us with our bareness.

    'Tis not the many oaths that makes the truth, but the plain single vow that is vowed true. What is not holy, that we swear not by, but take the high'st to witness; then, pray you, tell me: if I should swear by Jove's great attributes I loved you dearly, would you believe my oaths when I did love you ill? This has no holding, to swear by Him whom I protest to love that I will work against Him. Therefore your oaths are words, and poor conditions but unsealed — at least in my opinion.

Act 4 scene 3, lines 235–252

PAROLLES:
[As for Captain Dumaine?] — Sir, he would steal anything that wasn't tied down. As for raping and ravishing — he rivals Don Juan. He makes it a point to not keep his oaths; and he breaks them with the strength of Hercules. He lies so convincingly, sir, that you would swear the truth had no credibility; drunkenness is his best virtue, for he can be drunk as a skunk, and when he's asleep he doesn't do much harm, except to his bed linens; but everybody knows that so they make him sleep in the hay. I have a little more to say about his honesty: he has everything that an honest man should not have; and those things an honest man should have, he has none.

Act 4 scene 3, lines 235–252

PAROLLES:
[This Captain Dumaine?] He will steal, sir, an egg out of a cloister. For rapes and ravishments he parallels Nessus. He professes not keeping of oaths; in breaking 'em he is stronger than Hercules. He will lie, sir, with such volubility that you would think truth were a fool; drunkenness is his best virtue, for he will be swine-drunk, and in his sleep he does little harm, save to his bedclothes about him; but they know his conditions and lay him in straw. I have but little more to say, sir, of his honesty: he has everything that an honest man should not have; what an honest man should have, he has nothing.

Act 2 scene 1, lines 1–17 (cut)

DUKE SENIOR:
Now, my companions and fellow exiles,
haven't these simple pleasures made the life we lead here sweeter
than our life of artificial splendor? Aren't these woods
freer from danger than was the back-stabbing royal court?
Here we get to feel as Adam did when he was expelled from Eden —
and the changing seasons, with the icy stings
and rough rebukes of the winter's wind,
which, when it nips and blows upon my body
until I shiver with cold, makes me smile and say
'There's nothing phony here' — these are the things that teach
my senses to come alive and prove to me that I am human.
There is pleasure in learning from adversity;
and our life here, secluded as we are,
teaches us to hear the voice of the trees, the stories told by the
    babbling brooks,
to learn lessons from the stones, and to see the good in all things.
I would not change it.

Act 2 scene 1, lines 1–17 (cut)

DUKE SENIOR:
Now, my co-mates and brothers in exile,
Hath not old custom made this life more sweet
Than that of painted pomp? Are not these woods
More free from peril than the envious court?
Here feel we not the penalty of Adam,
The seasons' difference, as the icy fang
And churlish chiding of the winter's wind,
Which, when it bites and blows upon my body
Even till I shrink with cold, I smile and say
'This is no flattery' — these are counsellors
That feelingly persuade me what I am.
Sweet are the uses of adversity;
And this our life, exempt from public haunt,
Finds tongues in trees, books in the running brooks,
Sermons in stones, and good in everything.
I would not change it.

Now, my co-mates and brothers in exile, hath not old custom made this life more sweet than that of painted pomp? Are not these woods more free from peril than the envious court?

Here feel we not the penalty of Adam — the seasons' difference, (as the icy fang and churlish chiding of the winter's wind, which, when it bites and blows upon my body even till I shrink with cold), I smile and say 'This is no flattery' — these are counsellors that feelingly persuade me what I am.

Sweet are the uses of adversity; and this our life, exempt from public haunt, finds tongues in trees, books in the running brooks, sermons in stones, and good in everything. I would not change it.

Act 2 scene 7, lines 106–119

ORLANDO:
Why do you speak so politely? Pardon me, please —
I thought that everything here was savage,
and therefore I tried to appear as cruel as I
was able. But whoever you are
here in this deserted place,
standing in the shade of these gloomy branches,
whiling away your time —
if ever you have experienced better times;
if ever you've heard church bells ring;
if ever you've dined at an honest man's table;
if ever you've shed a tear,
and know how it feels to pity and to be pitied —
then let me win you to my cause like a gentleman;
and hoping that I can, I blush and put away my sword.

Act 2 scene 7, lines 106–119

ORLANDO:

Speak you so gently? Pardon me, I pray you —
I thought that all things had been savage here,
And therefore put I on the countenance
Of stern commandment. But whate'er you are
That in this desert inaccessible,
Under the shade of melancholy boughs,
Lose and neglect the creeping hours of time —
If ever you have looked on better days;
If ever been where bells have knolled to church;
If ever sat at any good man's feast;
If ever from your eyelids wiped a tear,
And know what 'tis to pity and be pitied —
Let gentleness my strong enforcement be;
In the which hope I blush, and hide my sword.

Speak you so gently? Pardon me, I pray you — I thought that all things had been savage here, and therefore put I on the countenance of stern commandment.

But whate'er you are that in this desert inaccessible, under the shade of melancholy boughs, lose and neglect the creeping hours of time, if ever you have looked on better days; if ever been where bells have knolled to church; if ever sat at any good man's feast; if ever from your eyelids wiped a tear, and know what 'tis to pity and be pitied, let gentleness my strong enforcement be; in the which hope I blush, and hide my sword.

Act 3 scene 2, lines 359–379 (combined)

ROSALIND:
Love is simply a form of madness, and I tell you, lovers
should be locked up and whipped just like madmen are:
and the reason why they are not treated and
cured in this manner, is that the lunacy is so universal that
those who should be treating the ailment
are in love themselves. But I profess curing
it with therapy. [I once cured] someone, using this technique.
He was supposed to imagine that I was his love, his lady;
and I instructed him to woo me every day — at which time
I would (since I was merely a fickle youth) grieve, be
effeminate, whimsical, capricious and loving, proud,
outrageous, silly, shallow, inconstant, tearful,
smiling; for each passion I did something but
for not one single passion did I portray anything truthfully (since
    boys and women,
for the most part, are known to act like this): I would
like him for a moment, then loathe him; then permit him to
    woo me, then
reject him; sometimes I'd tearfully lead him on, then I'd spit at him;
so that I drove my suitor out of his madness of love
and into your everyday sort of madness that he could live with —
which caused him to remove himself from the normal stream of
life and shut himself up
like a hermit. And so I cured him; and in this same manner
will I take it upon myself to cleanse your heart as
pure as a healthy sheep's, so that there won't be one spot
of love left in it.

Act 3 scene 2, lines 359–379 (combined)

ROSALIND:
Love is merely a madness, and I tell you, deserves
as well a dark house and a whip as madmen do:
and the reason why they are not so punished and
cured is that the lunacy is so ordinary that the
whippers are in love too. Yet I profess curing
it by counsel. [I did cure] one, and in this manner.
He was to imagine me his love, his mistress;
and I set him every day to woo me: at which time
would I, being but a moonish youth, grieve, be
effeminate, changeable, longing and liking, proud,
fantastical, apish, shallow, inconstant, full of tears,
full of smiles; for every passion something and
for no passion truly anything, as boys and women are,
for the most part, cattle of this color: would now
like him, now loathe him; then entertain him, then
forswear him; now weep for him, then spit at him;
that I drave my suitor from his mad humor of love
to a living humor of madness — which was, to forswear
the full stream of the world and to live in a nook
merely monastic. And thus I cured him; and this way
will I take upon me to wash your liver as clean as a
sound sheep's heart, that there shall not be one spot
of love in't.

Act 3 scene 5, lines 8–27

PHEBE:
I won't be your executioner.
I'll leave you, because I don't want to hurt you.
You say to me that there is murder in my eye —
oh what a clever thought, for sure, and very probable,
that eyes, which are the frailest and softest of things,
which shut their delicate lids tight against the tiniest bits of dust,
should have the power to be tyrants, butchers, murderers!
I'm frowning on you now with all my heart,
and if my eyes could wound, they should now be killing you;
you should be swooning now; now falling down;
so, if you're not dying, shame on you, shame on you,
don't lie and say that my eyes are murderers!
Show me the wound that my eye has made in you.
If I scratch you with a pin, there'd remain
some scar; if you lean on a bamboo mat
the pattern of it and some actual impression
remains for a moment on your palm; and yet my eyes,
which I have darted at you, have not hurt you one bit,
nor, I am certain, is there any such power in eyes
that could do any harm.

Act 3 scene 5, lines 8–27

PHEBE:
I would not be thy executioner.
I fly thee, for I would not injure thee.
Thou tell'st me there is murder in mine eye.
'Tis pretty sure, and very probable,
That eyes, that are the frail'st and softest things,
Who shut their coward gates on atomies,
Should be called tyrants, butchers, murderers!
Now I do frown on thee with all my heart,
And if mine eyes can wound, now let them kill thee;
Now counterfeit to swoon; why now fall down,
Or if thou canst not, O for shame, for shame,
Lie not, to say mine eyes are murderers!
Now show the wound mine eye hath made in thee.
Scratch thee but with a pin, and there remains
Some scar of it; lean upon a rush,
The cicatrice and capable impressure
Thy palm some moment keeps; but now mine eyes,
Which I have darted at thee, hurt thee not,
Nor, I am sure, there is no force in eyes
That can do hurt.

I would not be thy executioner. I fly thee, for I would not injure thee.

Thou tell'st me there is murder in mine eye. 'Tis pretty sure, and very probable, that eyes, that are the frail'st and softest things, who shut their coward gates on atomies, should be called tyrants, butchers, murderers!

Now I do frown on thee with all my heart, and if mine eyes can wound, now let them kill thee; now counterfeit to swoon; why now fall down — or if thou canst not, O for shame, for shame, lie not, to say mine eyes are murderers!

Now show the wound mine eye hath made in thee. Scratch thee but with a pin, and there remains some scar of it; lean upon a rush, the cicatrice and capable impressure thy palm some moment keeps; but now mine eyes, which I have darted at thee, hurt thee not, nor, I am sure, there is no force in eyes that can do hurt.

Act 3 scene 5, lines 35–60 (cut)

ROSALIND:
And why, I ask you? Who do you think you are,
that you think you can insult and condescend to
this poor wretched fellow? What, though you're not
    even good-looking —
for, surely, I think you'd be wise to turn out the lights
before getting into bed with anyone —
can you still be so conceited and so heartless?
Why, what does this mean? Why are you looking at me?
I see nothing more in you than in the average
work of nature. Oh, dear god,
I think she's trying to win me over too!
No, truly, proud missy, don't even think it.
It won't be your dark eyebrows nor your creamy cheeks,
that will win over my spirits to adore you.
You foolish shepherd, why do you run after her?
You're a thousand times a better looking man
than she is a woman.
It's not her mirror, but you, that builds up her ego,
and because of you she thinks she's prettier
than any of her features show her to be.
So mistress, get hip to yourself. Get down on your knees,
be penitent, and thank heaven that you've got a good
    man to love you;
'cause I'll whisper it to you like a friend in your ear,
take him while you can, you're not going to get many chances.

Act 3 scene 5, lines 35–60 (cut)

ROSALIND:
And why, I pray you? Who might be your mother,
That you insult, exult, and all at once,
Over the wretched? What, though you have no beauty
(As by my faith, I see no more in you
Than without candle may go dark to bed)
Must you be therefore proud and pitiless?
Why, what means this? Why do you look on me?
I see no more in you than in the ordinary
Of nature's sale-work. 'Od's my little life,
I think she means to tangle my eyes too!
No, faith, proud mistress, hope not after it;
'Tis not your inky brows, nor your cheek of cream
That can entame my spirits to your worship.
You foolish shepherd, wherefore do you follow her?
You are a thousand times a properer man
Than she a woman.
'Tis not her glass, but you, that flatters her,
And out of you she sees herself more proper
Than any of her lineaments can show her.
But mistress, know yourself. Down on your knees,
And thank heaven, fasting, for a good man's love;
For I must tell you friendly in your ear,
Sell when you can, you are not for all markets.

And why, I pray you? Who might be your mother, that you insult, exult, and all at once, over the wretched? What, though you have no beauty (as by my faith, I see no more in you than without candle may go dark to bed) must you be therefore proud and pitiless?

Why, what means this? Why do you look on me? I see no more in you than in the ordinary of nature's sale-work. 'Od's my little life, I think she means to tangle my eyes too!

No, faith, proud mistress, hope not after it; 'tis not your inky brows, nor your cheek of cream that can entame my spirits to your worship.

You foolish shepherd, wherefore do you follow her? You are a thousand times a properer man than she a woman. 'Tis not her glass, but you, that flatters her, and out of you she sees herself more proper than any of her lineaments can show her.

But mistress, know yourself. Down on your knees, and thank heaven, fasting, for a good man's love; for I must tell you friendly in your ear — sell when you can, you are not for all markets.

Act 5 scene 1, lines 39–55 (combined)

TOUCHSTONE:
Then let me teach you this: If you *have* something, you *have* it!
Now, it's a rhetorical argument that water, when poured out of a
cup and into a glass (thereby filling the glass), empties the cup.
Now, all writers agree that *ipse* means 'he.' Now, you are not *ipse*,
because I am 'he.' 'He' sir, that is meant to marry this woman.
Therefore, you clown, abandon (which in the vernacular means,
'leave') the society (or as you might say, 'company') of this female
(which you commonly call 'woman'). Which, put all together is,
'abandon the society of this female,' or, clown, you perish! Or, to
make that even clearer, you die; or, that is to say, I'll kill you, do
away with you, translate your life into death, your liberty into
everlasting bondage. I will deal in poison with you, or in beating,
or in dueling. I will conspire against you; I will overwhelm you with
strategy, I will kill you a hundred and fifty ways. Therefore tremble
and depart.

Act 5 scene 1, lines 39–55 (combined)

TOUCHSTONE:
Then learn this of me: to have, is to have! For it is a figure in rhetoric that drink, being poured out of a cup into a glass, by filling the one doth empty the other. For all your writers do consent that *ipse* is he. Now, you are not *ipse*, for I am he. He, sir, that must marry this woman. Therefore, you clown, abandon (which is in the vulgar, 'leave') the society (which in the boorish is, 'company') of this female (which in the common is, 'woman'). Which together is — 'abandon the society of this female,' or, clown, thou perishest! Or, to thy better understanding, diest; or, to wit, I kill thee, make thee away, translate thy life into death, thy liberty into bondage. I will deal in poison with thee, or in bastinado, or in steel. I will bandy with thee in faction; I will o'errun thee with policy; I will kill thee a hundred and fifty ways. Therefore tremble and depart.

Act 3 scene 2, lines 41–66 (cut, starts midspeech)

IMOGEN: *(reading)*
'Dearest of creatures, take note that I am in Cambria, at
Milford Haven. Whatever your love urges you to do with this information,
follow it. So, he who remains loyal to his word, wishes you
every happiness and the strengthening of your love,
Leonatus Posthumus.'
Oh, what I'd give for a horse with wings! Do you hear, Pisanio?
He is at Milford Haven. Look it up, and tell me
how far it is there. If someone not in a big hurry
can plod there in a week, why can't I
glide there in a day? Then, loyal Pisanio,
who longs as I do to see my lord, who longs —
oh let me rephrase that — not quite like me — still who longs
but in a less extreme manner — oh, not like me at all,
for mine's beyond beyond; tell me, and tell me quickly —
                    how far it is
to this same blessed Milford. And while you're at it
tell me how Wales got so lucky
to be the possessor of such a heavenly spot. But first of all,
tell me how we may sneak out of here; and, to cover up our
absence from here while we go there, what kind of excuse
we can come up with; but first, how we get there:
why should we have deliver the excuse before we've hatched the plan?
We'll talk about that later. Say something!

Act 3 scene 2, lines 41–66 (cut, starts midspeech)

IMOGEN: *(reading)*
'Dearest of creatures, take notice that I am in Cambria, at
Milford Haven. What your own love will out of this advise
you, follow. So he wishes you all happiness, that remains
loyal to his vow, and your increasing in love,
Leonatus Posthumus.'
O for a horse with wings! Hear'st thou, Pisanio?
He is at Milford Haven. Read, and tell me
How far 'tis thither. If one of mean affairs
May plod it in a week, why may not I
Glide thither in a day? Then, true Pisanio,
Who long'st like me to see thy lord, who long'st —
O let me bate — but not like me — yet long'st
But in a fainter kind — O, not like me,
For mine's beyond beyond; say, and speak thick —
                how far it is
To this same blessèd Milford. And by th'way
Tell me how Wales was made so happy as
T''inherit such a haven. But first of all,
How we may steal from hence; and for the gap
That we shall make in time from our hence-going
Till our return, to excuse; but first, how get hence.
Why should excuse be born or ere begot?
We'll talk of that hereafter. Prithee speak!

'Dearest of creatures, take notice that I am in Cambria, at Milford Haven. What your own love will out of this advise you, follow. So he wishes you all happiness, that remains loyal to his vow, and your increasing in love, Leonatus Posthumus.'

O for a horse with wings! Hear'st thou, Pisanio? He is at Milford Haven. Read, and tell me how far 'tis thither. If one of mean affairs may plod it in a week, why may not I glide thither in a day? Then, true Pisanio, who long'st like me to see thy lord, who long'st — O let me bate — but not like me — yet long'st but in a fainter kind — O, not like me, for mine's beyond beyond; say, and speak thick –how far it is to this same blessèd Milford. And by th'way tell me how Wales was made so happy as t'inherit such a haven.

But first of all, how we may steal from hence; and for the gap that we shall make in time from our hence-going till our return, to excuse; but first, how get hence. Why should excuse be born or ere begot? We'll talk of that hereafter. Prithee speak!

Act 1 scene 1, lines 162–186 (cut and combined)

BERNARDO/MARCELLUS/HORATIO:
It was just about to speak, when the cock crowed.
And then it darted off, like some guilty person
hearing an alarm bell ring. I have heard
that the cock, who announces the morning's arrival,
with his high-pitched and shrill-sounding voice,
awakens the sun; and at this signal
all the demons of the night hurry off
to their hiding places.
Some claim that just prior to the season
when our Savior's birth is celebrated,
the bird of dawn sings all night long;
and then, they say, no spirits dare to venture forth,
the nights are safe, at that time comets don't streak,
fairies have no power to entrance, and witches' charms are ineffective,
that's how holy and how blessed that time is.
Oh look, the morning, with its reddish hue,
is rising over that high dew-clad eastern hill.
Let's break up the watch; and I suggest
we tell what we have seen tonight
to young Hamlet; because, on my life,
this spirit, who won't speak to us, will speak to him.

Act 1 scene 1, lines 163–186 (cut and combined)

BERNARDO/MARCELLUS/HORATIO:
It was about to speak, when the cock crew.
And then it started, like a guilty thing
Upon a fearful summons. I have heard
The cock, that is the trumpet to the morn,
Doth with his lofty and shrill-sounding throat
Awake the god of day; and at his warning,
The extravagant and erring spirit hies
To his confine.
Some say that ever 'gainst that season comes
Wherein our Saviour's birth is celebrated,
The bird of dawning singeth all night long;
And then, they say, no spirit dare stir abroad,
The nights are wholesome, then no planets strike,
No fairy takes, nor witch hath power to charm,
So hallowed and so gracious is the time.
But look, the morn, in russet mantle clad,
Walks o'er the dew of yon high eastern hill.
Break we our watch up; and by my advice
Let us impart what we have seen tonight
Unto young Hamlet; for, upon my life,
This spirit, dumb to us, will speak to him.

It was about to speak, when the cock crew. And then it started, like a guilty thing upon a fearful summons. I have heard the cock, that is the trumpet to the morn, doth with his lofty and shrill-sounding throat awake the god of day; and at his warning, the extravagant and erring spirit hies to his confine. Some say that ever 'gainst that season comes wherein our Saviour's birth is celebrated, the bird of dawning singeth all night long; and then, they say, no spirit dare stir abroad, the nights are wholesome, then no planets strike, no fairy takes, nor witch hath power to charm, so hallowed and so gracious is the time.

But look, the morn, in russet mantle clad, walks o'er the dew of yon high eastern hill. Break we our watch up; and by my advice let us impart what we have seen tonight unto young Hamlet; for, upon my life, this spirit, dumb to us, will speak to him.

Act 1, scene 2, lines 208–234 (combined)

HORATIO:
For two nights running these gentlemen,
Marcellus and Bernardo, have during their watch
in the deep dark middle of the night
been encountered in this manner. A figure like your father,
looking exactly like him, from head to foot,
appears before them and very solemnly
walks slowly and majestically by them. Three times he walked
past their stunned and fearful gazes,
within the length of his royal staff; while they, turned
almost to jelly by their fear,
stood silent and uttered not a sound. They told me
all this in utmost secrecy,
and I stood watch with them on the third night;
when, just as they had told me, as to the time,
the look of the thing, proving what they'd said true,
the apparition appears. I knew your father:
as identical as my hands are to each other, it was to your father.
    [I spoke to it]
but it did not answer. Yet once I thought
it lifted up its head and made
a move, as if it was about to speak;
but just then the morning cock crowed loudly,
and at the sound it shrunk away in haste
and vanished from view.

Act 1 scene 2, lines 208–234 (combined)

HORATIO:
Two nights together had these gentlemen,
Marcellus and Bernardo, on their watch
In the dead vast and middle of the night
Been thus encountered. A figure like your father,
Armed at point exactly, cap-a-pie,
Appears before them and with solemn march
Goes slow and stately by them. Thrice he walked
By their oppressed and fear-surprisèd eyes,
Within his truncheon's length; whilst they, distilled
Almost to jelly with the act of fear,
Stand dumb and speak not to him. This to me
In dreadful secrecy impart they did,
And I with them the third night kept the watch;
Where, as they had delivered, both in time,
Form of the thing, each word made true and good,
The apparition comes. I knew your father:
These hands are not more like. [I spoke to it]
But answer made it none. Yet once methought
It lifted up it head and did address
Itself to motion, like as it would speak;
But even then the morning cock crew loud,
And at the sound it shrunk in haste away
And vanished from our sight.

Two nights together had these gentlemen, Marcellus and Bernardo, on their watch in the dead vast and middle of the night been thus encountered. A figure like your father, armed at point exactly, cap-a-pie, appears before them and with solemn march goes slow and stately by them. Thrice he walked by their oppressed and fear-surprisèd eyes, within his truncheon's length; whilst they, distilled almost to jelly with the act of fear, stand dumb and speak not to him. This to me in dreadful secrecy impart they did, and I with them the third night kept the watch; where, as they had delivered, both in time, form of the thing, each word made true and good, the apparition comes.

I knew your father: these hands are not more like. [I spoke to it] but answer made it none. Yet once methought it lifted up it head and did address itself to motion, like as it would speak; but even then the morning cock crew loud, and at the sound it shrunk in haste away and vanished from our sight.

Act 2 scene 1, lines 86–111 (cut and combined)

OPHELIA:
My lord, as I was sewing in my room,
Lord Hamlet, with his jacket all unbuttoned,
bare-headed, with dirty stockings,
unhitched, and falling down around his ankles;
looking as pale as his shirt, with his knees knocking against each other,
and with such a pitiful look about him
as if he had been sent from hell
to tell of horrible things, he comes to me.
He took me by the wrist and held me firmly;
then he holds me at arm's length from him,
and, holding his other hand above his brow,
he starts to scrutinize my face
as though he were about to draw it. This continued for a long time.
Finally, he shook my arm a few times,
and three times nodded his head up and down,
then he let forth a sigh so pitiful and deeply felt
that it seemed like it might split him to pieces
and end his life. After that, he let me go,
and keeping his head towards me, he turned,
and seemed to find his way without using his eyes,
and so out the door he went without looking,
all the time keeping his eyes fixed on me.

Act 2 scene 1, lines 86–111 (cut and combined)

OPHELIA:
My lord, as I was sewing in my closet,
Lord Hamlet, with his doublet all unbraced,
No hat upon his head, his stockings fouled,
Ungartered, and down-gyved to his ankle;
Pale as his shirt, his knees knocking each other,
And with a look so piteous in purport
As if he had been loosèd out of hell
To speak of horrors, he comes before me.
He took me by the wrist and held me hard;
Then goes he to the length of all his arm,
And, with his other hand thus o'er his brow,
He falls to such perusal of my face
As he would draw it. Long stayed he so.
At last, a little shaking of mine arm,
And thrice his head thus waving up and down,
He raised a sigh so piteous and profound
As it did seem to shatter all his bulk
And end his being. That done, he lets me go,
And with his head over his shoulder turned,
He seemed to find his way without his eyes,
For out o' doors he went without their help
And to the last bended their light on me.

My lord, as I was sewing in my closet, Lord Hamlet, with his doublet all unbraced, no hat upon his head, his stockings fouled, ungartered, and down-gyved to his ankle; pale as his shirt, his knees knocking each other, and with a look so piteous in purport as if he had been loosèd out of hell to speak of horrors, he comes before me.

He took me by the wrist and held me hard; then goes he to the length of all his arm, and, with his other hand thus o'er his brow, he falls to such perusal of my face as he would draw it. Long stayed he so. At last, a little shaking of mine arm, and thrice his head thus waving up and down, he raised a sigh so piteous and profound as it did seem to shatter all his bulk and end his being. That done, he lets me go, and with his head over his shoulder turned, he seemed to find his way without his eyes, for out o' doors he went without their help and to the last bended their light on me.

Act 4 scene 3, lines 19–40 (cut and combined)

HAMLET:

[Where's Polonius?] — At supper. Not where he's eating, but where he's being eaten. A certain assemblage of civic-minded worms are occupied with him right now. Your worm is your only real top-dog when it comes to dining. We fatten all other creatures to feed ourselves, and we are food for maggots. Your fat king and your lean beggar are merely variations — two dishes, but on the same table. Same end for both. A man may fish with the worm that has eaten a king, and eat the fish that has fed on that worm. [But as for Polonius? He's] in heaven. Send someone there to check. If your messenger doesn't find him there, go to the other place yourself to look. But surely, if you don't find him within a month, you'll start smelling him as you go up the stairs into the lobby. He'll stay there till you come.

Act 4 scene 3, lines 19–40 (cut and combined)

HAMLET:
[Where's Polonius?] — At supper. Not where he eats, but where he is eaten. A certain convocation of politic worms are e'en at him. Your worm is your only emperor for diet. We fat all creatures else to fat us, and we fat ourselves for maggots. Your fat king and your lean beggar is but variable service — two dishes, but to one table. That's the end. A man may fish with the worm that hath eat of a king, and eat of the fish that hath fed of that worm. [But for Polonius? He's] in heaven. Send thither to see. If your messenger find him not there, seek him i' the other place yourself. But indeed, if you find him not within this month, you shall nose him as you go up the stairs into the lobby. He will stay till you come.

Act 4 scene 5, lines 2–14 (combined)

GENTLEMAN:
                    She is anxious,
almost beside herself; her anxiety must be pitied.
She talks a lot about her father; she says she's heard
there's mischief afoot, and hems and haws, and beats her breast;
jumps at the slightest movement; she speaks vaguely,
and only half of it makes sense. Her speech is unintelligible,
yet ambiguous as it is, it makes one attempt to make
sense of it; they try to guess at the meaning,
and piece the words together as they see fit;
her words, along with the winks and nods and gestures she uses,
makes one believe that there is sense in it all,
and enigmatic as it is, it shows deep unhappiness.

Act 4 scene 5, lines 2–14 (combined)

GENTLEMAN:*
                    She is importunate,
Indeed distract; Her mood will needs be pitied.
She speaks much of her father; says she hears
There's tricks i'th' world, and hems, and beats her heart;
Spurns enviously at straws; speaks things in doubt,
That carry but half sense. Her speech is nothing,
Yet the unshapèd use of it doth move
The hearers to collection; they aim at it,
And botch the words up fit to their own thoughts;
Which, as her winks and nods and gestures yield them,
Indeed would make one think there might be thought,
Though nothing sure, yet much unhappily.

      She is importunate, indeed distract; her mood will needs be pitied. She speaks much of her father; says she hears there's tricks i'th' world, and hems, and beats her heart; spurns enviously at straws; speaks things in doubt, that carry but half sense. Her speech is nothing, yet the unshapèd use of it doth move the hearers to collection; they aim at it, and botch the words up fit to their own thoughts; which, as her winks and nods and gestures yield them, indeed would make one think there might be thought, though nothing sure, yet much unhappily.

---

*Sometimes attributed to Horatio.

Act 4 scene 7, lines 181–201 (combined)

GERTRUDE:
One disaster follows on another's heels,
they come so quickly. Your sister's drowned, Laertes.
There is a willow that hangs over a brook
reflecting its silvery leaves in the glassy stream.
She came there with fantastic garlands,
composed of crowflowers, nettles, daisies, and long purples —
which crude shepherds call by a vulgar name, —
but our chaste maidens call 'dead men's fingers.'
When, upon the overhanging boughs, her crown of weeds
she climbed up to hang, a spiteful branch broke off.
Then down the garland of weeds and she
fell into the weeping brook. Her clothes spread out wide
and like a mermaid, for a while, they bore her aloft;
during which time she chanted bits of old tunes,
as though she were unaware of the danger she was in,
or as if she were a native creature, at home
in that element; but it wasn't long
until her garments, drenched with water,
pulled the poor wretch from her musical perch
down to a muddy death.

Act 4 scene 7, lines 181–201 (combined)

GERTRUDE:
One woe doth tread upon another's heel,
So fast they follow. Your sister's drowned, Laertes.
There is a willow grows aslant a brook,
That shows his hoar leaves in the glassy stream.
There with fantastic garlands did she come
Of crowflowers, nettles, daisies, and long purples,
That liberal shepherds give a grosser name,
But our cold maids do dead-men's-fingers call them.
There on the pendent boughs her coronet weeds
Clamb'ring to hang, an envious sliver broke,
When down her weedy trophies and herself
Fell in the weeping brook. Her clothes spread wide
And, mermaid-like, awhile they bore her up;
Which time she chanted snatches of old tunes,
As one incapable of her own distress,
Or like a creature native and indued
Unto that element; but long it could not be
Till that her garments, heavy with their drink,
Pulled the poor wretch from her melodious lay
To muddy death.

One woe doth tread upon another's heel, so fast they follow. Your sister's drowned, Laertes. There is a willow grows aslant a brook, that shows his hoar leaves in the glassy stream. There with fantastic garlands did she come of crowflowers, nettles, daisies, and long purples, that liberal shepherds give a grosser name, but our cold maids do dead-men's-fingers call them.

There on the pendent boughs her coronet weeds clamb'ring to hang, an envious sliver broke, when down her weedy trophies and herself fell in the weeping brook. Her clothes spread wide and, mermaid-like, awhile they bore her up; which time she chanted snatches of old tunes, as one incapable of her own distress, or like a creature native and indued unto that element; but long it could not be till that her garments, heavy with their drink, pulled the poor wretch from her melodious lay to muddy death.

Act 5 scene 2, lines 163–181 or 226–245

HAMLET:
Pardon me, sir, I have wronged you;
pardon me, as you are a gentleman.
Everyone here knows,
as you no doubt have heard, how I've been afflicted
with a sort of madness. Whatever I have done
which your being and sense of honor has taken
such strong exception to, I must proclaim was done out of madness.
Was it Hamlet who wronged Laertes? Not Hamlet.
If Hamlet was not himself,
and while he was not himself he wronged Laertes,
then it's not Hamlet who did it. Hamlet denies doing it.
Who did it then? His madness. If this is so,
Hamlet himself has been wronged.
His madness is poor Hamlet's enemy.
Sir, in the hearing of these people,
permit my disavowal of any intentional evil
help me to gain your forgiveness
insomuch as I have unwittingly acted
to hurt my brother.

Act 5 scene 2, lines 163–181 or 226–245

HAMLET:
Give me your pardon, sir, I have done you wrong;
But pardon't, as you are a gentleman.
This presence knows,
And you must needs have heard, how I am punished
With sore distraction. What I have done
That might your nature, honor, and exception
Roughly awake, I here proclaim was madness.
Was't Hamlet wronged Laertes? Never Hamlet.
If Hamlet from himself be ta'en away,
And when he's not himself does wrong Laertes,
Then Hamlet does it not, Hamlet denies it.
Who does it, then? His madness. If't be so,
Hamlet is of the faction that is wronged;
His madness is poor Hamlet's enemy.
Sir, in this audience,
Let my disclaiming from a purposed evil
Free me so far in your most generous thoughts
That I have shot my arrow o'er the house
And hurt my brother.

Give me your pardon, sir, I have done you wrong; but pardon't, as you are a gentleman. This presence knows, and you must needs have heard, how I am punished with sore distraction. What I have done that might your nature, honor, and exception roughly awake, I here proclaim was madness.

Was't Hamlet wronged Laertes? Never Hamlet. If Hamlet from himself be ta'en away, and when he's not himself does wrong Laertes, then Hamlet does it not, Hamlet denies it. Who does it, then? His madness. If't be so, Hamlet is of the faction that is wronged; his madness is poor Hamlet's enemy.

Sir, in this audience, let my disclaiming from a purposed evil free me so far in your most generous thoughts that I have shot my arrow o'er the house and hurt my brother.

Act 1 scene 2, lines 173–195

PRINCE:
I know you all, and will for now put up with
the extreme frivolousness of your behavior.
Yet in doing this, I will be like the sun,
which sometimes allows poisonous, smoky clouds
to conceal its radiance from the world,
so that, when it wishes to reveal itself again,
when it is needed, it will be even more appreciated
after breaking through the dark and ugly mists
of vapors that had seemed to choke it off.
If all the year were made up of holidays,
play would become as boring as work.
But when they are rare, they are looked forward to
and nothing is more pleasing than these rare occurrences.
So, when I finally drop my debauched habits
and assume the role no one thought I ever would,
so much better will I then appear,
so much more shall I dash my detractor's hopes.
And, as a bit of metal appears to shine against a dull background,
my transformation, will shine so brightly as to conceal
    my past faults,
and will appear more wonderful and attract more attention
than if it had nothing contrasting with which to set it off.
I'll offend so much, that I will perfect offending to an art,
and then redeem myself when men least expect I will.

Act 1 scene 2, lines 173–195

PRINCE:
I know you all, and will a while uphold
The unyoked humor of your idleness.
Yet herein will I imitate the sun,
Who doth permit the base contagious clouds
To smother up his beauty from the world,
That, when he please again to be himself,
Being wanted, he may be more wondered at
By breaking through the foul and ugly mists
Of vapors that did seem to strangle him.
If all the year were playing holidays,
To sport would be as tedious as to work.
But when they seldom come, they wished-for come,
And nothing pleaseth but rare accidents.
So, when this loose behavior I throw off
And pay the debt I never promisèd,
By how much better than my word I am,
By so much shall I falsify men's hopes.
And like bright metal on a sullen ground,
My reformation, glittering o'er my fault,
Shall show more goodly and attract more eyes
Than that which hath no foil to set it off.
I'll so offend, to make offense a skill,
Redeeming time when men think least I will.

I know you all, and will a while uphold the unyoked humor of your idleness. Yet herein will I imitate the sun, who doth permit the base contagious clouds to smother up his beauty from the world, that, when he please again to be himself, being wanted, he may be more wondered at by breaking through the foul and ugly mists of vapors that did seem to strangle him.

If all the year were playing holidays, to sport would be as tedious as to work. But when they seldom come, they wished-for come, and nothing pleaseth but rare accidents. So, when this loose behavior I throw off and pay the debt I never promisèd, by how much better than my word I am, by so much shall I falsify men's hopes. And like bright metal on a sullen ground, my reformation, glittering o'er my fault, shall show more goodly and attract more eyes than that which hath no foil to set it off. I'll so offend, to make offense a skill, redeeming time when men think least I will.

Act 1 scene 3, lines 29–69 (cut)

HOTSPUR:
My king, I did not refuse to send you those prisoners.
But I remember, when the fighting was over,
when I was worn out from the battle and was incredibly exhausted,
out of breath and faint, leaning upon my sword,
there appeared this particular lord, neat, and finely dressed.
He was all perfumed like a fashion designer,
and between his finger and his thumb he held
a perfume bottle, which every now and then
he held up to his nose and then took it away again —
and as the soldiers carried dead bodies by,
he called them ignorant fools, ill-mannered,
to bring such a smelly ugly corpse
downwind of his own fine person.
With many fancy and ladylike phrases
he talked to me, and somewhere along the way, he demanded
my prisoners in your Majesty's behalf.
I then, still in pain with my untreated wounds hurting,
answered without thinking something or other,
he should, or he should not; for it made me mad
to see him look so dapper and smell so sweet,
and talk so like a prissy little lady
of guns and drums and wounds — God damn him!
And I beg you, not to let what he said
be given any credence as an accusation
of the loyalty I have for your Majesty.

Act 1 scene 3, lines 29–69 (cut)

HOTSPUR:
My liege, I did deny no prisoners.
But I remember, when the fight was done,
When I was dry with rage and extreme toil,
Breathless and faint, leaning upon my sword,
Came there a certain lord, neat, and trimly dressed.
He was perfumèd like a milliner,
And 'twixt his finger and his thumb he held
A pouncet box, which ever and anon
He gave his nose and took't away again —
And as the soldiers bore dead bodies by,
He called them untaught knaves, unmannerly,
To bring a slovenly unhandsome corse
Betwixt the wind and his nobility.
With many holiday and lady terms
He questioned me, amongst the rest, demanded
My prisoners in your Majesty's behalf.
I then, all smarting with my wounds being cold,
Answered neglectingly I know not what,
He should, or he should not; for he made me mad
To see him shine so brisk, and smell so sweet,
And talk so like a waiting gentlewoman
Of guns and drums and wounds — God save the mark!
And I beseech you, let not his report
Come current for an accusation
Betwixt my love and your high Majesty.

My liege, I did deny no prisoners. But I remember, when the fight was done, when I was dry with rage and extreme toil, breathless and faint, leaning upon my sword, came there a certain lord, neat, and trimly dressed. He was perfumèd like a milliner, and 'twixt his finger and his thumb he held a pouncet box, which ever and anon he gave his nose and took't away again — and as the soldiers bore dead bodies by, he called them untaught knaves, unmannerly, to bring a slovenly unhandsome corse betwixt the wind and his nobility.

With many holiday and lady terms he questioned me, amongst the rest, demanded my prisoners in your Majesty's behalf. I then, all smarting with my wounds being cold, answered neglectingly I know not what, he should, or he should not; for he made me mad to see him shine so brisk, and smell so sweet, and talk so like a waiting gentlewoman of guns and drums and wounds — God save the mark! And I beseech you, let not his report come current for an accusation betwixt my love and your high Majesty.

Act 1 scene 3, lines 212–231 (combined)

HOTSPUR:
      [My prisoners!] I'll keep all of them!
By God, he shall not get a Scotsman of them.
No, if a Scot could save his soul, he wouldn't get one.
I'll keep them, I swear it. Yes, I will, that's certain.
He said he would not ransom Mortimer,
and forbade me to even mention Mortimer.
But I will find him when he's sleeping,
and in his ear I'll scream 'Mortimer!'
Not only that, I'll get a bird to be taught to say
nothing but 'Mortimer,' and I'll give it to him,
to keep him hopping mad.
I will concentrate on nothing else,
except to find ways to irritate Bolingbroke.
And that same hot-shot Prince of Wales —
if it weren't for the fact that his father doesn't love him
and would be happy if something were to happen to him —
I would have him poisoned with a pint of beer.

Act 1 scene 3, lines 212–231 (combined)

HOTSPUR:
      [My prisoners!] I'll keep them all!
By God, he shall not have a Scot of them.
No, if a Scot would save his soul, he shall not.
I'll keep them, by this hand. Nay, I will, that's flat.
He said he would not ransom Mortimer,
Forbade my tongue to speak of Mortimer.
But I will find him when he lies asleep,
And in his ear I'll holloa 'Mortimer!'
Nay, I'll have a starling shall be taught to speak
Nothing but 'Mortimer,' and give it him,
To keep his anger still in motion.
All studies here I solemnly defy,
Save how to gall and pinch this Bolingbroke.
And that same sword-and-buckler Prince of Wales —
But that I think his father loves him not
And would be glad he met with some mischance —
I would have him poisoned with a pot of ale.

    [My prisoners!] I'll keep them all! By God, he shall not have a Scot of them. No, if a Scot would save his soul, he shall not. I'll keep them, by this hand. Nay, I will, that's flat. He said he would not ransom Mortimer, forbade my tongue to speak of Mortimer. But I will find him when he lies asleep, and in his ear I'll holloa 'Mortimer!' Nay, I'll have a starling shall be taught to speak nothing but 'Mortimer,' and give it him, to keep his anger still in motion.

    All studies here I solemnly defy, save how to gall and pinch this Bolingbroke. And that same sword-and-buckler Prince of Wales — but that I think his father loves him not and would be glad he met with some mischance — I would have him poisoned with a pot of ale.

Act 2 scene 3, lines 31–58 (cut)

LADY PERCY:
Oh my dear lord, why do you keep to yourself?
What have I done that for two weeks now
you've kept me out of your bed?   •
Tell me, sweet lord, what's caused you to lose
your appetite, your joy of life, and kept you from sleeping?
Why do you stare at the ground,
and seem to jump when you're just sitting by yourself?
Why do your cheeks look so pale,
and why have you traded our precious intimate moments together
for meditation and depressing thoughts?
During your restless slumbering I have stood by,
and heard you muttering words of war,
giving instructions to your bounding steed,
crying out 'Courage! To the field!' And you've talked
about raids and retreats, about trenches, tents,
about prisoners' ransom, and about dead soldiers,
and of all the other events of a fierce battle.
Your spirits have been so at war
that beads of sweat have formed upon your brow,
like bubbles is a recently disturbed stream.
And your face has contorted into strange expressions,
like one sees when men hold their breath
before attempted some incredible feat. Oh, what does this all mean?
My lord is pondering some important matters,
and I must be made aware of them, or else he doesn't love me.

Act 2 scene 3, lines 31–58 (cut)

LADY PERCY:
O my good lord, why are you thus alone?
For what offense have I this fortnight been
A banished woman from my Harry's bed?
Tell me, sweet lord, what is't that takes from thee
Thy stomach, pleasure, and thy golden sleep?
Why dost thou bend thine eyes upon the earth,
And start so often when thou sit'st alone?
Why hast thou lost the fresh blood in thy cheeks,
And given my treasures and my right of thee
To thick-eyed musing and cursed melancholy?
In thy faint slumbers I by thee have watched,
And heard thee murmur tales of iron wars,
Speak terms of manage to thy bounding steed,
Cry 'Courage! To the field!' And thou hast talked
Of sallies and retires, of trenches, tents,
Of prisoners' ransom, and of soldiers slain,
And all the currents of a heady fight.
Thy spirit within thee hath been so at war
That beads of sweat have stood upon thy brow,
Like bubbles in a late-disturbèd stream.
And in thy face strange motions have appeared,
Such as we see when men restrain their breath
On some great sudden hest. Oh, what portents are these?
Some heavy business hath my lord in hand,
And I must know it, else he loves me not.

O my good lord, why are you thus alone? For what offense have I this fortnight been a banished woman from my Harry's bed? Tell me, sweet lord, what is't that takes from thee thy stomach, pleasure, and thy golden sleep? Why dost thou bend thine eyes upon the earth, and start so often when thou sit'st alone? Why hast thou lost the fresh blood in thy cheeks, and given my treasures and my right of thee to thick-eyed musing and cursed melancholy?

In thy faint slumbers I by thee have watched, and heard thee murmur tales of iron wars, speak terms of manage to thy bounding steed, cry 'Courage! To the field!' And thou hast talked of sallies and retires, of trenches, tents, of prisoners' ransom, and of soldiers slain, and all the currents of a heady fight. Thy spirit within thee hath been so at war that beads of sweat have stood upon thy brow, like bubbles in a late-disturbèd stream. And in thy face strange motions have appeared, such as we see when men restrain their breath on some great sudden hest. Oh, what portents are these? Some heavy business hath my lord in hand, and I must know it, else he loves me not.

Act 3 scene 2, lines 130–159 (cut)

PRINCE:
> God forgive all those who have so colored
your Majesty's opinion of me!
I will redeem myself by killing Percy,
and at the conclusion of that glorious day
be bold enough to call myself your son.
And that shall be the day, whenever it comes,
that this example of honor and renown,
this gallant Hotspur, this acclaimed knight,
and your disregarded Harry happen to meet.
I wish that the honors heaped upon him
could be multiplied, and that my shames
might be doubled! For the time will come
when I shall force this northern star to exchange
his glories for my indignities.
This, in the name of God, I promise.
The which (if I perform and I survive)
I do hope your Majesty can forgive
the pain I've caused with my intemperance.
If not, death cancels all debts,
and I will die a hundred thousand deaths
before I'd break one iota of this vow.

Act 3 scene 2, lines 130–159 (cut)

PRINCE:

        God forgive them that so much have swayed
Your Majesty's good thoughts away from me!
I will redeem all this on Percy's head,
And in the closing of some glorious day
Be bold to tell you that I am your son.
And that shall be the day, whene'er it lights,
That this same child of honor and renown,
This gallant Hotspur, this all-praisèd knight,
And your unthought-of Harry chance to meet.
For every honor sitting on his helm,
Would they were multitudes, and on my head
My shames redoubled! For the time will come
That I shall make this Northern youth exchange
His glorious deeds for my indignities.
And I will call him to so strict account
That he shall render every glory up.
This, in the name of God, I promise here.
The which (if I perform and do survive),*
I do beseech your Majesty may salve
The long-grown wounds of my intemperance.
If not, the end of life cancels all bands,
And I will die a hundred thousand deaths
Ere break the smallest parcel of this vow.

      God forgive them that so much have swayed your Majesty's good thoughts away from me!
I will redeem all this on Percy's head, and in the closing of some glorious day be bold to tell you
that I am your son. And that shall be the day, whene'er it lights, that this same child of honor
and renown, this gallant Hotspur, this all-praisèd knight, and your unthought-of Harry chance
to meet.

      For every honor sitting on his helm, would they were multitudes, and on my head my
shames redoubled! For the time will come that I shall make this Northern youth exchange his
glorious deeds for my indignities. And I will call him to so strict account that he shall render
every glory up. This, in the name of God, I promise here. The which (if I perform and do survive),* I do beseech your Majesty may salve the long-grown wounds of my intemperance. If not,
the end of life cancels all bands, and I will die a hundred thousand deaths ere break the smallest
parcel of this vow.

---

*This is how this part of the line reads in the First Folio.

Act 2 scene 3, lines 10–44 (cut)

LADY PERCY:
Oh, pause, for God's sake do not go to these wars!
In the past, Father, you broke your word
when you had stronger reasons for keeping it than now —
when your own Percy, when my beloved Harry,
kept looking northward hoping to see his father
bringing up his troops, but he looked in vain.
Who was it then that persuaded you to stay at home?
That day, two reputations were lost, yours and your son's.
As for yours, God in heaven will have to restore that!
But for his, it remained in him as the sun
keeps shining in the sky, and by his example
all the knights of England were inspired
to attempt brave acts. He was truly the model
which the noble youths attempted to imitate.
He was the pattern and mirror, image and guidebook,
which others copied. And him — oh, wonderful him!
second to none, yet unassisted by you,
never, oh, never, do his ghost the wrong
to protect your dignity more scrupulously
in others eyes than you did in his!

Act 2 scene 3, lines 10–44 (cut)

LADY PERCY:
Oh, yet, for God's sake, go not to these wars!
The time was, Father, that you broke your word
When you were more endeared to it than now —
When your own Percy, when my heart's dear Harry,
Threw many a northward look to see his father
Bring up his powers, but he did long in vain.
Who then persuaded you to stay at home?
There were two honors lost, yours and your son's.
For yours the God of Heaven brighten it!
For his, it stuck upon him as the sun
In the gray vault of heaven, and by his light
Did all the chivalry of England move
To do brave acts. He was indeed the glass
Wherein the noble youth did dress themselves.
He was the mark and glass, copy and book,
That fashioned others. And him — oh, wondrous him!
Second to none, unseconded by you,
Never, oh, never, do his ghost the wrong
To hold your honor more precise and nice
With others than with him!

Oh, yet, for God's sake, go not to these wars! The time was, Father, that you broke your word when you were more endeared to it than now — when your own Percy, when my heart's dear Harry, threw many a northward look to see his father bring up his powers, but he did long in vain. Who then persuaded you to stay at home? There were two honors lost, yours and your son's. For yours the God of Heaven brighten it!

For his, it stuck upon him as the sun in the gray vault of heaven, and by his light did all the chivalry of England move to do brave acts.

He was indeed the glass wherein the noble youth did dress themselves. He was the mark and glass, copy and book, that fashioned others. And him — oh, wondrous him! Second to none, unseconded by you, never, oh, never, do his ghost the wrong to hold your honor more precise and nice with others than with him!

Act 1 scene 1, lines 103–139 (cut and combined)

THIRD MESSENGER:
My gracious lords, to add to your grief,
I must inform you of a dismal battle
between bold Lord Talbot and the French
      in which Lord Talbot was defeated.
Last August tenth, this awe-inspiring lord,
having not more than six thousand in his troop,
was surrounded by twenty-three thousand French
soldiers and was attacked.
The fighting continued for more than three hours;
during which valiant Talbot, acting superhuman,
performed amazing feats with his sword and lance.
Here, there, and everywhere, enraged he killed.
The entire army was astounded by him.
His soldiers, witnessing his fearless spirit,
cried out with all their might, 'Talbot! Talbot!'
and rushed into the heart of the battle.
At this moment the conquest would have been guaranteed,
if Sir John Falstaff had not displayed his cowardice.
He fled, without having struck one blow.
What followed was widespread destruction and a massacre.
They were encircled by the enemy.
A mere nobody, to win the Dolphin's favor,
stabbed Talbot in the back with a spear —
a man whom not one of the strongest and best of the Frenchmen
dared to even look in face.

Act 1 scene 1, lines 103–139 (cut and combined)

THIRD MESSENGER:
My gracious lords, to add to your laments,
I must inform you of a dismal fight
Betwixt the stout Lord Talbot and the French
        wherein Lord Talbot was o'erthrown.
The tenth of August last, this dreadful lord,
Having full scarce six thousand in his troop,
By three and twenty thousand of the French
Was round encompassèd and set upon.
More than three hours the fight continuèd;
Where valiant Talbot, above human thought,
Enacted wonders with his sword and lance.
Here, there, and everywhere, enraged he slew.
All the whole army stood agazed on him.
His soldiers, spying his undaunted spirit,
'A Talbot! a Talbot!' cried out amain,
And rushed into the bowels of the battle.
Here had the conquest fully been sealed up,
If Sir John Falstaff had not played the coward.
He fled, not having struck one stroke.
Hence grew the general wrack and massacre.
Enclosèd were they with their enemies.
A base villain, to win the Dolphin's grace,
Thrust Talbot with a spear into the back,
Whom all France, with their chief assembled strength,
Durst not presume to look once in the face.

     My gracious lords, to add to your laments, I must inform you of a dismal fight betwixt the stout Lord Talbot and the French wherein Lord Talbot was o'erthrown. The tenth of August last, this dreadful lord, having full scarce six thousand in his troop, — by three and twenty thousand of the French was round encompassèd and set upon. More than three hours the fight continuèd; where valiant Talbot, above human thought, enacted wonders with his sword and lance. Here, there, and everywhere, enraged he slew. All the whole army stood agazed on him. His soldiers, spying his undaunted spirit, 'A Talbot! a Talbot!' cried out amain, and rushed into the bowels of the battle.

     Here had the conquest fully been sealed up, if Sir John Falstaff had not played the coward. He fled, not having struck one stroke. Hence grew the general wrack and massacre. Enclosèd were they with their enemies. A base villain, to win the Dolphin's grace, thrust Talbot with a spear into the back, whom all France, with their chief assembled strength, durst not presume to look once in the face.

Act 1 scene 2, lines 72–92

JOAN LA PUCELLE:
I am by birth a shepherd's daughter,
I have not been educated in any way.
Heaven and the Virgin Mary have taken pleasure
in blessing my lowly circumstances.
Look, while I was tending to my young lambs,
as the sun's parching heat tanned my cheeks,
God's mother deigned to appear to me
and, in a glorious vision,
prompted me to leave my lowly occupation
and free my country from its misery.
She promised her aid and assured success.
She revealed herself in her total magnificence;
and, whereas I was sunburned and dark-complected before,
once having been bathed in the purifying rays that she cast on me,
I now am blessed with the beauty that you see.
Ask me whatever question you wish,
and I will answer with complete honesty;
try my courage in combat, if you dare,
and you will find that I surpass what you'd expect from a woman.
Consider this, you will have success
if you accept me as your comrade in war.

Act 1 Scene 2, lines 72–92

JOAN LA PUCELLE:
      I am by birth a shepherd's daughter,
My wit untrained in any kind of art.
Heaven and our Lady gracious hath it pleased
To shine on my contemptible estate.
Lo, whilst I waited on my tender lambs,
And to sun's parching heat displayed my cheeks,
God's mother deignèd to appear to me
And, in a vision full of majesty,
Willed me to leave my base vocation
And free my country from calamity.
Her aid she promised, and assured success.
In complete glory she revealed herself;
And, whereas I was black and swart before,
With those clear rays which she infused on me,
That beauty am I blessed with, which you may see.
Ask me what question thou canst possible,
And I will answer unpremeditated;
My courage try by combat, if thou dar'st,
And thou shalt find that I exceed my sex.
Resolve on this, thou shalt be fortunate
If thou receive me for thy warlike mate.

    I am by birth a shepherd's daughter, my wit untrained in any kind of art. Heaven and our Lady gracious hath it pleased to shine on my contemptible estate. Lo, whilst I waited on my tender lambs, and to sun's parching heat displayed my cheeks, God's mother deignèd to appear to me and, in a vision full of majesty, willed me to leave my base vocation and free my country from calamity. Her aid she promised, and assured success. In complete glory she revealed herself; and, whereas I was black and swart before, with those clear rays which she infused on me, that beauty am I blessed with, which you may see.

    Ask me what question thou canst possible, and I will answer unpremeditated; my courage try by combat, if thou dar'st, and thou shalt find that I exceed my sex. Resolve on this, thou shalt be fortunate if thou receive me for thy warlike mate.

Act 1 scene 1, lines 214–260 (cut)

YORK:
Anjou and Maine have been given to the French;
we've lost Paris; the state of Normandy
hangs by a thread now that they are lost.
So now York must sit, and fret and keep silent,
while deals are made using his lands.
Anjou and Maine both given to the French!
Bad news for me because I'd hoped to conquer France,
just as I hope to take over the rich English lands.
The day will come when York will claim what is his;
and, when I see an opportunity, [I'll] claim the crown,
for that's the reward I'm seeking to gain.
Then, York, be patient, till the time is right:
keep watch and stay alert while others sleep,
till Henry is wasted by his indulgence in the joys of love,
with his new bride, England's overpriced Queen,
and Humphrey is at odds with his fellow noblemen:
then I will raise on high the milk-white rose
whose sweet smell shall perfume the air,
and on my banner emblazon this symbol of the Yorks,
and go to battle against the house of Lancaster;
and, by force, I'll make him give up the crown
whose school-boy regime has brought lovely England down.

Act 1 scene 1, lines 214–260 (cut)

YORK:
Anjou and Maine are given to the French;
Paris is lost; the state of Normandy
Stands on a tickle point now they are gone.
So York must sit, and fret and bite his tongue,
While his own lands are bargained for and sold.
Anjou and Maine both given unto the French!
Cold news for me, for I had hope of France,
Even as I have of fertile England's soil.
A day will come when York shall claim his own;
And, when I spy advantage, [I'll] claim the crown,
For that's the golden mark I seek to hit.
Then, York, be still awhile, till time do serve:
Watch thou and wake, when others be asleep,
Till Henry, surfeiting in the joys of love,
With his new bride and England's dear-bought Queen,
And Humphrey with the peers be fall'n at jars:
Then will I raise aloft the milk-white rose,
With whose sweet smell the air shall be perfumed,
And in my standard bear the arms of York,
To grapple with the house of Lancaster;
And, force perforce, I'll make him yield the crown,
Whose bookish rule hath pulled fair England down.

Anjou and Maine are given to the French; Paris is lost; the state of Normandy stands on a tickle point now they are gone. So York must sit, and fret and bite his tongue, while his own lands are bargained for and sold.

Anjou and Maine both given unto the French! Cold news for me, for I had hope of France, even as I have of fertile England's soil. A day will come when York shall claim his own; and, when I spy advantage, [I'll] claim the crown, for that's the golden mark I seek to hit.

Then, York, be still awhile, till time do serve: watch thou and wake, when others be asleep, till Henry, surfeiting in the joys of love, with his new bride and England's dear-bought Queen, and Humphrey with the peers be fall'n at jars: then will I raise aloft the milk-white rose, with whose sweet smell the air shall be perfumed, and in my standard bear the arms of York, to grapple with the house of Lancaster; and, force perforce, I'll make him yield the crown, whose bookish rule hath pulled fair England down.

Act 1 scene 3, lines 77–89

QUEEN:
Of all these lords, not one of them irks me half as much
as that haughty dame, the Lord Protector's wife.
She sweeps through the court with her retinue of women
acting more like an empress than a Duke's wife,
so that newcomers to court think that she's the Queen.
She spends all the duke's income on her clothes
and secretly looks down on us for being poor.
I hope I may live to be revenged on her!
Despicable low-born slut that she is,
she boasted to her hangers-on the other day
that the train of her least expensive dress
was worth more than all of my father's lands,
before Suffolk gave him the two dukedoms for his daughter.

Act 1 scene 3, lines 77–89

QUEEN:
Not all these lords do vex me half so much
As that proud dame, the Lord Protector's wife.
She sweeps it through the court with troops of ladies,
More like an empress than Duke Humphrey's wife,
Strangers in court do take her for the Queen.
She bears a duke's revenues on her back,
And in her heart she scorns our poverty.
Shall I not live to be avenged on her?
Contemptuous base-born callet as she is,
She vaunted 'mongst her minions t'other day,
The very train of her worst wearing gown
Was better worth than all my father's lands,
Till Suffolk gave two dukedoms for his daughter.

Not all these lords do vex me half so much as that proud dame, the Lord Protector's wife. She sweeps it through the court with troops of ladies, more like an empress than Duke Humphrey's wife, — strangers in court do take her for the Queen. She bears a duke's revenues on her back, and in her heart she scorns our poverty.

Shall I not live to be avenged on her? Contemptuous base-born callet as she is, she vaunted 'mongst her minions t'other day, the very train of her worst wearing gown was better worth than all my father's lands, till Suffolk gave two dukedoms for his daughter.

Act 3 scene1, lines 4–38 (cut)

QUEEN:
Can't you see? Or do you just refuse to observe
how much he's changed?
How regally he now carries himself,
how insolent he's recently become,
how proud, how bold, and unlike himself?
We remember when he was gentle and pleasant,
when, if we should so much as look askance at him,
he would immediately be down on his knee kneeling to us,
so that everyone in court admired his humility.
But encounter him now,
he wrinkles his brow and looks angrily
and walks by without so much as a nod,
refusing to pay the respects that are due to us.
When a lapdog barks nobody's afraid,
but when a lion roars, even a King is fearful;
And Humphrey is not an unimportant man in England.
Therefore I think it is bad policy,
that he should be allowed anywhere near your royal self.
The high regard I have for my lord
forces me to point out these dangerous attitudes of the Duke's.
If it seems foolish, call it women's intuition —
and these intuitions — if they can be proved unfounded,
I will acknowledge, and admit I was wrong about the Duke.

Act 3 scene 1, lines 4–38 (cut)

QUEEN:
Can you not see? Or will ye not observe
The strangeness of his altered countenance?
With what a majesty he bears himself,
How insolent of late he is become,
How proud, how peremptory, and unlike himself?
We know the time since he was mild and affable,
And if we did but glance a far-off look,
Immediately he was upon his knee,
That all the court admired him for submission.
But meet him now,
He knits his brow and shows an angry eye
And passeth by with stiff unbowèd knee,
Disdaining duty that to us belongs.
Small curs are not regarded when they grin,
But great men tremble when the lion roars;
And Humphrey is no little man in England.
Me seemeth then it is no policy,
That he should come about your royal person.
The reverent care I bear unto my lord
Made me collect these dangers in the Duke.
If it be fond, call it a woman's fear-
Which fear, if better reasons can supplant,
I will subscribe, and say I wronged the Duke.

Can you not see? Or will ye not observe the strangeness of his altered countenance? With what a majesty he bears himself, how insolent of late he is become, how proud, how peremptory, and unlike himself? We know the time since he was mild and affable, and if we did but glance a far-off look, immediately he was upon his knee, that all the court admired him for submission. But meet him now, he knits his brow and shows an angry eye and passeth by with stiff unbowèd knee, disdaining duty that to us belongs.

Small curs are not regarded when they grin, but great men tremble when the lion roars; and Humphrey is no little man in England. Me seemeth then it is no policy, that he should come about your royal person. The reverent care I bear unto my lord made me collect these dangers in the Duke. If it be fond, call it a woman's fear, which fear, if better reasons can supplant, I will subscribe, and say I wronged the Duke.

Act 3 scene 1, lines 332–383 (cut)

YORK:
Now, York, or never, do away with your fearful thoughts,
and convert any doubts to unbridled courage.
Become what you hope to be, or surrender yourself
to death; it is not worth living otherwise.
Let lily-livered fear affect the average man,
and allow it no place in a royal heart.
Faster than a springtime rain comes thought after thought,
and not a single thought that's not about the kingship.
My brain, busier than a spider spinning webs
weaves intricate traps to ensnare my enemies.
Good, my noble friends, good; how very clever of you,
to send me off with an army;
it was an army that I lacked, and you have given me one;
how very kind of you; yet be well assured
you're putting dangerous weapons into a madman's hands.
While I'm in Ireland training my fearsome force,
I will foment such riots back in England
that it will send ten thousand souls to heaven or to hell;
and these riots will continue to rage
until the golden crown sitting upon my head,
shining like the sun's luminescent beams,
can calm the passions that have been stirred up.
For with Humphrey dead, as he soon will be,
and Henry deposed, the kingship goes to me.

Act 3 scene 1, lines 332–383 (cut)

YORK:
Now, York, or never, steel thy fearful thoughts,
And change misdoubt to resolution:
Be that thou hop'st to be, or what thou art
Resign to death; it is not worth th'enjoying.
Let pale-faced fear keep with the mean-born man,
And find no harbor in a royal heart.
Faster than spring-time show'rs comes thought on thought,
And not a thought but thinks on dignity.
My brain more busy than the laboring spider
Weaves tedious snares to trap mine enemies.
Well, nobles, well; 'tis politicly done,
To send me packing with an host of men.
'Twas men I lacked, and you will give them me;
I take it kindly; yet be well assured
You put sharp weapons in a madman's hands.
Whiles I in Ireland nourish a mighty band,
I will stir up in England some black storm
Shall blow ten thousand souls to heaven or hell;
And this fell tempest shall not cease to rage
Until the golden circuit on my head,
Like to the glorious sun's transparent beams,
Do calm the fury of this mad-bred flaw.
For Humphrey being dead, as he shall be,
And Henry put apart, the next for me.

Now, York, or never, steel thy fearful thoughts, and change misdoubt to resolution: be that thou hop'st to be, or what thou art resign to death; it is not worth th'enjoying. Let pale-faced fear keep with the mean-born man, and find no harbor in a royal heart.

Faster than spring-time show'rs comes thought on thought, and not a thought but thinks on dignity. My brain more busy than the laboring spider weaves tedious snares to trap mine enemies.

Well, nobles, well; 'tis politicly done, to send me packing with an host of men. 'Twas men I lacked, and you will give them me; I take it kindly; yet be well assured you put sharp weapons in a madman's hands.

Whiles I in Ireland nourish a mighty band, I will stir up in England some black storm shall blow ten thousand souls to heaven or hell; and this fell tempest shall not cease to rage until the golden circuit on my head, — like to the glorious sun's transparent beams, do calm the fury of this mad-bred flaw. For Humphrey being dead, as he shall be, and Henry put apart, the next for me.

Act 3 scene 2, lines 160–195 (cut)

WARWICK:
See how the blood has all coagulated in his face.
I have often seen someone who's died of natural causes,
looking ashen, emaciated, pale, and bloodless —
the blood having all rushed down to the fast-beating heart,
which, in its struggle to keep alive,
the heart attracts to assist in its fight for life —
the blood then remains there and cools in the heart never to return
to redden and beautify the cheeks again.
But look, his face is blackened and filled with blood,
his eyeballs are popping further out than when he was alive,
and they have the ghastly stare of a strangled man;
his hair is standing on end, his nostrils flared with his struggling;
his hands spread wide apart, as if he grasped
and tugged for life and was forcefully subdued.
There is no other explanation but he was murdered:
the least of these indications prove it.

Act 3 scene 2, lines 160–195 (cut)

WARWICK:
See how the blood is settled in his face.
Oft have I seen a timely-parted ghost,
Of ashy semblance, meager, pale, and bloodless,
Being all descended to the laboring heart,
Who, in the conflict that it holds with death,
Attracts the same for aidance 'gainst the enemy;
Which with the heart there cools, and ne'er returneth
To blush and beautify the cheek again.
But see, his face is black and full of blood,
His eyeballs further out than when he lived,
Staring full ghastly like a strangled man;
His hair upreared, his nostrils stretched with struggling;
His hands abroad displayed, as one that grasped
And tugged for life, and was by strength subdued.
It cannot be but he was murdered here:
The least of all these signs were probable.

See how the blood is settled in his face. Oft have I seen a timely-parted ghost, of ashy semblance, meager, pale, and bloodless — being all descended to the laboring heart, who, in the conflict that it holds with death, attracts the same for aidance 'gainst the enemy; which with the heart there cools, and ne'er returneth to blush and beautify the cheek again.

But see, his face is black and full of blood, his eyeballs further out than when he lived, staring full ghastly like a strangled man; his hair upreared, his nostrils stretched with struggling; his hands abroad displayed, as one that grasped and tugged for life, and was by strength subdued.

It cannot be but he was murdered here: the least of all these signs were probable.

Act 4 scene 2, lines 34–84 (cut and combined)

CADE:
I, John Cade, so named after my *supposed* father — demand silence. My real father was a Mortimer — my mother a Plantagenet — my wife is descended of the Lacies — therefore I come from an honorable house. I am valiant. I will not give up. I am fearless. Be brave, then because your leader is brave, and vows to bring change. Under my rule in England, seven loaves of half-cent bread will sell for one penny; when you ask for a glass of beer, you'll be given a quart; it will be a crime to remain sober. All the lands shall be publicly owned, and when I am King, as King I will be — there won't be any money; everyone will eat and drink on me. [The first thing we'll do, is kill all the lawyers.] Yup, that's what I'll do. Isn't it a shame, that the skin of an innocent lamb should be turned into parchment paper? And that paper, when it's written on, can cause a man's downfall? Some say bees sting; but I say it's the bee's wax: because I once put my seal on a piece of paper, and I lost everything I owned.

Act 4 scene 2, lines 34–84 (cut and combined)

CADE:
We, John Cade, so termed of our supposèd father — command silence. My father was a Mortimer — my mother a Plantagenet — my wife descended of the Lacies — therefore am I of an honorable house. Valiant I am. I am able to endure much. I fear neither sword nor fire. Be brave, then; for your captain is brave, and vows reformation. There shall be in England seven halfpenny loaves sold for a penny; the three-hooped pot shall have ten hoops; and I will make it felony to drink small beer. All the realm shall be in common, and when I am King, as King I will be — there shall be no money; all shall eat and drink on my score. [The first thing we do, let's kill all the lawyers.] Nay, that I mean to do. Is not this a lamentable thing, that of the skin of an innocent lamb should be made parchment? That parchment, being scribbled o'er, should undo a man? Some say the bee stings; but I say, 'tis the bee's wax: for I did but seal once to a thing, and I was never mine own man since.

Act 5 scene 1, lines 87–105 (cut)

YORK:
What's this! Is Somerset still free?
Then, York, unlock what's in your mind,
let your tongue express what you feel.
Shall I have to look Somerset in the eye?
Deceitful King, why have you broken your word to me,
knowing that I cannot tolerate being lied to?
Did I call you a King? No, you are not King,
you're not fit to govern and rule the people.
That head of yours is not worthy to wear a crown;
your hand was meant to grasp a religious pilgrim's walking stick
and not to hold the awe-inspiring royal scepter.
That crown should be encircling my forehead.
My hand should be holding a scepter up
and using it to enact the laws of the land.
Make way! I swear, you will no longer rule
over me whom heaven created to be your ruler.

Act 5 scene 1, lines 87–105 (cut)

YORK:
How now! Is Somerset at liberty?
Then, York, unloose thy long-imprisoned thoughts,
And let thy tongue be equal with thy heart.
Shall I endure the sight of Somerset?
False King, why hast thou broken faith with me,
Knowing how hardly I can brook abuse?
King did I call thee? No, thou art not King,
Not fit to govern and rule multitudes.
That head of thine doth not become a crown;
Thy hand is made to grasp a palmer's staff,
And not to grace an awful princely scepter.
That gold must round engirt these brows of mine.
Here is a hand to hold a scepter up
And with the same to act controlling laws.
Give place! By heaven, thou shalt rule no more
O'er him whom heaven created for thy ruler.

How now! Is Somerset at liberty? Then, York, unloose thy long-imprisoned thoughts, and let thy tongue be equal with thy heart. Shall I endure the sight of Somerset? False King, why hast thou broken faith with me,
knowing how hardly I can brook abuse?
King did I call thee? No, thou art not King, not fit to govern and rule multitudes. That head of thine doth not become a crown; thy hand is made to grasp a palmer's staff, and not to grace an awful princely scepter. That gold must round engirt these brows of mine. Here is a hand to hold a scepter up and with the same to act controlling laws. Give place! By heaven, thou shalt rule no more o'er him whom heaven created for thy ruler.

Act 1 scene 1, lines 33–56

MARULLUS:
Why are you celebrating? What booty has he captured?
What prisoners are following him into Rome
marching in captivity alongside his chariot?
You blockheads, you morons, you worse than inanimate objects!
Oh you hard-hearted, cruel men of Rome,
don't you remember Pompey? How often
did you climb up on the walls and the battlements,
the lookout towers and the windows, yes, even to the chimney tops,
with your babies in your arms, and sat there
the whole day long, patiently looking forward,
to catching a single glimpse of great Pompey passing through the
        streets of Rome.
And when you saw his chariot appear,
didn't you let forth such a great cheer,
that the Tiber quivered within her banks
with the echoes of your shouts
reverberating in her hollowed-out shores?
And are you now donning your finest clothes?
And are you now making a new holiday?
And are you now strewing flowers in his path
who comes in triumph over Pompey?
Leave!
Run to your houses, get down upon your knees,
and pray to the gods to hold back the plague
that would no doubt come as a result of your ingratitude.

Act 1 scene 1, lines 33–56

MARULLUS:
Wherefore rejoice? What conquest brings he home?
What tributaries follow him to Rome,
To grace in captive bonds his chariot wheels?
You blocks, you stones, you worse than senseless things!
O you hard hearts, you cruel men of Rome,
Knew you not Pompey? Many a time and oft
Have you climbed up to walls and battlements,
To towers and windows, yea, to chimney tops,
Your infants in your arms, and there have sat
The livelong day, with patient expectation,
To see great Pompey pass the streets of Rome.
And when you saw his chariot but appear,
Have you not made an universal shout,
That Tiber trembled underneath her banks
To hear the replication of your sounds
Made in her concave shores?
And do you now put on your best attire?
And do you now cull out a holiday?
And do you now strew flowers in his way
That comes in triumph over Pompey's blood?
Be gone!
Run to your houses, fall upon your knees,
Pray to the gods to intermit the plague
That needs must light on this ingratitude.

Wherefore rejoice? What conquest brings he home? What tributaries follow him to Rome, to grace in captive bonds his chariot wheels?

You blocks, you stones, you worse than senseless things! O you hard hearts, you cruel men of Rome, knew you not Pompey? Many a time and oft have you climbed up to walls and battlements, to towers and windows, yea, to chimney tops, your infants in your arms, and there have sat the livelong day, with patient expectation, to see great Pompey pass the streets of Rome. And when you saw his chariot but appear, have you not made an universal shout, that Tiber trembled underneath her banks to hear the replication of your sounds made in her concave shores?

And do you now put on your best attire? And do you now cull out a holiday? And do you now strew flowers in his way that comes in triumph over Pompey's blood? Be gone! Run to your houses, fall upon your knees, pray to the gods to intermit the plague that needs must light on this ingratitude.

Act 1 scene 2, lines 92–118 (cut)

CASSIUS:
I cannot say what other men
think about life, but as for me,
I'd sooner not exist, then live to have to
revere a mere mortal such as myself.
I was born as free as Caesar; so were you.
We've both been fed the same, and we can both
endure the winter's cold as well as he:
for once, on a raw and gusty day,
when the raging Tiber was overflowing her banks,
Caesar said to me, 'Do you dare, Cassius, to
leap with me into this angry river,
and swim to that point?' Immediately,
with everything I had on, I plunged in
and told him to follow: and so he did.
The current surged, and we fought it
with vigorous strength, pushing through it
making headway with spirited competitiveness.
But before we could arrive at the appointed place,
Caesar cried, 'Help me, Cassius, or I'll drown!'
I, just as our famous ancestor, Aeneas,
rescued old Anchises when Troy was burning,
by carrying him upon his shoulders, thus from the waves of the Tiber
did I rescue the exhausted Caesar. And this man
is now turned into a god, and I, Cassius, am
merely a lowly being, and must bow to him
if Caesar throws a careless glance my way.

Act 1 scene 2, lines 92–118 (cut)

CASSIUS:
I cannot tell what you and other men
Think of this life, but for my single self,
I had as lief not be, as live to be
In awe of such a thing as I myself.
I was born free as Caesar; so were you.
We both have fed as well, and we can both
Endure the winter's cold as well as he:
For once, upon a raw and gusty day,
The troubled Tiber chafing with her shores,
Caesar said to me 'Dar'st thou, Cassius, now
Leap in with me into this angry flood,
And swim to yonder point?' Upon the word,
Accout'red as I was, I plungèd in
And bade him follow: so indeed he did.
The torrent roared, and we did buffet it
With lusty sinews, throwing it aside
And stemming it with hearts of controversy.
But ere we could arrive the point proposed,
Caesar cried 'Help me, Cassius, or I sink!'
I, as Aeneas, our great ancestor,
Did from the flames of Troy upon his shoulder
The old Anchises bear, so from the waves of Tiber
Did I the tired Caesar. And this man
Is now become a god, and Cassius is
A wretched creature, and must bend his body
If Caesar carelessly but nod on him.

I cannot tell what you and other men think of this life, but for my single self, I had as lief not be, as live to be in awe of such a thing as I myself.

I was born free as Caesar; so were you. We both have fed as well, and we can both endure the winter's cold as well as he: for once, upon a raw and gusty day, the troubled Tiber chafing with her shores, Caesar said to me 'Dar'st thou, Cassius, now leap in with me into this angry flood, and swim to yonder point?' Upon the word, accout'red as I was, I plungèd in and bade him follow: so indeed he did.

The torrent roared, and we did buffet it with lusty sinews, throwing it aside and stemming it with hearts of controversy. But ere we could arrive the point proposed, Caesar cried 'Help me, Cassius, or I sink!' I, as Aeneas, our great ancestor, did from the flames of Troy upon his shoulder the old Anchises bear, — so from the waves of Tiber did I the tired Caesar.

And this man is now become a god, and Cassius is a wretched creature, and must bend his body if Caesar carelessly but nod on him.

Act 1 scene 2, lines 63–65 and 162–175 (combined)

BRUTUS:
Into what sort of trouble are you trying to lead me, Cassius,
that you want me to search within myself
for something which doesn't exist in me?
That you're my true friend, I have no doubts.
What you're trying to persuade me to do, I have some inkling.
What I think of this, and of our current situation,
we'll discuss later. As for now,
I would not like to (I ask in all friendship)
be pushed any further. What you have said to me
I will consider; what you have yet to say to me
I will patiently hear, and find a suitable time
to listen to and discuss these important matters.
Till then, my noble friend, think about this:
Brutus would rather be a peasant
than one of the foremost citizens of Rome
considering the unbearable rules that these times
are likely to force on us.

Act 1 scene 2, lines 63–65 and 162–175 (combined)

BRUTUS:
Into what dangers would you lead me, Cassius,
That you would have me seek into myself
For that which is not in me?
That you do love me I am nothing jealous.
What you would work me to, I have some aim.
How I have thought of this, and of these times,
I shall recount hereafter. For this present,
I would not so (with love I might entreat you)
Be any further moved. What you have said
I will consider; what you have to say
I will with patience hear, and find a time
Both meet to hear and answer such high things.
Till then, my noble friend, chew upon this:
Brutus had rather be a villager
Than to repute himself a son of Rome
Under these hard conditions as this time
Is like to lay upon us.

Into what dangers would you lead me, Cassius, that you would have me seek into myself for that which is not in me?

That you do love me I am nothing jealous. What you would work me to, I have some aim. How I have thought of this, and of these times, I shall recount hereafter. For this present, I would not so (with love I might entreat you) be any further moved.

What you have said I will consider; what you have to say I will with patience hear, and find a time both meet to hear and answer such high things. Till then, my noble friend, chew upon this: Brutus had rather be a villager than to repute himself a son of Rome under these hard conditions as this time is like to lay upon us.

Act 1 scene 2, lines 191–213 (combined)

CAESAR:
Let me be surrounded by men who are fat,
well-groomed men, who sleep well at night.
Cassius over there has a lean and hungry look;
he thinks too much: men like him are dangerous.
I wish he were fatter! But I don't fear him.
Yet, if I were the sort who could feel fear,
I don't know anyone I would want to avoid
as quickly as that lean Cassius. He reads a lot,
he's always aware of what's going on, and he's able to
see right through to men's motives. He doesn't like theater,
as you do, Antony; he doesn't listen to music;
he seldom smiles, and when he does
it's as if he's smirking to himself, and hating himself
for having been moved to smile at anything.
Men like him never rest easy in their hearts
as long as anyone else holds a position higher than they themselves.
And therefore they are very dangerous.
I'm only telling you what should be feared
and not what I fear; for remember I am Caesar.

Act 1 scene 2, lines 191–213 (combined)

CAESAR:
Let me have men about me that are fat,
Sleek-headed men, and such as sleep a-nights.
Yond Cassius has a lean and hungry look;
He thinks too much: such men are dangerous.
Would he were fatter! But I fear him not.
Yet if my name were liable to fear,
I do not know the man I should avoid
So soon as that spare Cassius. He reads much,
He is a great observer, and he looks
Quite through the deeds of men. He loves no plays,
As thou dost, Antony; he hears no music;
Seldom he smiles, and smiles in such a sort
As if he mocked himself, and scorned his spirit
That could be moved to smile at anything.
Such men as he be never at heart's ease
Whiles they behold a greater than themselves,
And therefore are they very dangerous.
I rather tell thee what is to be feared
Than what I fear; for always I am Caesar.

Let me have men about me that are fat, sleek-headed men, and such as sleep a-nights. Yond Cassius has a lean and hungry look; he thinks too much: such men are dangerous. Would he were fatter! But I fear him not.

Yet if my name were liable to fear, I do not know the man I should avoid so soon as that spare Cassius. He reads much, he is a great observer, and he looks quite through the deeds of men. He loves no plays, as thou dost, Antony; he hears no music; seldom he smiles, and smiles in such a sort as if he mocked himself, and scorned his spirit that could be moved to smile at anything. Such men as he be never at heart's ease whiles they behold a greater than themselves, and therefore are they very dangerous.

I rather tell thee what is to be feared than what I fear; for always I am Caesar.

Act 1 scene 2, lines 220–250 (cut and combined)

CASCA:
Well, there was a crown offered to him; and when offered, he pushed it away with the back of his hand, like this; and then the people started shouting. He pushed it away three times, each time more gently than before; and each time he pushed it away everyone around me shouted. I saw Mark Antony offer him this crown — yet it wasn't actually a crown, it was a sort of laurel wreath — and, as I said, he pushed it away once; but still, to my way of thinking, he would rather have taken it. Then he offered it to him again; and then he pushed it away again; but to my way of thinking, he was very reluctant to take his hands off it. And then he offered it a third time. He pushed it away a third time; and even as he refused it, the masses whooped and clapped their chapped hands and threw their sweaty caps into the air, and let out such a lot of stinking breath because Caesar had refused the crown, that it practically choked Caesar; he swooned and fainted from it. And as for me, I didn't dare laugh, because I was too afraid of opening my mouth and breathing in all that smelly breath.

Act 1 scene 2, lines 220–250 (cut and combined)

CASCA:
Why, there was a crown offered him; and being offered him, he put it by with the back of his hand, thus; and then the people fell a-shouting. He put it by thrice, every time gentler than other; and at every putting-by mine honest neighbors shouted. I saw Mark Antony offer him a crown, yet 'twas not a crown neither, 'twas one of these coronets; and, as I told you, he put it by once; but for all that, to my thinking, he would fain have had it. Then he offered it to him again; then he put it by again; but to my thinking, he was very loath to lay his fingers off it. And then he offered it the third time. He put it the third time by; and still as he refused it, the rabblement hooted, and clapped their chopt hands, and threw up their sweaty nightcaps, and uttered such a deal of stinking breath because Caesar refused the crown, that it had, almost, choked Caesar; for he swounded and fell down at it. And for mine own part, I durst not laugh, for fear of opening my lips and receiving the bad air.

Act 1 scene 3, lines 3–33 (cut and combined)

CASCA:
Aren't you troubled, when the entire earth
shakes like a ball on a string? Oh Cicero,
I have been in storms when the whipping winds
have split old oak trees, and I have seen
the raging oceans swell and rage and foam
till they raise up as high as the threatening clouds;
but never till tonight, never till now,
did I go through a hailstorm that rained down fire.
Either there is a civil war in the heavens,
or else the world, having been too insolent to the gods,
has enraged them so that they want to destroy us.
An ordinary slave — you'd know him by sight —
held up his left hand, which flamed and burned
like twenty torches joined together, and yet his hand,
not even feeling the fire, remained unburned.
And yesterday the night owl sat
at noontime in the market place,
hooting and shrieking. When such omens
all come at once, don't listen to men who say,
'This is the cause, it's perfectly normal,'
for I believe these are ominous signs
that are directed toward our nation.

Act 1 scene 3, lines 3–33 (cut and combined)

CASCA:
Are not you moved, when all the sway of earth
Shakes like a thing unfirm? O Cicero,
I have seen tempests, when the scolding winds
Have rived the knotty oaks, and I have seen
Th'ambitious ocean swell and rage and foam,
To be exalted with the threat'ning clouds;
But never till tonight, never till now,
Did I go through a tempest dropping fire.
Either there is a civil strife in heaven,
Or else the world, too saucy with the gods,
Incenses them to send destruction.
A common slave — you know him well by sight —
Held up his left hand, which did flame and burn
Like twenty torches joined, and yet his hand,
Not sensible of fire, remained unscorched.
And yesterday the bird of night did sit
Even at noonday upon the market place,
Hooting and shrieking. When these prodigies
Do so conjointly meet, let not men say,
'These are their reasons, they are natural,'
For I believe they are portentous things
Unto the climate that they point upon.

Are not you moved, when all the sway of earth shakes like a thing unfirm? O Cicero, I have seen tempests, when the scolding winds have rived the knotty oaks, and I have seen th'ambitious ocean swell and rage and foam, to be exalted with the threat'ning clouds; but never till tonight, never till now, did I go through a tempest dropping fire. Either there is a civil strife in heaven, or else the world, too saucy with the gods, incenses them to send destruction.

A common slave — you know him well by sight — held up his left hand, which did flame and burn like twenty torches joined, and yet his hand, not sensible of fire, remained unscorched. And yesterday the bird of night did sit even at noonday upon the market place, hooting and shrieking. When these prodigies do so conjointly meet, let not men say, 'These are their reasons, they are natural,' for I believe they are portentous things unto the climate that they point upon.

Act 2 scene 1, lines 10–34

BRUTUS:
The only course is to kill him; yet for my part,
I have no personal justification to do it,
except for the good of the public. He wants to be crowned.
How that might change him, that is the question.
It is the limelight that brings forth those who wish to be the center
    of attention and power,
and that creates the need for caution. If he is crowned,
it seems to me we are simply giving him the power
to control us anytime he pleases.
The misuse of greatness comes when the element of compassion
is removed from those who have power; but to speak truly of Caesar
I have never known him to be ruled by his passions
more than his reason. But it is well known
that one often pretends to be humble in the process of
climbing the ladder of success;
but once one has reached the top of that ladder
he often forgets where he has come from,
and seeks only more power, scorning all those
who helped him on his way. So might Caesar.
And, in case he might, we must prevent him. And, since the
    complaint against him
will appear to have no apparent justification as it stands,
we will have to put it this way: that who he would become, if he
    were made all-powerful,
would tend to these very excesses.
And therefore we have to imagine him as a serpent's egg
which when hatched, would (as snakes do) become dangerous,
and therefore we must kill him before he emerges from his shell.

Act 2 scene 1, lines 10–34

BRUTUS:
It must be by his death; and for my part,
I know no personal cause to spurn at him,
But for the general. He would be crowned.
How that might change his nature, there's the question.
It is the bright day that brings forth the adder,
And that craves wary walking. Crown him that,
And then I grant we put a sting in him
That at his will he may do danger with.
Th'abuse of greatness is, when it disjoins
Remorse from power. And to speak truth of Caesar,
I have not known when his affections swayed
More than his reason. But 'tis a common proof
That lowliness is young ambition's ladder,
Whereto the climber upward turns his face;
But when he once attains the upmost round,
He then unto the ladder turns his back,
Looks in the clouds, scorning the base degrees
By which he did ascend. So Caesar may.
Then lest he may, prevent. And since the quarrel
Will bear no color for the thing he is,
Fashion it thus: that what he is, augmented,
Would run to these and these extremities;
And therefore think him as a serpent's egg,
Which, hatched, would as his kind grow mischievous,
And kill him in the shell.

It must be by his death; and for my part, I know no personal cause to spurn at him, but for the general. He would be crowned. How that might change his nature, there's the question. It is the bright day that brings forth the adder, and that craves wary walking. Crown him that, and then I grant we put a sting in him that at his will he may do danger with.

Th'abuse of greatness is, when it disjoins remorse from power. And to speak truth of Caesar, I have not known when his affections swayed more than his reason. But 'tis a common proof that lowliness is young ambition's ladder, whereto the climber upward turns his face; but when he once attains the upmost round, he then unto the ladder turns his back, looks in the clouds, scorning the base degrees by which he did ascend. So Caesar may. Then lest he may, — prevent. And since the quarrel will bear no color for the thing he is, fashion it thus: that what he is, augmented, would run to these and these extremities; and therefore think him as a serpent's egg, which, hatched, would as his kind grow mischievous, and kill him in the shell.

Act 2 scene 1, lines 236–256

PORTIA:
             You have rudely, Brutus,
left my bed. And last night at supper
you suddenly stood up and walked around,
deep in thought, sighing, with your arms folded;
and when I asked you what was wrong
you stared at me unkindly.
I persisted: then you scratched your head
and stamped your foot impatiently.
Yet I persevered, and still you didn't answer
but with an angry gesture of your hand
signaled me to leave. So I did,
afraid of reinforcing your anger
which seemed much too inflamed already, and at the same time
hoping it was only a temporary moodiness,
which at one time or another effects every man.
Bur it will not let you eat, nor talk, nor sleep;
and if it could have as much effect upon your appearance
as it has had upon your disposition,
I would not even recognize you, Brutus. My dear lord,
tell me what is bothering you so.

Act 2 scene 1, lines 236–256

PORTIA:

                    Y'have ungently, Brutus,
Stole from my bed. And yesternight at supper
You suddenly arose and walked about,
Musing and sighing with your arms across;
And when I asked you what the matter was,
You stared upon me with ungentle looks.
I urged you further; then you scratched your head
And too impatiently stamped with your foot.
Yet I insisted; yet you answered not,
But with an angry wafter of your hand
Gave sign for me to leave you. So I did,
Fearing to strengthen that impatience
Which seemed too much enkindled, and withal
Hoping it was but an effect of humor,
Which sometime hath his hour with every man.
It will not let you eat, nor talk, nor sleep,
And could it work so much upon your shape
As it hath much prevailed on your condition,
I should not know you, Brutus. Dear my lord,
Make me acquainted with your cause of grief.

    Y'have ungently, Brutus, stole from my bed. And yesternight at supper you suddenly arose and walked about, musing and sighing with your arms across; and when I asked you what the matter was, you stared upon me with ungentle looks.

    I urged you further; then you scratched your head and too impatiently stamped with your foot. Yet I insisted; yet you answered not, but with an angry wafter of your hand gave sign for me to leave you. So I did, fearing to strengthen that impatience which seemed too much enkindled, and withal hoping it was but an effect of humor, which sometime hath his hour with every man.

    It will not let you eat, nor talk, nor sleep, and could it work so much upon your shape as it hath much prevailed on your condition, I should not know you, Brutus. Dear my lord, make me acquainted with your cause of grief.

Act 2 scene 1, lines 258–287 (cut and combined)

PORTIA:
Brutus is wise, and if he were not in good health,
he would do what is required to become cured.
Is Brutus sick, and is it medically sound
to walk with your shirt unbuttoned breathing in the dampness
of the dank morning? Tell me, is Brutus sick
and will he sneak out of his warm bed,
to go wandering about in the night,
risking the chills and germs of the outdoors
to add to his sickness? No, my Brutus;
you have some harmful sickness within your mind,
which by my rights as your wife
I should be informed of; and on my knees
I beg you, by my once-praised beauty,
by all your vows of love, and by that great vow
which united us and made us one,
that you reveal to me, your other self, your other half,
why you are so miserable.
Within the contract of marriage, tell me, Brutus,
do you reserve the right to keep secrets from me
about issues that pertain to you? Am I your partner
but, only as it were, up to a point?
To eat meals with you, sleep in your bed,
and talk to you sometimes? Am I merely an ornament
for your pleasure? If this is the case,
Portia is Brutus's whore, not his wife.

Act 2 scene 1, lines 258–287 (cut and combined)

PORTIA:
Brutus is wise and, were he not in health,
He would embrace the means to come by it.
Is Brutus sick, and is it physical
To walk unbracèd and suck up the humors
Of the dank morning? What, is Brutus sick,
And will he steal out of his wholesome bed
To dare the vile contagion of the night,
And tempt the rheumy and unpurgèd air,
To add unto his sickness? No, my Brutus;
You have some sick offense within your mind,
Which by the right and virtue of my place
I ought to know of; and upon my knees
I charm you, by my once commended beauty,
By all your vows of love, and that great vow
Which did incorporate and make us one,
That you unfold to me, your self, your half,
Why you are heavy.
Within the bond of marriage, tell me, Brutus,
Is it excepted I should know no secrets
That appertain to you? Am I your self
But, as it were, in sort or limitation?
To keep with you at meals, comfort your bed,
And talk to you sometimes? Dwell I but in the suburbs
Of your good pleasure? If it be no more,
Portia is Brutus' harlot, not his wife.

Brutus is wise and, were he not in health, he would embrace the means to come by it. Is Brutus sick, and is it physical to walk unbracèd and suck up the humors of the dank morning? What, is Brutus sick, and will he steal out of his wholesome bed to dare the vile contagion of the night, and tempt the rheumy and unpurgèd air, to add unto his sickness?

No, my Brutus; you have some sick offense within your mind, which by the right and virtue of my place I ought to know of; and upon my knees I charm you, by my once commended beauty, by all your vows of love, and that great vow which did incorporate and make us one, that you unfold to me, your self, your half, why you are heavy.

Within the bond of marriage, tell me, Brutus, is it excepted I should know no secrets that appertain to you? Am I your self but, as it were, in sort or limitation? To keep with you at meals, comfort your bed, and talk to you sometimes? Dwell I but in the suburbs of your good pleasure? If it be no more, Portia is Brutus' harlot, not his wife.

Act 2 scene 2, lines 8–54 (cut and combined)

CALPURNIA:
What do you mean, Caesar? You're not thinking of leaving?
You shall not stir out of your house today.
Caesar, I've never believed in omens,
but now they frighten me. There is someone inside,
who in addition to what we've heard and seen,
tells of horrid sights seen by the watchmen.
A lioness gave birth in the streets,
and graves have opened wide and spit out their dead.
Fierce fiery warriors fight upon the clouds
in ranks and squadrons and proper military formation,
and the clouds drizzled blood on the Capital;
the noise of the battle hurled through the air,
horses neighed, and dying men groaned,
and ghosts shrieked and squealed in the streets.
Oh Caesar, these things are too extraordinary,
and I'm afraid of them.
When a beggar dies, no comets are seen;
these meteor showers occur only for the death of a prince.
Your confidence is overriding your wisdom!
Do not go out today! Say it is my fear
that keeps you home and not your own.
On my knees, I beg you to let me persuade you in this.

Act 2 scene 2, lines 8–54 (cut and combined)

CALPURNIA:
What mean you, Caesar? Think you to walk forth?
You shall not stir out of your house today.
Caesar, I never stood on ceremonies,
Yet now they fright me. There is one within,
Besides the things that we have heard and seen,
Recounts most horrid sights seen by the watch.
A lioness hath whelpèd in the streets,
And graves have yawned and yielded up their dead.
Fierce fiery warriors fought upon the clouds
In ranks and squadrons and right form of war,
Which drizzled blood upon the Capital.
The noise of battle hurtled in the air,
Horses did neigh, and dying men did groan,
And ghosts did shriek and squeal about the streets.
O Caesar, these things are beyond all use,
And I do fear them.
When beggars die there are no comets seen;
The heavens themselves blaze forth the death of princes.
Your wisdom is consumed in confidence!
Do not go forth today! Call it my fear
That keeps you in the house and not your own.
Let me upon my knee prevail in this.

What mean you, Caesar? Think you to walk forth? You shall not stir out of your house today. Caesar, I never stood on ceremonies, yet now they fright me. There is one within, besides the things that we have heard and seen, recounts most horrid sights seen by the watch. A lioness hath whelpèd in the streets, and graves have yawned and yielded up their dead. Fierce fiery warriors fought upon the clouds in ranks and squadrons and right form of war, which drizzled blood upon the Capital. The noise of battle hurtled in the air, horses did neigh, and dying men did groan, and ghosts did shriek and squeal about the streets.

O Caesar, these things are beyond all use, and I do fear them. When beggars die there are no comets seen; the heavens themselves blaze forth the death of princes. Your wisdom is consumed in confidence! Do not go forth today! Call it my fear that keeps you in the house and not your own. Let me upon my knee prevail in this.

Act 3 scene 1, lines 123–137

SERVANT:
In this fashion, Brutus, my master instructed me to kneel;
in this fashion Mark Antony instructed me to fall down
and being prostrate, he told me to say this:
Brutus is noble, wise, valiant, and honest;
Caesar was mighty, bold, royal, and loving.
Say I love Brutus and I honor him;
say I feared Caesar, honored him, and loved him.
If Brutus will deign to allow Antony
to safely come to him and be convinced to his satisfaction
that Caesar deserved to lie here dead,
Mark Antony shall not love dead Caesar
as well as he will love living Brutus; and he will align
himself on the side of noble Brutus
to face the dangers of this uncertain state of affairs
with all faithfulness. So says my master Antony.

Act 3 scene 1, lines 123–137

SERVANT:
Thus, Brutus, did my master bid me kneel;
Thus did Mark Antony bid me fall down;
And being prostrate, thus he bade me say:
Brutus is noble, wise, valiant, and honest;
Caesar was mighty, bold, royal, and loving.
Say I love Brutus and I honor him;
Say I feared Caesar, honored him, and loved him.
If Brutus will vouchsafe that Antony
May safely come to him and be resolved
How Caesar hath deserved to lie in death,
Mark Antony shall not love Caesar dead
So well as Brutus living; but will follow
The fortunes and affairs of noble Brutus
Thorough the hazards of this untrod state
With all true faith. So says my master Antony.

    Thus, Brutus, did my master bid me kneel; thus did Mark Antony bid me fall down; and being prostrate, thus he bade me say: Brutus is noble, wise, valiant, and honest; Caesar was mighty, bold, royal, and loving.
    Say I love Brutus and I honor him; say I feared Caesar, honored him, and loved him.
    If Brutus will vouchsafe that Antony may safely come to him and be resolved how Caesar hath deserved to lie in death, Mark Antony shall not love Caesar dead so well as Brutus living; but will follow the fortunes and affairs of noble Brutus thorough the hazards of this untrod state with all true faith. So says my master Antony.

Act 3 scene 1, lines 148–164

ANTONY:
Oh mighty Caesar! Have you been brought down so far?
Are all your conquests, glories, triumphs, spoils of war,
reduced to this tiny heap? Farewell to you.
I don't know, gentlemen, what your intentions are,
who else's blood must be shed, who else is considered corrupt.
If I am, there is no time as fitting
as the moment of Caesar's death, nor no weapons
half as worthy as your swords, made more worthy
being covered with the noblest blood in all the world.
I beg you, if you hold anything against me,
now, while your hands still reek with warm blood,
do what you will. If I live a thousand years,
I will not find myself so ready to die,
no place, nor no means of death, will please me so
as here by Caesar, and executed by you,
the finest and the principal forces of our time.

Act 3 scene 1, lines 148–164

ANTONY:
O mighty Caesar! dost thou lie so low?
Are all thy conquests, glories, triumphs, spoils,
Shrunk to this little measure? Fare thee well.
I know not, gentlemen, what you intend,
Who else must be let blood, who else is rank.
If I myself, there is no hour so fit
As Caesar's death's hour; nor no instrument
Of half that worth as those your swords, made rich
With the most noble blood of all this world.
I do beseech ye, if you bear me hard,
Now, whilst your purpled hands do reek and smoke,
Fulfill your pleasure. Live a thousand years,
I shall not find myself so apt to die;
No place will please me so, no mean of death,
As here by Caesar, and by you cut off,
The choice and master spirits of this age.

O mighty Caesar! dost thou lie so low? Are all thy conquests, glories, triumphs, spoils, shrunk to this little measure? Fare thee well.

I know not, gentlemen, what you intend, who else must be let blood, who else is rank. If I myself, there is no hour so fit as Caesar's death's hour; nor no instrument of half that worth as those your swords, made rich with the most noble blood of all this world. I do beseech ye, if you bear me hard, now, whilst your purpled hands do reek and smoke, fulfill your pleasure. Live a thousand years, I shall not find myself so apt to die; no place will please me so, no mean of death, as here by Caesar, and by you cut off, the choice and master spirits of this age.

Act 2 scene 1, lines 373–396 (cut)

BASTARD:
I swear, these scoundrels from Angiers are making fun of you, kings,
and are confidently standing upon their battlements
as if in a theater, gaping and pointing
at your fervent scenes and your heroics.
Your royal highnesses listen to me.
Be allies for a while and join forces
to bring this town to its knees.
Then, in the east and the west let France and England station
their fully loaded battering cannons,
until their appalling reverberations shake down
the very walls of this contemptuous city.
I'd fire repeatedly upon these asses,
until they are totally defenseless
and then leave them as unprotected as the air we all breathe.
When that's done, tear up your pact,
and go your separate ways once again;
then turn face to face and point your bloody swords at each other.
Until the time comes when good fortune
shall smile on one of your sides,
and pick one of you to win the day,
and grant that one a glorious victory.
So how do you like my daring advice, mighty kings?
Doesn't it have the true ring of politics in action?

Act 2 scene 1, lines 373–396 (cut)

BASTARD:
By heaven, these scroyles of Angiers flout you, kings,
And stand securely on their battlements
As in a theater, whence they gape and point
At your industrious scene and acts of death.
Your royal presences be ruled by me.
Be friends awhile and both conjointly bend
Your sharpest deeds of malice on this town.
By east and west let France and England mount
Their battering cannon chargèd to the mouths,
Till their soul-fearing clamors have brawled down
The flinty ribs of this contemptuous city.
I'd play incessantly upon these jades,
Even till unfencèd desolation
Leave them as naked as the vulgar air.
That done, dissever your united strengths,
And part your mingled colors once again;
Turn face to face and bloody point to point.
Then in a moment Fortune shall cull forth
Out of one side her happy minion,
To whom in favor she shall give the day,
And kiss him with a glorious victory.
How like you this wild counsel, mighty states?
Smacks it not something of the policy?

By heaven, these scroyles of Angiers flout you, kings, and stand securely on their battlements as in a theater, whence they gape and point at your industrious scene and acts of death.

Your royal presences be ruled by me. Be friends awhile and both conjointly bend your sharpest deeds of malice on this town. By east and west let France and England mount their battering cannon chargèd to the mouths, till their soul-fearing clamors have brawled down the flinty ribs of this contemptuous city. I'd play incessantly upon these jades, even till unfencèd desolation leave them as naked as the vulgar air.

That done, dissever your united strengths, and part your mingled colors once again; turn face to face and bloody point to point. Then in a moment Fortune shall cull forth out of one side her happy minion, to whom in favor she shall give the day, and kiss him with a glorious victory.

How like you this wild counsel, mighty states? Smacks it not something of the policy?

Act 3 scene 1, lines 1–26 (cut)

CONSTANCE:
Gone off to be married! Gone off to swear to a peace!
Deceitful blood to deceitful blood wed! Gone to be allies!
Shall Lewis have Blanche, and Blanche have those provinces?
It can't be; you have misspoke, you've heard wrong.
Be certain of what you're saying, tell me your story again.
It can't be true; you're only saying it's so.
I know you're not trustworthy, because your word
is only the empty bluster of a nobody.
Truly, I don't believe you, man;
I have a king's word to the contrary.
You shall be punished for scaring me like this,
because I am sick and susceptible to fears,
overwhelmed with wrongs, and therefore full of fears,
a widow, without a husband, subject to fears,
a woman, therefore naturally I am fearful;
and even if you now confessed that you had jested,
I am so upset I couldn't even forgive you,
I will continue to quake and tremble all day.
What do you mean by this shaking of your head?
Why are you looking so mournfully upon my son?
Why do you have your hand upon your breast?
Are these signs of sadness which confirm your words?
If so tell me again, not everything you said before,
just one thing, whether your tale is true.

Act 3 scene 1, lines 1–26 (cut)

CONSTANCE:
Gone to be married! Gone to swear a peace!
False blood to false blood joined! Gone to be friends!
Shall Lewis have Blanche, and Blanche those provinces?
It is not so; thou hast misspoke, misheard.
Be well advised, tell o'er thy tale again.
It cannot be; thou dost but say 'tis so.
I trust I may not trust thee, for thy word
Is but the vain breath of a common man.
Believe me, I do not believe thee, man;
I have a king's oath to the contrary.
Thou shalt be punished for thus frighting me,
For I am sick and capable of fears,
Oppressed with wrongs, and therefore full of fears,
A widow, husbandless, subject to fears,
A woman, naturally born to fears;
And though thou now confess thou didst but jest,
With my vexed spirits I cannot take a truce,
But they will quake and tremble all this day.
What dost thou mean by shaking of thy head?
Why dost thou look so sadly on my son?
What means that hand upon that breast of thine?
Be these sad signs confirmers of thy words?
Then speak again, not all thy former tale,
But this one word, whether thy tale be true.

Gone to be married! Gone to swear a peace! False blood to false blood joined! Gone to be friends! Shall Lewis have Blanche, and Blanche those provinces? It is not so; thou hast misspoke, misheard. Be well advised, tell o'er thy tale again. It cannot be; thou dost but say 'tis so. I trust I may not trust thee, for thy word is but the vain breath of a common man. Believe me, I do not believe thee, man; I have a king's oath to the contrary.

Thou shalt be punished for thus frighting me, for I am sick and capable of fears, oppressed with wrongs, and therefore full of fears, — a widow, husbandless, subject to fears, a woman, naturally born to fears; and though thou now confess thou didst but jest, with my vexed spirits I cannot take a truce, but they will quake and tremble all this day.

What dost thou mean by shaking of thy head? Why dost thou look so sadly on my son? What means that hand upon that breast of thine? Be these sad signs confirmers of thy words? Then speak again, not all thy former tale, but this one word, whether thy tale be true.

Act 3 scene 1, lines 326–336

BLANCHE:
The sun's covered with blood. Good-bye, good times!
Which side do I go with?
I am allied with both. Each army has one of my hands,
and as they rage, I who have hold of them both,
will be spun apart and dismembered.
Husband, I cannot pray for you to win.
Uncle, I have to pray that you should lose.
Father, I may not wish you good fortune.
Grandmother, I will not wish that your wishes prevail.
Whoever wins, I am still the loser;
I am assured of a loss before the game is even played.

Act 3 scene 1, lines 326–336

BLANCHE:
The sun's o'ercast with blood. Fair day, adieu!
Which is the side that I must go withal?
I am with both. Each army hath a hand,
And in their rage, I having hold of both,
They whirl asunder and dismember me.
Husband, I cannot pray that thou mayst win.
Uncle, I needs must pray that thou mayst lose.
Father, I may not wish the fortune thine.
Grandam, I will not wish thy wishes thrive.
Whoever wins, on that side shall I lose;
Assurèd loss before the match be played.

The sun's o'ercast with blood. Fair day, adieu! Which is the side that I must go withal? I am with both. Each army hath a hand, and in their rage, (I having hold of both), they whirl asunder and dismember me.

Husband, I cannot pray that thou mayst win. Uncle, I needs must pray that thou mayst lose. Father, I may not wish the fortune thine. Grandam, I will not wish thy wishes thrive. Whoever wins, on that side shall I lose; assurèd loss before the match be played.

Act 3 scene 4, lines 38–60 (cut and combined)

CONSTANCE:
If only my tongue could have the power of thunder!
Then I would make the earth shake with my passion.
I'm not mad; I know this hair I'm tearing out is mine.
I know my name is Constance; I know I was Geoffrey's wife.
And that young Arthur is my son, and that he is doomed!
I am not mad. I wish to God I was,
because then it's likely I could forget who I am.
Oh, if only I could, what grief would I then forget!
Preach to me a philosophy that would drive me mad,
and you shall be canonized, cardinal.
Because, since I am not mad but aware of my grief,
my sane self reasonably shows me
how I can relieve myself of my woes,
and tells me to kill or hang myself.
If I were mad, I should forget my son,
or madly think that some rag doll were him.
I am not mad. Too well, oh too well am I aware
of the unique horror of each disaster.

Act 3 scene 4, lines 38–60 (cut and combined)

CONSTANCE:
O that my tongue were in the thunder's mouth!
Then with a passion would I shake the world,
And rouse from sleep that fell anatomy
Which cannot hear a lady's feeble voice,
Which scorns a modern invocation.
I am not mad; this hair I tear is mine.
My name is Constance; I was Geoffrey's wife.
Young Arthur is my son, and he is lost!
I am not mad. I would to God I were,
For then 'tis like I should forget myself.
O, if I could, what grief should I forget!
Preach some philosophy to make me mad,
And thou shalt be canonized, cardinal.
For, being not mad but sensible of grief,
My reasonable part produces reason
How I may be delivered of these woes,
And teaches me to kill or hang myself.
If I were mad, I should forget my son,
Or madly think a babe of clouts were he.
I am not mad. Too well, too well I feel
The different plague of each calamity.

O that my tongue were in the thunder's mouth! Then with a passion would I shake the world, and rouse from sleep that fell anatomy which cannot hear a lady's feeble voice, which scorns a modern invocation.

I am not mad; this hair I tear is mine. My name is Constance; I was Geoffrey's wife. Young Arthur is my son, and he is lost! I am not mad. I would to God I were, for then 'tis like I should forget myself. O, if I could, what grief should I forget!

Preach some philosophy to make me mad, and thou shalt be canonized, cardinal. For, being not mad but sensible of grief, my reasonable part produces reason how I may be delivered of these woes, and teaches me to kill or hang myself. If I were mad, I should forget my son, or madly think a babe of clouts were he.

I am not mad. Too well, too well I feel the different plague of each calamity.

Act 4 scene 1, lines 39–58 (cut)

ARTHUR:
Must you burn out both my eyes with hot pokers?
                    And would you do it?
Have you the heart? When you had a headache,
I tied my handkerchief around your forehead —
the finest one I had, a princess had made it for me —
and I never even asked you for it back again;
and held your head in my hands at midnight,
asking, 'What do you need?' and 'Where are you hurting?'
or 'What can I do for you?'
Most poor men's sons would have just stayed still,
and never even spoken a kind word to you,
but you had a prince at your sickbed.
Now, you may think my love was calculated,
and call it sly; do so if you want.
If it pleases heaven for you to treat me ill,
why then you have to. Will you poke out my eyes?
These eyes that never did nor never would
even so much as frown at you?

Act 4 scene 1, lines 39–58 (cut and combined)

ARTHUR:
Must you with hot irons burn out both mine eyes?
                    And will you?
Have you the heart? When your head did but ache,
I knit my handkerchief about your brows —
The best I had, a princess wrought it me —
And I did never ask it you again;
And with my hand at midnight held your head,
Saying, 'What lack you?' and 'Where lies your grief?'
Or 'What good love may I perform for you?'
Many a poor man's son would have lain still,
And ne'er have spoke a loving word to you,
But you at your sick service had a prince.
Nay, you may think my love was crafty love,
And call it cunning; do and if you will.
If heaven be pleased that you must use me ill,
Why then you must. Will you put out mine eyes?
These eyes that never did nor never shall
So much as frown on you?

Must you with hot irons burn out both mine eyes? And will you? Have you the heart? When your head did but ache, I knit my handkerchief about your brows — the best I had, a princess wrought it me — and I did never ask it you again; and with my hand at midnight held your head, saying, 'What lack you?' and 'Where lies your grief?' or 'What good love may I perform for you?' Many a poor man's son would have lain still, and ne'er have spoke a loving word to you, but you at your sick service had a prince.

Nay, you may think my love was crafty love, and call it cunning; do and if you will. If heaven be pleased that you must use me ill, why then you must. Will you put out mine eyes? These eyes that never did nor never shall so much as frown on you?

Act 4 scene 2, lines 208–242 (cut and combined)

KING JOHN:
It is the curse of kings to be surrounded
by lackeys who interpret their very whims as an authorization
to commit murder.
How often the mere perception that an ill deed can be done
leads to that ill deed being done! Had you not stood there,
a fellow whose very appearance,
cries out to commit crimes,
the idea of this murder would not have come into my mind;
but by taking note of the horrible sight of you,
seeing that you were capable of this bloody deed,
suitable, willing to do it,
I merely mentioned the killing of Arthur;
and you, in order to suck up to a king,
didn't hesitate for a moment to destroy a prince.
Had you merely shook your head or considered for a moment
when I vaguely mentioned what I had in mind,
or looked doubtfully upon me,
as if to say, 'Spell it out to me,'
deep shame would have silenced me, made me stop,
and your doubts might have instilled some
        doubt in me.
But you understood my intimations
and did by intimation agree to the crime;
yes, unhesitatingly, you wholeheartedly consented to it,
and afterwards allowed your brutal hand to commit
that deed which neither of our tongues dared mention.
Get out of my sight, and never let me see you again!

Act 4 scene 2, lines 208–242 (cut and combined)

KING JOHN:
It is the curse of kings to be attended
By slaves that take their humors for a warrant
To break within the bloody house of life.
How oft the sight of means to do ill deeds
Makes deeds ill done! Hadst not thou been by,
A fellow by the hand of nature marked,
Quoted and signed to do a deed of shame,
This murder had not come into my mind;
But taking note of thy abhorred aspect,
Finding thee fit for bloody villainy,
Apt, liable to be employed in danger,
I faintly broke with thee of Arthur's death;
And thou, to be endearèd to a king,
Made it no conscience to destroy a prince.
Hadst thou but shook thy head or made a pause
When I spake darkly what I purposèd,
Or turned an eye of doubt upon my face,
As bid me tell my tale in express words,
Deep shame had struck me dumb, made me break off,
And those thy fears might have wrought fears in me.
But thou didst understand me by my signs
And didst in signs again parley with sin;
Yea, without stop, didst let thy heart consent,
And consequently thy rude hand to act
The deed which both our tongues held vile to name.
Out of my sight, and never see me more!

It is the curse of kings to be attended by slaves that take their humors for a warrant to break within the bloody house of life. How oft the sight of means to do ill deeds makes deeds ill done! Hadst not thou been by, — a fellow by the hand of nature marked, quoted and signed to do a deed of shame, — this murder had not come into my mind; but taking note of thy abhorred aspect, finding thee fit for bloody villainy, apt, liable to be employed in danger, I faintly broke with thee of Arthur's death; and thou, to be endearèd to a king, made it no conscience to destroy a prince.

Hadst thou but shook thy head or made a pause when I spake darkly what I purposèd, or turned an eye of doubt upon my face, as bid me tell my tale in express words, deep shame had struck me dumb, made me break off, and those thy fears might have wrought fears in me.

But thou didst understand me by my signs and didst in signs again parley with sin; yea, without stop, didst let thy heart consent, and consequently thy rude hand to act the deed which both our tongues held vile to name. Out of my sight, and never see me more!

Act 5 scene 1, lines 44–61

BASTARD:
Why are you depressed? Why do you look so sad?
Be as daring in your actions, as you have been in your thoughts.
Don't let the world see fear and self-doubt
shake the confidence of a king's demeanor.
Have the energy to face the moment; fight fire with fire.
Threaten anyone who appears a threat, and look fear in the eye
and stare it down. So shall the masses,
who imitate the behavior of those above them,
become inspired by your example and adopt
an invincible spirit of undaunted courage.
Go now, and shine as the god of war does
when he is about to grace the battlefield with his presence.
Show courage and self-assurance.
What, shall they find the lion in his den
and frighten him there? And make him cower there?
Oh, don't let that ever be said! Seek out your prey, and venture forth
to meet the enemy far from your doorstep,
and grapple with him before he dares to come so near.

Act 5 scene 1, lines 44–61

BASTARD:
But wherefore do you droop? Why look you sad?
Be great in act, as you have been in thought.
Let not the world see fear and sad distrust
Govern the motion of a kingly eye.
Be stirring as the time; be fire with fire.
Threaten the threat'ner, and outface the brow
Of bragging horror. So shall inferior eyes,
That borrow their behaviors from the great,
Grow great by your example and put on
The dauntless spirit of resolution.
Away, and glisten like the god of war
When he intendeth to become the field.
Show boldness and aspiring confidence.
What, shall they seek the lion in his den
And fright him there? And make him tremble there?
O, let it not be said! Forage, and run
To meet displeasure farther from the doors,
And grapple with him ere he come so nigh.

But wherefore do you droop? Why look you sad? Be great in act, as you have been in thought. Let not the world see fear and sad distrust govern the motion of a kingly eye. Be stirring as the time; be fire with fire.

Threaten the threat'ner, and outface the brow of bragging horror. So shall inferior eyes, that borrow their behaviors from the great, grow great by your example and put on the dauntless spirit of resolution.

Away, and glisten like the god of war when he intendeth to become the field. Show boldness and aspiring confidence. What, shall they seek the lion in his den and fright him there? And make him tremble there? O, let it not be said! Forage, and run to meet displeasure farther from the doors, and grapple with him ere he come so nigh.

Act 5 scene 2, lines 78–108 (cut)

LEWIS:
Your grace must pardon me; I will not retreat.
I am too nobly born to be used as a pawn,
to be made a puppet
to any princely power in the world.
Your words first fueled the fires of war
between this half-beaten kingdom and myself,
and you added even more fuel to feed that fire;
and now it's far too huge to be blown out.
And do you come to me now to tell me that John has made
peace with the church? What does that peace mean to me?
I, by right of my marriage,
after young Arthur, am next in line to the throne,
and, now that the battle is half won, must I retreat
because John has made peace with Rome?
Am I Rome's slave? What expenses has Rome paid,
how many men has it provided, what military hardware has it sent,
to help with this war? Wasn't it I
who paid for all this? Who else but I.
And now don't I hold the best cards in this game
to win this easy match being played for a crown?
And shall I now give back what I have won?
No, no, on my soul, it will never happen.

Act 5 scene 2, lines 78–108 (cut)

LEWIS:
Your grace shall pardon me; I will not back.
I am too highborn to be propertied,
To be a secondary at control,
To any sovereign state throughout the world.
Your breath first kindled the dead coal of wars
Between this chastised kingdom and myself,
And brought in matter that should feed this fire;
And now 'tis far too huge to be blown out.
And come ye now to tell me John hath made
His peace with Rome? What is that peace to me?
I, by the honor of my marriage bed,
After young Arthur, claim this land for mine,
And, now it is half-conquered, must I back
Because that John hath made his peace with Rome?
Am I Rome's slave? What penny hath Rome borne,
What men provided, what munition sent,
To underprop this action? Is't not I
That undergo this charge? Who else but I.
Have I not here the best cards for the game
To win this easy match played for a crown?
And shall I now give o'er the yielded set?
No, no, on my soul, it never shall be said.

Your grace shall pardon me; I will not back. I am too highborn to be propertied, to be a secondary at control, to any sovereign state throughout the world. Your breath first kindled the dead coal of wars between this chastised kingdom and myself, and brought in matter that should feed this fire; and now 'tis far too huge to be blown out. And come ye now to tell me John hath made his peace with Rome?

What is that peace to me? I, by the honor of my marriage bed, — after young Arthur, — claim this land for mine, and, now it is half-conquered, must I back because that John hath made his peace with Rome? Am I Rome's slave? What penny hath Rome borne, what men provided, what munition sent, to underprop this action? Is't not I that undergo this charge? Who else but I.

Have I not here the best cards for the game to win this easy match played for a crown? And shall I now give o'er the yielded set? No, no, on my soul, it never shall be said.

Act 1 scene 1, lines 91–110 (cut and combined)

CORDELIA:
Nothing, my lord. Nothing.
As much as it saddens me, I cannot force
my heart into my mouth. I love your Majesty
according to my duty, no more nor less.
                         My good lord,
you have fathered me, raised me, loved me; I
return those duties back as is properly fit,
I obey you, love you, and most of all honor you.
Why do my sisters have husbands, if, as they say
they love you only? Hopefully, when I shall wed,
the lord who takes my hand in wedlock shall take
half my love with him, half my care and duty.
Hopefully I shall never marry like my sisters,
to love my father only.

Act 1 scene 1, lines 91–110 (cut and combined)

CORDELIA:
Nothing, my lord. Nothing.
Unhappy that I am, I cannot heave
My heart into my mouth. I love your Majesty
According to my bond, no more nor less.
                              Good my lord,
You have begot me, bred me, loved me; I
Return those duties back as are right fit,
Obey you, love you, and most honor you.
Why have my sisters husbands, if they say
They love you all? Happily, when I shall wed,
That lord whose hand must take my plight shall carry
Half my love with him, half my care and duty.
Sure I shall never marry like my sisters,
To love my father all.

Nothing, my lord. Nothing. Unhappy that I am, I cannot heave my heart into my mouth. I love your Majesty according to my bond, no more nor less.

Good my lord, you have begot me, bred me, loved me; I return those duties back as are right fit, obey you, love you, and most honor you. Why have my sisters husbands, if they say they love you all? Happily, when I shall wed, that lord whose hand must take my plight shall carry half my love with him, half my care and duty. Sure I shall never marry like my sisters, to love my father all.

Act 1 scene 1, lines 250–261

FRANCE:
Fairest Cordelia, who is very rich, though she has no wealth,
perfect, though she's been abandoned; and as deeply loved, as she
    is despised!
Yourself and your virtues I take to my heart.
It is lawful that I may claim as my own what has been thrown away.
Oh god, god! It's odd that the cold shoulder received from them
should cause a burning love to spark in me.
Your daughter with no dowry, King, cast to me by fortune,
is queen to me, to my people, and to all of France.
Not all the dukes of soggy Burgundy
could purchase this unappreciated, yet precious maiden from me.
Bid them farewell, Cordelia, even though they are unkind,
you're leaving this place, but a better place you'll find.

Act 1 scene 1, lines 250–261

FRANCE:
Fairest Cordelia, that art most rich, being poor;
Most choice, forsaken; and most loved, despised!
Thee and thy virtues here I seize upon.
Be it lawful I take up what's cast away.
Gods, gods! 'Tis strange that from their coldest neglect
My love should kindle to inflamed respect.
Thy dowerless daughter, King, thrown to my chance,
Is queen of us, of ours, and our fair France.
Not all the dukes of waterish Burgundy
Can buy this unprized precious maid of me.
Bid them farewell, Cordelia, though unkind,
Thou losest here, a better where to find.

Fairest Cordelia, that art most rich, being poor; most choice, forsaken; and most loved, despised! Thee and thy virtues here I seize upon. Be it lawful I take up what's cast away.

Gods, gods! 'Tis strange that from their coldest neglect my love should kindle to inflamed respect. Thy dowerless daughter, King, thrown to my chance, is queen of us, of ours, and our fair France. Not all the dukes of waterish Burgundy can buy this unprized precious maid of me.

Bid them farewell, Cordelia, though unkind, thou losest here, a better where to find.

Act 1 scene 2, lines 1–22

EDMOND:
Nature, you are the goddess to whom I pray — to your laws
I am committed. Why then should I
be subjected to tortuous customs and allow
the squeamishness of people to disinherit me,
just because I am some twelve or fourteen months
younger than my brother? Why am I called bastard? How am I base?
When I am as well proportioned,
as noble minded, and as like my father,
as any married woman's offspring? Why do they brand us
with base? with baseness? with bastardy? base, base?
When we, who in those stolen moments of lust, inherit
more of the constitution and energetic qualities
than could be passed on (on a boring, loveless passionless bed)
to a whole tribe of dunces
who are conceived by the half-asleep? Well then,
legitimate Edgar, I must have your inheritance.
Our father loves the bastard Edmund
as much as his legitimate son. Fine word, 'legitimate'!
Well, my legitimate, if this letter succeeds,
and my plan prospers, Edmund, the base
surpass the legitimate. I will thrive; I will prosper.
Now, gods, stand up for bastards!

Act 1 scene 2, lines 1–22

EDMOND:
Thou, Nature, art my goddess — to thy law
My services are bound. Wherefore should I
Stand in the plague of custom and permit
The curiosity of nations to deprive me,
For that I am some twelve or fourteen moonshines
Lag of a brother? Why bastard? wherefore base?
When my dimensions are as well compact;
My mind as generous, and my shape as true,
As honest madam's issue? Why brand they us
With base? with baseness? bastardy? base, base?
Who, in the lusty stealth of nature, take
More composition and fierce quality
Than doth, within a dull, stale tired bed,
Go to the creating a whole tribe of fops
Got 'tween asleep and wake? Well then,
Legitimate Edgar, I must have your land.
Our father's love is to the bastard Edmund
As to the legitimate. Fine word, 'legitimate'!
Well, my legitimate, if this letter speed
And my invention thrive, Edmund, the base
Shall top the legitimate; I grow; I prosper.
Now, gods, stand up for bastards!

Thou, Nature, art my goddess — to thy law my services are bound. Wherefore should I stand in the plague of custom and permit the curiosity of nations to deprive me, for that I am some twelve or fourteen moonshines lag of a brother?

Why bastard? wherefore base? when my dimensions are as well compact; my mind as generous, and my shape as true, as honest madam's issue? Why brand they us with base? with baseness? bastardy? base, base? who, in the lusty stealth of nature, take more composition and fierce quality than doth, — within a dull, stale tired bed, — go to the creating a whole tribe of fops got 'tween asleep and wake?

Well then, legitimate Edgar, I must have your land. Our father's love is to the bastard Edmund as to the legitimate. Fine word, 'legitimate'! Well, my legitimate, if this letter speed and my invention thrive, Edmund, the base shall top the legitimate; I grow; I prosper.

Act 1 scene 3, lines 4–21 (combined)

GONERIL:
Day and night he does me wrong! Every hour
he bursts out with some offensive action or other,
that puts us all on edge. I'll not endure it!
His knights grow wilder, and he himself reproaches us
for every little thing. When he returns from hunting,
I will not speak to him. Tell him I'm sick.
If you let down in your care of him,
that would be just fine; I'll personally answer for it.
Treat him as negligently as you please,
you and your fellow servants. I'd just as soon he questions me
    about it.
If he doesn't like it, let him go to my sister's,
who I know is in full agreement with me,
and will not be swayed. Silly old man,
who still wants to keep the power
that he has already delegated! Now, by my life,
old fools are like babies, and must be
rebuked, not flattered when they become too full of themselves.
Remember what I have said.

Act 1 scene 3, lines 4–21 (combined)

GONERIL:
By day and night, he wrongs me! Every hour
He flashes into one gross crime or other
That sets us all at odds. I'll not endure it!
His knights grow riotous, and himself upbraids us
On every trifle. When he returns from hunting,
I will not speak with him. Say I am sick.
If you come slack of former services,
You shall do well; the fault of it I'll answer.
Put on what weary negligence you please,
You and your fellows. I'd have it come to question.
If he distaste it, let him to my sister,
Whose mind and mine I know in that are one,
Not to be overruled. Idle old man,
That still would manage those authorities
That he hath given away! Now, by my life,
Old fools are babes again, and must be used
With checks as flatteries, when they are seen abused.
Remember what I have said.

By day and night, he wrongs me! Every hour he flashes into one gross crime or other that sets us all at odds. I'll not endure it! His knights grow riotous, and himself upbraids us on every trifle.

When he returns from hunting, I will not speak with him. Say I am sick. If you come slack of former services, you shall do well; the fault of it I'll answer. Put on what weary negligence you please, you and your fellows. I'd have it come to question. If he distaste it, let him to my sister, whose mind and mine I know in that are one, not to be overruled.

Idle old man, that still would manage those authorities that he hath given away! Now, by my life, old fools are babes again, and must be used with checks as flatteries, when they are seen abused. Remember what I have said.

Act 4 scene 2, lines 35–76 (cut and combined)

ALBANY:
                    Oh Goneril,
you are not worth the dust the rude wind
blows in your face. What have you done?
You are tigers, not daughters, What have you accomplished?
A father, and a gracious old man — you have driven mad.
Could my good brother-in-law have stood back and let you do it?
A man, a prince, who had received so much from him?
If the gods don't send powerful messengers
quickly down to punish these vile offenses,
do not doubt it will come! Look at yourself, you devil!
                    If I could
allow my hands to obey my heart,
they would be likely to dislocate and tear apart
your flesh and bones. But however fiendish you are,
you're protected because you have the shape of a woman.

Act 4 scene 2, lines 35–76 (cut and combined)

ALBANY:

                    O Goneril,
You are not worth the dust which the rude wind
Blows in your face. What have you done?
Tigers not daughters, what have you performed?
A father, and a gracious agèd man have you madded.
Could my good brother suffer you to do it?
A man, a prince, by him so benefited?
If that the heavens do not their visible spirits
Send quickly down to tame these vile offences,
It will come! — See thyself, devil!
                 Were't my fitness
To let these hands obey my blood,
They are apt enough to dislocate and tear
Thy flesh and bones; howe'er thou art a fiend,
A woman's shape doth shield thee.

O Goneril, you are not worth the dust which the rude wind blows in your face. What have you done? Tigers not daughters, what have you performed? A father, and a gracious agèd man have you madded.

Could my good brother suffer you to do it? A man, a prince, by him so benefited? If that the heavens do not their visible spirits send quickly down to tame these vile offences, it will come!

See thyself, devil! Were't my fitness to let these hands obey my blood, they are apt enough to dislocate and tear thy flesh and bones; howe'er thou art a fiend, a woman's shape doth shield thee.

Act 4 scene 7, lines 26–42 (combined)

CORDELIA:
Oh my dear father! Give my lips
the power to restore your health, and let this kiss
repair the massive injuries that my two sisters
have inflicted on your most revered self!
If you had not been their father, your white hairs
would have caused them to feel pity. Was this a face
to be exposed to the harsh elements?
to be left out in a crashing thunderstorm?
in the most terrible, flashing strikes
of swift, jagged lightning? to stand watch — poor lost soul! —
with hardly a hat on your head? My enemy's dog,
even if he'd bitten me, would have been offered the warmth
of my fire that night. And you were forced, poor father,
to huddle with pigs and vagabonds,
in bits of moldy straw? Oh, god, oh, god!
It's amazing that both your life and mind
were not lost. He's awakening; speak to him.

Act 4 scene 7, lines 26–42 (combined)

CORDELIA:
O my dear father! Restoration hang
Thy medicine on my lips, and let this kiss
Repair those violent harms that my two sisters
Have in thy reverence made!
Had you not been their father, these white flakes
Did challenge pity of them. Was this a face
To be opposed against the warring winds?
To stand against the deep dread-bolted thunder?
In the most terrible and nimble stroke
Of quick, cross lightning? To watch — poor perdu! —
With this thin helm? Mine enemy's dog,
Though he had bit me, should have stood that night
Against my fire; and wast thou fain, poor father,
To hovel thee with swine and rogues forlorn,
In short and musty straw? Alack, alack!
'Tis wonder that thy life and wits at once
Had not concluded all. He wakes; speak to him.

O my dear father! Restoration hang thy medicine on my lips, and let this kiss repair those violent harms that my two sisters have in thy reverence made! Had you not been their father, these white flakes did challenge pity of them. Was this a face to be opposed against the warring winds? To stand against the deep dread-bolted thunder? In the most terrible and nimble stroke of quick, cross lightning? To watch — poor perdu! — with this thin helm?

Mine enemy's dog, though he had bit me, should have stood that night against my fire; and wast thou fain, poor father, to hovel thee with swine and rogues forlorn, in short and musty straw? Alack, alack! 'Tis wonder that thy life and wits at once had not concluded all.

He wakes; speak to him.

Act 5 scene 1, lines 55–70

EDMOND:
To both of these sisters I have made love;
each is jealous of the other, like one who's been bitten and is
wary of snakes. Which of them shall be mine?
Both? one? or neither? Neither could be enjoyed
if the other remains alive: if I choose the widow
it would anger and madden her sister Goneril;
and I could hardly do as I please with her,
if her husband remains alive. For now though, I'll need
his support on the battlefield; after which,
it'll be up to her, who wants to get rid of him, to devise
a plan to quickly do it. As for his intention
to have mercy on Lear and Cordelia —
when the war is over, and when they are in my care,
they'll never see his pardon; for I myself must act
to achieve my ends, not debate the morality of it.

Act 5 scene 1 lines 55–70

EDMOND:
To both these sisters have I sworn my love;
Each jealous of the other, as the stung
Are of the adder. Which of them shall I take?
Both? one? or neither? Neither can be enjoyed
If both remain alive: to take the widow
Exasperates, makes mad her sister Goneril;
And hardly shall I carry out my side,
Her husband being alive. Now then, we'll use
His countenance for the battle; which being done,
Let her who would be rid of him devise
His speedy taking off. As for the mercy
Which he intends to Lear and to Cordelia,
The battle done, and they within our power,
Shall never see his pardon; for my state
Stands on me to defend, not to debate.

To both these sisters have I sworn my love; each jealous of the other, as the stung are of the adder.

Which of them shall I take? Both? one? or neither? Neither can be enjoyed if both remain alive: to take the widow exasperates, makes mad her sister Goneril; and hardly shall I carry out my side, her husband being alive. Now then, we'll use his countenance for the battle; which being done, let her who would be rid of him devise his speedy taking off.

As for the mercy which he intends to Lear and to Cordelia, the battle done, and they within our power, shall never see his pardon; for my state stands on me to defend, not to debate.

Act 1 scene 1, lines 34–69 (cut, combined, and rearranged)

BEROWNE:
I can only repeat what they have vowed.
That is, to live and study here for three years.
But there are some other strict regulations,
such as to not see a woman during that time,
which I sincerely hope is not listed in the rules;
and one day a week to eat no food,
and only one meal a day on all other days,
which I hope is not listed in the rules;
and then to sleep only three hours a night,
and not to nod off at all during the day,
which I certainly hope is not listed in the rules.
Oh, these are useless rules, too hard to keep,
not to see ladies, study, fast, not sleep.
What is the result of study, tell me that?
[Why, to know things we might not otherwise know.]
All right then; I will swear to study like this,
to learn things I might otherwise miss;
such as — to study where one may dine
when eating is expressly forbidden;
or study where to meet some lady who is fine
when the rules state that feminine contact is not permitted;
or, having sworn to keep a foolish oath,
study how to break it without losing face.
If this is what's gained through study, and if my premise is so,
swear me to this pursuit, and I would never say no.

Act 1 scene 1, lines 33–69 (cut, combined, and rearranged)

BEROWNE:
I can but say their protestation over.
That is, to live and study here three years.
But there are other strict observances,
As not to see a woman in that term,
Which I hope well is not enrollèd there;
And one day in a week to touch no food,
And but one meal on every day beside,
The which I hope is not enrollèd there;
And then to sleep but three hours in the night,
And not be seen to wink of all the day,
Which I hope well is not enrollèd there.
O, these are barren tasks, too hard to keep,
Not to see ladies, study, fast, not sleep!
What is the end of study, let me know?
[Why, that to know which else we should not know.]
Come on, then; I will swear to study so,
To know the thing I am forbid to know,
As thus, — to study where I well may dine
When I to feast expressly am forbid;
Or study where to meet some mistress fine
When mistresses from common sense are hid;
Or, having sworn too hard a keeping oath,
Study to break it and not break my troth.
If study's gain be thus, and this be so,
Swear me to this, and I will ne'er say no.

I can but say their protestation over. That is, to live and study here three years. But there are other strict observances, as not to see a woman in that term, which I hope well is not enrollèd there; and one day in a week to touch no food, and but one meal on every day beside, the which I hope is not enrollèd there; and then to sleep but three hours in the night, and not be seen to wink of all the day, which I hope well is not enrollèd there. O, these are barren tasks, too hard to keep, not to see ladies, study, fast, not sleep!

What is the end of study, let me know? [Why, that to know which else we should not know.] Come on, then; I will swear to study so, to know the thing I am forbid to know, as thus, — to study where I well may dine when I to feast expressly am forbid; or study where to meet some mistress fine when mistresses from common sense are hid; or, having sworn too hard a keeping oath, study to break it and not break my troth. If study's gain be thus, and this be so, swear me to this, and I will ne'er say no.

Act 4 scene 3, lines 324–397 (cut, combined, and rearranged)

BEROWNE:
Listen to me, love's warriors!
Think about what you first swore to:
to fast, to study, and to see no woman;
totally contrary to the very nature of youth!
For when would you, my lord, or you, or you,
have discovered the basis of study's importance
if you'd never seen the beauty of woman's face?
The love that we discover looking into a lady's eyes,
doesn't just exist as a memory in the brain,
but, with the power of the whole universe,
like thinking itself, it influences every sense,
and gives our senses super powers.
A lover's eye can see more clearly than an eagle;
a lover's ear can hear the faintest sound,
love feels with more delicacy and perception
than the sensitive antenna of a snail in its shell.
And when Love speaks through us, it's as if the voices of
    all the gods
were singing a lullaby to the heavens in perfect harmony.
Then what fools you were to swear to renounce women;
and, if you keep your oaths, you'll prove even bigger fools.
For wisdom's sake — a word that all men love to have —
or for Love's sake — a word that all men love to feel —
let us lose these oaths and thereby find our true selves.
From women's eyes I can deduce this principle:
they are the very basis, the manuals, the schools,
from which springs the true inspiration of man,
they reflect, contain, and nourish all the world.
Then when we see ourselves reflected in ladies' eyes,
don't we likewise see all that is worth knowing there?

Act 4 scene 3, lines 324–397(cut, combined, and rearranged)

BEROWNE:
Have at you then, affection's men-at-arms!
Consider what you first did swear unto:
To fast, to study, and to see no woman —
Flat treason 'gainst the kingly state of youth!
For when would you, my lord, or you, or you,
Have found the ground of study's excellence
Without the beauty of a woman's face?
Love, first learnèd in a lady's eyes,
Lives not alone immurèd in the brain,
But with the motion of all elements
Courses as swift as thought in every power,
And gives to every power a double power.
A lover's eyes will gaze an eagle blind.
A lover's ear will hear the lowest sound,
Love's feeling is more soft and sensible
Than are the tender horns of cockled snails.
And when Love speaks, the voice of all the gods
Make heaven drowsy with the harmony.
Then fools you were these women to forswear;
Or keeping what is sworn, you will prove fools.
From women's eyes this doctrine I derive:
They are the ground, the books, the academes,
From whence doth spring the true Promethean fire,
That show, contain, and nourish all the world.
Then when ourselves we see in ladies' eyes,
Do we not likewise see our learning there?

Have at you then, affection's men-at-arms! Consider what you first did swear unto: to fast, to study, and to see no woman — flat treason 'gainst the kingly state of youth! For when would you, my lord, or you, or you, have found the ground of study's excellence without the beauty of a woman's face? Love, first learnèd in a lady's eyes, lives not alone immurèd in the brain, but with the motion of all elements courses as swift as thought in every power, and gives to every power a double power. A lover's eyes will gaze an eagle blind. A lover's ear will hear the lowest sound, love's feeling is more soft and sensible than are the tender horns of cockled snails.

And when Love speaks, the voice of all the gods make heaven drowsy with the harmony. Then fools you were these women to forswear; or keeping what is sworn, you will prove fools. From women's eyes this doctrine I derive: they are the ground, the books, the academes, from whence doth spring the true Promethean fire, that show, contain, and nourish all the world. Then when ourselves we see in ladies' eyes, do we not likewise see our learning there?

Act 1 scene 2, lines 7–23

CAPTAIN:

Things looked doubtful,
as they do for two exhausted swimmers who, clinging to each other,
hinder each other's progress. The merciless Macdonwald
(fit to be a rebel, since he possesses
all the ever-increasingly hideous qualities
nature has to offer) is reinforced from Ireland
with foot soldiers and horsemen;
and good fortune (that whore) seemed to be smiling
on the damned rebel's side. But it wasn't enough;
for brave Macbeth — how well he deserves that title —
disdaining fortune, brandishing his sword,
which still steamed with the enemies' blood,
like the bravest of the brave, carved out a path
till he came face to face with the wretch;
no formalities, no farewells;
he simply ripped him from his navel to his jaw,
and stuck his head on the castle tower.

Act 1 scene 2, lines 7–23

CAPTAIN:
> Doubtful it stood,
As two spent swimmers, that do cling together
And choke their art. The merciless Macdonwald
(Worthy to be a rebel, for to that
The multiplying villainies of nature
Do swarm upon him) from the Western Isles
Of kerns and gallowglasses is supplied;
And Fortune, on his damnèd quarrel smiling,
Show'd like a rebel's whore. But all's too weak;
For brave Macbeth — well he deserves that name —
Disdaining Fortune, with his brandished steel,
Which smoked with bloody execution,
Like Valor's minion carved out his passage
Till he faced the slave;
Which ne'er shook hands, nor bade farewell to him,
Till he unseamed him from the nave to th'chops,
And fixed his head upon our battlements.

Doubtful it stood, (as two spent swimmers, that do cling together and choke their art. The merciless Macdonwald (worthy to be a rebel, for to that the multiplying villainies of nature do swarm upon him) from the Western Isles of kerns and gallowglasses is supplied; and Fortune, on his damnèd quarrel smiling, show'd like a rebel's whore.

But all's too weak; for brave Macbeth — well he deserves that name — disdaining fortune, with his brandished steel, which smoked with bloody execution, like Valor's minion carved out his passage till he faced the slave; — which ne'er shook hands, nor bade farewell to him, till he unseamed him from the nave to th'chops, and fixed his head upon our battlements.

Act 1 scene 3, lines 127–142 (cut)

MACBETH:

Two truths have been told,
as glorious preludes to the wonderful finale
of what will be a royal theme.
These supernatural enticements
cannot be ill, cannot be good. If ill,
why have they given me a promise of success
which has proven to be true? I am Thane of Cawdor.
If good, why am I drawn to that thought
whose horrible image makes my hair stand on end
and causes my heart to beat against my ribs
so unnaturally? Facing true horrors
is easier than dealing with imaginary ones.
My thoughts, merely conceiving an imaginary murder,
so unnerve me to the very core,
that I can barely function,
and can no longer distinguish the boundaries of reality.

Act 1 scene 3, lines 127–142 (cut)

MACBETH:

                      Two truths are told,
As happy prologues to the swelling act
Of the imperial theme.
This supernatural soliciting
Cannot be ill, cannot be good; if ill,
Why hath it given me earnest of success,
Commencing in a truth? I am Thane of Cawdor.
If good, why do I yield to that suggestion
Whose horrid image doth unfix my hair
And make my seated heart knock at my ribs,
Against the use of nature? Present fears
Are less than horrible imaginings.
My thought, whose murder yet is but fantastical,
Shakes so my single state of man
That function is smothered in surmise,
And nothing is but what is not.

     Two truths are told, as happy prologues to the swelling act of the imperial theme. This supernatural soliciting cannot be ill, cannot be good; if ill, why hath it given me earnest of success, commencing in a truth? I am Thane of Cawdor. If good, why do I yield to that suggestion whose horrid image doth unfix my hair and make my seated heart knock at my ribs, against the use of nature?

     Present fears are less than horrible imaginings. My thought, whose murder yet is but fantastical, shakes so my single state of man that function is smothered in surmise, and nothing is but what is not.

Act 1 scene 5, lines 38–54

LADY MACBETH:
                    Even the messenger sounded ominous
who announced the fatal arrival of Duncan
under my roof. Come you spirits
who deal in thoughts of mortality, remove all traces of
    feminine weakness,
and fill me from head to toe, full up
with the most dire cruelty! Thicken my blood,
stop up any passageways where remorse might enter,
so no pangs of conscience
can interfere with my deadly intentions, nor keep me from doing
the deed and gaining my ends! Come, to my womanly breasts,
and replace my milk with gall, you powers who aid in murder,
wherever in the unseen universe you are waiting
to make your mischief! Come, dark night,
and wrap yourself in the thickest smoke from hell,
so my sharp knife cannot see the wound it will make,
nor heaven be able to peer through that blanket of darkness,
to cry out, 'Stop, stop!'

Act 1 scene 5, lines 38–54

LADY MACBETH:

                    The raven himself is hoarse
That croaks the fatal entrance of Duncan
Under my battlements. Come, you spirits
That tend on mortal thoughts, unsex me here,
And fill me from the crown to the toe, top-full
Of direst cruelty! Make thick my blood,
Stop up th'access and passage to remorse,
That no compunctious visitings of nature
Shake my fell purpose, nor keep peace between
Th'effect and it! Come to my woman's breasts,
And take my milk for gall, you murd'ring ministers,
Wherever in your sightless substances
You wait on nature's mischief. Come, thick night,
And pall thee in the dunnest smoke of hell,
That my keen knife see not the wound it makes,
Nor Heaven peep through the blanket of the dark,
To cry 'Hold, hold!'

The raven himself is hoarse that croaks the fatal entrance of Duncan under my battlements.

Come, you spirits that tend on mortal thoughts, unsex me here, and fill me from the crown to the toe, top-full of direst cruelty! Make thick my blood, — stop up th'access and passage to remorse, that no compunctious visitings of nature shake my fell purpose, nor keep peace between th'effect and it!

Come to my woman's breasts, and take my milk for gall, you murd'ring ministers, wherever in your sightless substances you wait on nature's mischief. Come, thick night, and pall thee in the dunnest smoke of hell, that my keen knife see not the wound it makes, nor Heaven peep through the blanket of the dark, to cry 'Hold, hold!'

Act 1 scene 7, lines 47–59

LADY MACBETH:

Then what monster was it
that forced you to disclose this plan to me?
When you dared to do it — then you were manly —
and to be greater than you were, you would then
be a truly great man. Neither the opportunity, nor the circumstances,
existed then, and yet you were willing to ignore that fact.
They now have made themselves apparent, and that,
    their very existence,
is proving your undoing. I have nursed, and know
how sweet it is to love the baby who's suckling;
I would while it was smiling up at me,
have plucked my nipple from its boneless gums
and dashed its brains out, if I had sworn
as you have sworn to this.

Act 1 scene 7, lines 47–59

LADY MACBETH:

What beast was't then
That made you break this enterprise to me?
When you durst do it, then you were a man.
And to be more than what you were, you would
be so much more the man. Nor time, nor place,
Did then adhere, and yet you would make both.
They have made themselves, and that — their fitness now —
Does unmake you. I have given suck and know
How tender 'tis to love the babe that milks me;
I would, while it was smiling in my face,
Have plucked my nipple from his boneless gums
And dashed the brains out, had I so sworn
As you have done to this.

What beast was't then that made you break this enterprise to me? When you durst do it, then you were a man. And to be more than what you were, you would be so much more the man. Nor time, nor place, did then adhere, and yet you would make both. They have made themselves, and that — their fitness now — does unmake you.

I have given suck and know how tender 'tis to love the babe that milks me; I would, while it was smiling in my face, have plucked my nipple from his boneless gums and dashed the brains out, had I so sworn as you have done to this.

Act 1 scene 7, lines 60–73

LADY MACBETH:
                    We fail?
Just gather up your courage,
and we'll not fail. When Duncan is asleep
(where inevitably his hard day's journey
will lead him), his two attendants
will I so undermine with wine and toasting,
that memory — the guardian of the brain —
shall be a mere vapor, and the brain itself,
an empty cask. While in this drunken stupor,
with their besotted selves lying as if they were dead,
what can't you and I then do to
the unguarded Duncan? What not blame upon
his sodden officers, who shall appear guilty
of our great feat?

Act 1 scene 7, lines 60–73

LADY MACBETH:

                                We fail?
But screw your courage to the sticking place,
And we'll not fail. When Duncan is asleep
(Whereto the rather shall his day's hard journey
Soundly invite him), his two chamberlains
Will I with wine and wassail so convince,
That memory, the warder of the brain,
Shall be a fume, and the receipt of reason
A limbeck only. When in swinish sleep
Their drenchèd natures lies as in a death,
What cannot you and I perform upon
Th'unguarded Duncan? What not put upon
His spongy officers who shall bear the guilt
Of our great quell?

We fail? But screw your courage to the sticking place, and we'll not fail.
When Duncan is asleep (whereto the rather shall his day's hard journey soundly invite him), his two chamberlains will I with wine and wassail so convince, that memory, the warder of the brain, shall be a fume, and the receipt of reason a limbeck only. When in swinish sleep their drenchèd natures lies as in a death, what cannot you and I perform upon th'unguarded Duncan? What not put upon his spongy officers who shall bear the guilt of our great quell?

Act 2 scene 3, lines 106–116

MACBETH:
Who can be wise, bewildered, calm and furious,
loyal and objective, at the same moment? No man.
The desire for action, spurred by my intense love,
won out over my reason. Here lay Duncan,
his pale skin crisscrossed with his royal blood;
and his gashes looked like passageways
for destruction to enter; there were the murderers,
covered in blood, their daggers
dripping with gore. Who could hold back,
who had a heart that loved him, and who had the
courage to act upon that love?

Act 2 scene 3, lines 106–116

MACBETH:
Who can be wise, amazed, temp'rate and furious,
Loyal and neutral, in a moment? No man.
The expedition of my violent love
Outrun the pauser, reason. Here lay Duncan,
His silver skin laced with his golden blood,
And his gashed stabs looked like a breach in nature
For ruin's wasteful entrance: there, the murderers,
Steeped in the colors of their trade, their daggers
Unmannerly breeched with gore. Who could refrain,
That had a heart to love, and in that heart
Courage to make's love known?

Who can be wise, amazed, temp'rate and furious, loyal and neutral, in a moment?
No man.
The expedition of my violent love outrun the pauser, reason. Here lay Duncan, his silver
skin laced with his golden blood, and his gashed stabs looked like a breach in nature for ruin's
wasteful entrance: there, the murderers, steeped in the colors of their trade, their daggers unmannerly breeched with gore.
Who could refrain, that had a heart to love, and in that heart courage to make's love
known?

Act 3 scene 1, lines 91–107

MACBETH:
Yes, if classified you'd fall into the category of men;
just as hounds and greyhounds, mongrels, spaniels, curs
shaggy dogs, poodles, and wolves are all listed
under the name 'dog': Their peculiarities —
be it swiftness, slowness, slyness,
a house-pet, a hunter — distinguishes each of them
according to the particular gift which nature
has given him, and makes him
stand out from all the rest
who appear merely ordinary: and so it is with men.
Now, if your distinguishing characteristics
place you above the lowest rank of manhood, say so,
and I will share with you an idea
which, when achieved, will eliminate your enemy,
and win a place for you in my heart,
which feels sickly while he lives,
but would feel perfect if he were dead.

Act 3 scene 1, lines 91–107

MACBETH:
Ay, in the catalogue ye go for men;
As hounds and greyhounds, mongrels, spaniels, curs,
Shoughs, water rugs and demiwolves, are clept
All by the name of dogs. The valued file
Distinguishes the swift, the slow, the subtle,
The housekeeper, the hunter, every one
According to the gift which bounteous nature
Hath in him closed, whereby he does receive
Particular addition, from the bill
That writes them all alike: and so of men.
Now if you have a station in the file,
Not i' the worst rank of manhood, say't,
And I will put that business in your bosoms
Whose execution takes your enemy off,
Grapples you to the heart and love of us,
Who wear our health but sickly in his life,
Which in his death were perfect.

Ay, in the catalogue ye go for men; as hounds and greyhounds, mongrels, spaniels, curs, shoughs, water rugs and demiwolves, are clept all by the name of dogs. The valued file distinguishes the swift, the slow, the subtle, the housekeeper, the hunter, — every one according to the gift which bounteous nature hath in him closed, whereby he does receive particular addition, from the bill that writes them all alike: and so of men.

Now if you have a station in the file, not i' the worst rank of manhood, say't, and I will put that business in your bosoms whose execution takes your enemy off, grapples you to the heart and love of us, who wear our health but sickly in his life, which in his death were perfect.

Act 3 scene 2, lines 13–26

MACBETH:
We have merely scratched the snake, not killed it.
She'll heal and be well while our ineffectual efforts
remain in danger of her former poisons.
But let the framework of the world fall apart, let heaven and
    earth suffer,
before we shall eat our meals in fear and endure
these terrible dreams that wake us every night.
It's better to be with the dead,
whom we, to achieve our peace, have sent to their peace,
than — because of our tortured minds — to lie
in such restless frenzy. Duncan is in his grave;
after life's ups and downs he sleeps peacefully.
The worst has happened. Neither swords, nor poison,
domestic strife, foreign wars, nothing
can disturb him now!

Act 3 scene 2, lines 13–26

MACBETH:
We have scorched the snake, not killed it.
She'll close and be herself whilst our poor malice
Remains in danger of her former tooth.
But let the frame of things disjoint, both the worlds suffer,
Ere we will eat our meal in fear, and sleep
In the affliction of these terrible dreams
That shake us nightly. Better be with the dead,
Whom we, to gain our peace, have sent to peace,
Than on the torture of the mind to lie
In restless ecstasy. Duncan is in his grave;
After life's fitful fever he sleeps well.
Treason has done his worst. Nor steel, nor poison,
Malice domestic, foreign levy, nothing,
Can touch him further!

We have scorched the snake, not killed it. She'll close and be herself whilst our poor malice remains in danger of her former tooth.

But let the frame of things disjoint, both the worlds suffer, ere we will eat our meal in fear, and sleep in the affliction of these terrible dreams that shake us nightly. Better be with the dead, whom we, to gain our peace, have sent to peace, than on the torture of the mind to lie in restless ecstasy.

Duncan is in his grave; after life's fitful fever he sleeps well. Treason has done his worst. Nor steel, nor poison, malice domestic, foreign levy, nothing, can touch him further!

Act 3 scene 2, lines 40–55 (cut and combined)

MACBETH:

Before the bat has flown
from his protected place, before the evil goddess of hell has ordered
the night bell to signal the end of day, there shall be done
a deed of awe-inspiring magnitude. Come, blinding night,
close up the eyes of fair-dealing day,
and with your bloody and invisible hand,
tear from me those feelings of pity and remorse
that weaken me with fear and indecision! Light grows dim and the crow
flies into the gloomy woods.
Good things of the day begin to droop and drift away,
while the evil agents of night awaken to their prey.
You marvel at my words, but keep still.
Things badly begun can be strengthened through the use of ill.

Act 3 scene 2, lines 40–55 (cut and combined)

MACBETH:

Ere the bat hath flown
His cloistered flight, ere to black Hecate summons
The shard-borne beetle with his drowsy hums
Hath rung night's yawning peal, there shall be done
A deed of dreadful note. Come, seeling night,
Scarf up the tender eye of pitiful day,
And with thy bloody and invisible hand
Cancel and tear to pieces that great bond
Which keeps me pale! Light thickens and the crow
Makes wing to th'rooky wood.
Good things of day begin to droop and drowse,
Whiles night's black agents to their preys do rouse.
Thou marvel'st at my words, but hold thee still.
Things bad begun, make strong themselves by ill.

Ere the bat hath flown his cloistered flight, ere to black Hecate summons the shard-borne beetle with his drowsy hums hath rung night's yawning peal, there shall be done a deed of dreadful note.

Come, seeling night, scarf up the tender eye of pitiful day, and with thy bloody and invisible hand cancel and tear to pieces that great bond which keeps me pale! Light thickens and the crow makes wing to th'rooky wood. Good things of day begin to droop and drowse, whiles night's black agents to their preys do rouse.

Thou marvel'st at my words, but hold thee still. Things bad begun, make strong themselves by ill.

Act 1 scene 2, lines 12–25

PORTIA:

If to do a thing, were as easy as knowing what was the right thing to do, then chapels would be churches, and poor men's cottages princes' palaces. It's the good teacher who follows his own advice; I could more easily teach twenty others to do right, than be one of those twenty who must follow my own teachings. The brain can create rules to live by, but hot-blooded instincts ignore cold-blooded reason; just as youthful madness is capable of evading his old counselors by leaping the bounds of reason. But logic of this sort will not help me choose a husband. Oh dear, that word 'choose'! For I can neither choose the one I want, nor refuse those I dislike, so is the will of a living daughter curbed by the will of a dead father. Isn't it awful, Nerissa, that I have neither the power to choose nor the chance to refuse?

Act 1 scene 2, lines 12–25

PORTIA:

If to do were as easy as to know what were good to do, chapels had been churches, and poor men's cottages princes' palaces. It is a good divine that follows his own instructions; I can easier teach twenty what were good to be done than to be one of the twenty to follow mine own teaching. The brain may devise laws for the blood, but a hot temper leaps o'er a cold decree; such a hare is madness the youth to skip o'er the meshes of good counsel the cripple. But this reasoning is not in the fashion to choose me a husband. O, me, the word 'choose'! I may neither choose who I would nor refuse who I dislike, so is the will of a living daughter curbed by the will of a dead father. Is it not hard, Nerissa, that I cannot choose one, nor refuse none?

Act 3 scene 2, lines 1–23

PORTIA:
I beg you to wait. Delay for a day or two
Before you attempt to win me, 'cause if you choose wrong
you will have to depart (we will have to part), therefore put it
    off for a while.
Something tells me, though not love of course,
that I don't want you to go; but you yourself know
hatred would never inspire such feelings.
But, in case you do not understand me clearly-
(yet a virgin has no way to convey this except to voice her thoughts)
I wish I could keep you here for a month or two
before you make your attempt. I could teach you
how to choose correctly, — but that would be cheating
something I would never do. But if I don't, you might not win me.
And if that happens, you'll make me wish I'd sinned —
that I had cheated. Damn your eyes!
they have looked upon me and divided my allegiance;
one half of me is yours; the other half . . . yours —
I would say mine; but whatever is mine is yours,
and so all yours! Oh, this is a horrid situation
which puts these obstacles between my heart and you who possess it!
And so, though I am yours in spirit, I'm not yours in body. If that
    would prove so,
let fortune go to hell for it, not me.
I talk too much, but it is in order to delay the moment of decision,
to stretch it and draw it out in length,
to keep you from choosing.

Act 3, scene 2, lines 1–23

PORTIA:
I pray you tarry. Pause a day or two
Before you hazard, for in choosing wrong
I lose your company. Therefore forbear awhile.
There's something tells me, but it is not love,
I would not lose you; and you know yourself
Hate counsels not in such a quality.
But lest you should not understand me well —
And yet a maiden hath no tongue but thought —
I would detain you here some month or two
Before you venture for me. I could teach you
How to choose right, but then I am forsworn.
So will I never be. So may you miss me.
But if you do, you'll make me wish a sin —
That I had been forsworn. Beshrow your eyes!
They have o'erlooked me and divided me;
One half of me is yours, the other half yours —
Mine own I would say; but if mine then yours,
And so all yours! O, these naughty times
Puts bars between the owners and their rights!
And so, though yours, not yours. Prove it so,
Let fortune go to hell for it, not I.
I speak too long, but 'tis to peize the time,
To eke it and to draw it out in length,
To stay you from election.

I pray you tarry. Pause a day or two before you hazard, for in choosing wrong I lose your company. Therefore forbear awhile. There's something tells me, but it is not love, I would not lose you; and you know yourself hate counsels not in such a quality.

But lest you should not understand me well — and yet a maiden hath no tongue but thought — I would detain you here some month or two before you venture for me. I could teach you how to choose right, but then I am forsworn. So will I never be. So may you miss me. But if you do, you'll make me wish a sin — that I had been forsworn.

Beshrow your eyes! They have o'erlooked me and divided me; one half of me is yours, the other half yours— mine own I would say; but if mine then yours, and so all yours! O these naughty times puts bars between the owners and their rights! And so, though yours, not yours.

Prove it so; let fortune go to hell for it, not I. I speak too long, but 'tis to peize the time, to eke it and to draw it out in length, to stay you from election.

Act 3 scene 2, lines 149–174

PORTIA:
You see me, Lord Bassanio, standing here,
as I am. And though for myself alone
I would not wish myself to be
other than I am, yet for you
I wish I were triple twenty times better,
a thousand times prettier, ten thousand times richer,
so that I might stand higher in your estimation,
I wish my virtues, beauty, fortune, friends,
could surpass all counts. But my personal worth
is worth something — which, to sum up,
is a naive girl, uneducated, inexperienced;
happy in that, she in not yet too old
to learn; happier still,
she is not so dull-witted that she can't learn;
happiest of all, is that her simple spirit
can join itself to yours to be taught,
as you become her lord, her director, her guide.
Myself and all that I possess I turn over to
your control. Till now I was the head
of this household, master of my servants,
my own person, but as of now, this moment,
this house, these servants, and I myself
are yours, my lord's. I give them away with this ring,
which if you ever part from, lose, or give away,
shall indicate the loss of your love
and be the signal for me to reproach you.

Act 3 scene 2, lines 149–174

PORTIA:
You see me, Lord Bassanio, where I stand,
Such as I am. Though for myself alone
I would not be ambitious in my wish
To wish myself much better, yet for you
I would be trebled twenty times myself,
A thousand times more fair, ten thousand times more rich,
That only to stand high in your account,
I might in virtues, beauties, livings, friends,
Exceed account. But the full sum of me
Is sum of something — which, to term in gross,
Is an unlessoned girl, unschooled, unpractised;
Happy in this, she is not yet so old
But she may learn; happier than this,
She is not bred so dull but she can learn;
Happiest of all, is that her gentle spirit
Commits itself to yours to be directed,
As from her lord, her governor, her king.
Myself and what is mine to you and yours
Is now converted. But now I was the lord
Of this fair mansion, master of my servants,
Queen o'er myself; and even now, but now,
This house, these servants, and this same myself
Are yours, my lord's. I give them with this ring,
Which when you part from, lose, or give away,
Let is presage the ruin of your love
And be my vantage to exclaim on you.

You see me, Lord Bassanio, where I stand, such as I am. Though for myself alone I would not be ambitious in my wish to wish myself much better, yet for you I would be trebled twenty times myself — a thousand times more fair, ten thousand times more rich — that only to stand high in your account, I might in virtues, beauties, livings, friends, exceed account.

But the full sum of me is sum of something, which, to term in gross, is an unlessoned girl, unschooled, unpractised; happy in this, she is not yet so old but she may learn; happier than this, she is not bred so dull but she can learn; happiest of all, is that her gentle spirit commits itself to yours to be directed, as from her lord, her governor, her king.

Myself and what is mine to you and yours is now converted. But now I was the lord of this fair mansion, master of my servants, queen o'er myself; and even now, but now, this house, these servants, and this same myself are yours, my lord's. I give them with this ring, which when you part from, lose, or give away, let is presage the ruin of your love and be my vantage to exclaim on you.

Act 3 scene 4, lines 62–78

PORTIA:
                                    I'll bet you anything,
when we are both dressed up like young men,
I'll show to be finer of the two,
and wear my dagger more gallantly,
and pitch my voice so that it sounds like it is
just changing, and turn my dainty little steps
into manly strides, and talk of battles
like a fine bragging youth, and tell wonderful tales,
about how honorable ladies sought my love,
and how, when I rejected them, they fell ill and died —
I couldn't help myself! Then I'll repent,
and wish, after all, that I hadn't killed them.
And twenty of these tall tales will I tell,
so that everyone will believe I've been out of school
for at least a year. I can think of
a thousand silly jokes I've heard from these boastful fellows,
which I'll try out.

Act 3 scene 4, lines 62–78

PORTIA:

I'll hold thee any wager,
When we are both accoutered like young men,
I'll prove the prettier fellow of the two,
And wear my dagger with the braver grace,
And speak between the change of man and boy
With a reed voice, and turn two mincing steps
Into a manly stride, and speak of frays
Like a fine bragging youth, and tell quaint lies,
How honorable ladies sought my love,
Which I denying, they fell sick and died —
I could not do withal! Then I'll repent,
And wish, for all that, that I had not killed them.
And twenty of these puny lies I'll tell,
That men shall swear I have discontinued school
Above a twelvemonth. I have within my mind
A thousand raw tricks of these bragging Jacks,
Which I will practice.

I'll hold thee any wager, when we are both accoutered like young men, I'll prove the prettier fellow of the two, and wear my dagger with the braver grace, and speak between the change of man and boy with a reed voice, and turn two mincing steps into a manly stride, and speak of frays like a fine bragging youth, and tell quaint lies, how honorable ladies sought my love, which I denying, they fell sick and died — I could not do withal!

Then I'll repent, and wish, for all that, that I had not killed them. And twenty of these puny lies I'll tell, that men shall swear I have discontinued school above a twelvemonth. I have within my mind a thousand raw tricks of these bragging Jacks, which I will practice.

Act 4 scene 1, lines 297–314 (combined)

PORTIA:
A pound of that very merchant's flesh is yours.
The court awards it, and it is legally yours.
And you must cut this flesh from off his breast.
The law permits this and the court has awarded it.
[But] wait just a moment; there is another matter.
This contract does not award you any blood;
it expressly states, 'a pound of flesh.'
Then take your award, take your pound of flesh;
but, if in cutting it, you should shed
one drop of this Christian's blood, your lands and possessions
will be, by the laws of Venice, confiscated
by the state of Venice.

Act 4 scene 1, lines 297–314 (combined)

PORTIA:
A pound of that same merchant's flesh is thine.
The court awards it, and the law doth give it.
And you must cut this flesh from off his breast.
The law allows it, and the court awards it.
[But] Tarry a little; there is something else.
This bond doth give thee here no jot of blood;
The words expressly are 'a pound of flesh.'
Take then thy bond, take thou thy pound of flesh;
But in the cutting it, if thou dost shed
One drop of Christian blood, thy lands and goods
Are by the laws of Venice confiscate
Unto the state of Venice.

A pound of that same merchant's flesh is thine. The court awards it, and the law doth give it. And you must cut this flesh from off his breast. The law allows it, and the court awards it.

[But] Tarry a little; there is something else. This bond doth give thee here no jot of blood; the words expressly are 'a pound of flesh.'

Take then thy bond, take thou thy pound of flesh; but in the cutting it, if thou dost shed one drop of Christian blood, thy lands and goods are by the laws of Venice confiscate unto the state of Venice.

Act 5 scene 1, lines 1–23 (cut and combined)

LORENZO:
The moon shines bright. On such a night as this,
when a delicate breeze gently caressed the trees
stirring not a sound, on such a night
I think Troilus did climb the walls of Troy
and poured forth his very soul towards the Greek tents
where Cressida slept that night. On such a night
Dido stood with a willow branch in her hand
upon the raging seashore, and beckoned her lover
to return to Carthage. On such a night
did Jessica sneak away from the wealthy Jew's house,
and with her good-for-nothing lover escape from Venice
and came to Belmont. On such a night
did pretty Jessica, like a little vixen,
slander her lover, and he forgave her for it.

Act 5 scene 1, lines 1–23 (cut and combined)

LORENZO:
The moon shines bright. In such a night as this,
When the sweet wind did gently kiss the trees
And they did make no noise, in such a night
Troilus methinks mounted the Troyan walls,
And sighed his soul toward the Grecian tents
Where Cressid lay that night. In such a night
Stood Dido with a willow in her hand
Upon the wild sea banks and waft her love
To come again to Carthage. In such a night
Did Jessica steal from the wealthy Jew,
And with an unthrift love did run from Venice
As far as Belmont. In such a night
Did pretty Jessica, like a little shrew,
Slander her love, and he forgave it her.

The moon shines bright. In such a night as this, when the sweet wind did gently kiss the trees and they did make no noise, in such a night Troilus methinks mounted the Troyan walls, and sighed his soul toward the Grecian tents where Cressid lay that night.

In such a night stood Dido with a willow in her hand upon the wild sea banks and waft her love to come again to Carthage.

In such a night did Jessica steal from the wealthy Jew, and with an unthrift love did run from Venice as far as Belmont.

In such a night did pretty Jessica, like a little shrew, slander her love, and he forgave it her.

Act 5 scene 1, lines 54–88 (cut and combined)

LORENZO:
How pleasantly the moonlight rests upon this ridge!
Here shall we sit and let the sounds of music
creep into our ears; the gentle silence and the night
are fitting to the sweet, harmonious strains.
Sit, Jessica. Look how the backdrop of the heavens
seems so richly inlaid with bright golden spheres.
The orbit of even the tiniest planet that you see
produces sounds like an angel singing,
serenading the youthful cherubins;
such harmony exists in our immortal souls,
but while we are trapped in our earthly bodies
of flesh, we're unable to hear it.
The man that has no music in himself,
nor is not moved by such sweet harmonies,
is fit only for treason, deceit, and destruction;
his impulses are as gloomy as night,
and his disposition as dismal as hell.
Let no such man be trusted. Listen to the music.

Act 5 scene 1, lines 54–88 (cut and combined)

LORENZO:
How sweet the moonlight sleeps upon this bank!
Here will we sit and let the sounds of music
Creep in our ears; soft stillness and the night
Become the touches of sweet harmony.
Sit, Jessica. Look how the floor of heaven
Is thick inlaid with patens of bright gold.
There's not the smallest orb which thou behold'st
But in his motion like an angel sings,
Still quiring to the young-eyed cherubins;
Such harmony is in immortal souls,
But whilst this muddy vesture of decay
Doth grossly close it in, we cannot hear it.
The man that hath no music in himself,
Nor is not moved with concord of sweet sounds,
Is fit for treasons, stratagems, and spoils;
The motions of his spirit are dull as night,
And his affections dark as Erebus.
Let no such man be trusted. Mark the music.

How sweet the moonlight sleeps upon this bank! Here will we sit and let the sounds of music creep in our ears; soft stillness and the night become the touches of sweet harmony. Sit, Jessica.

Look how the floor of heaven is thick inlaid with patens of bright gold. There's not the smallest orb which thou behold'st but in his motion like an angel sings, still quiring to the young-eyed cherubins; such harmony is in immortal souls, but whilst this muddy vesture of decay doth grossly close it in, we cannot hear it.

The man that hath no music in himself, nor is not moved with concord of sweet sounds, is fit for treasons, stratagems, and spoils; the motions of his spirit are dull as night, and his affections dark as Erebus. Let no such man be trusted. Mark the music.

Act 1 scene 1, lines 100–111

LYSANDER:
I am, my lord, from as good a family as he,
as well off: my love is stronger than his:
my fortunes are in every way equal,
if not greater than Demetrius':
but — more important than anything I might boast of —
I am beloved by beautiful Hermia.
Why should I not then pursue my claim to her?
Demetrius — I'll swear it to his face —
made love to Nedar's daughter, Helena,
and won her over; and she, sweet lady, dotes,
devoutly dotes, dotes adoringly,
on this tainted and fickle fellow.

Act 1 scene 1, lines 100–111

LYSANDER:
I am, my lord, as well derived as he,
As well possessed; my love is more than his;
My fortunes every way as fairly ranked,
If not with vantage, as Demetrius:
And — which is more than all these boasts can be —
I am beloved of beauteous Hermia.
Why should not I then prosecute my right?
Demetrius — I'll avouch it to his head —
Made love to Nedar's daughter, Helena,
And won her soul; and she, sweet lady, dotes,
Devoutly dotes, dotes in idolatry,
Upon this spotted and inconstant man.

I am, my lord, as well derived as he, as well possessed: my love is more than his: my fortunes every way as fairly ranked, if not with vantage, as Demetrius: And — which is more than all these boasts can be — I am beloved of beauteous Hermia. Why should not I then prosecute my right?

Demetrius — I'll avouch it to his head — made love to Nedar's daughter, Helena, and won her soul; and she, sweet lady, dotes, devoutly dotes, dotes in idolatry, upon this spotted and inconstant man.

Act 1 scene 1, lines 134–151 (combined)

LYSANDER;
Oh my! According to everything I've ever read,
or ever heard recounted or reported,
the course of true love never did run smooth;
sometimes it's because of a difference in backgrounds —
or else a mismatch by reason of age —
or else because it was based upon someone else's choosing —
or, if it was a mutually acceptable choice,
war, death, or sickness might seek to destroy it,
making it as momentary as a sound,
as fleeting as a shadow, as short as any dream,
as brief as the lightning in a pitch-black night,
that, in a sudden flash, reveals both heaven and earth;
and before a man is capable of saying, 'Look!'
the jaws of darkness have devoured it up:
so quickly, beautiful things can come to ruin.

Act 1 scene 1, lines 134–151 (combined)

LYSANDER:
Ay me! for aught that I could ever read,
Could ever hear by tale or history,
The course of true love never did run smooth;
But, either it was different in blood —
Or else misgraffèd in respect of years —
Or else it stood upon the choice of friends —
Or, if there were a sympathy in choice,
War, death, or sickness did lay siege to it,
Making it momentary as a sound,
Swift as a shadow, short as any dream,
Brief as the lightning in the collied night,
That, in a spleen, unfolds both heaven and earth;
And ere a man hath power to say, 'Behold!'
The jaws of darkness do devour it up:
So quick bright things come to confusion.

Ay me! for aught that I could ever read, could ever hear by tale or history, the course of true love never did run smooth; but, either it was different in blood — or else misgraffèd in respect of years — or else it stood upon the choice of friends — or, if there were a sympathy in choice, war, death, or sickness did lay siege to it, making it momentary as a sound, swift as a shadow, short as any dream, brief as the lightning in the collied night, that, in a spleen, unfolds both heaven and earth; and ere a man hath power to say, 'Behold!' the jaws of darkness do devour it up: so quick bright things come to confusion.

Act 1 scene 1, lines 168–178

HERMIA:

My good Lysander,
I swear to you by Cupid's strongest bow,
by his finest arrow tipped with gold,
by the purity of Venus' doves,
by that which combines souls and furthers love,
and by the passions which smoldered in Carthage's Queen,
when the disloyal Trojan sailed off and was never again seen,
by all the vows that men have ever broken
(a greater number than women have ever spoken),
in that very place where you have asked me to,
tomorrow, I will certainly meet with you.

Act 1 scene 1, lines 168–178

HERMIA:

My good Lysander,
I swear to thee by Cupid's strongest bow,
By his best arrow with the golden head,
By the simplicity of Venus' doves,
By that which knitteth souls and prospers loves,
And by that fire which burned the Carthage queen,
When the false Troyan under sail was seen,
By all the vows that ever men have broke
(In number more than ever women spoke),
In that same place thou hast appointed me,
Tomorrow truly will I meet with thee.*

My good Lysander, I swear to thee by Cupid's strongest bow, by his best arrow with the golden head, by the simplicity of Venus' doves, by that which knitteth souls and prospers loves, and by that fire which burned the Carthage queen, when the false Troyan under sail was seen, by all the vows that ever men have broke (in number more than ever women spoke), in that same place thou hast appointed me, tomorrow truly will I meet with thee.*

---

*Note: This is all one long run-on sentence; Helena barely takes a breath!

Act 1 scene 1, lines 181–194

HELENA:
You call me pretty? Take that 'pretty' back again.
Demetrius loves your looks. Oh, happy looks!
Your eyes are like stars, and your voice is musical,
more melodious than the lark's song to the shepherd's ear,
when the wheat is sprouting, when the hawthorn buds appear.
Sickness is catching. If only looks were catching too,
I would catch yours, lovely Hermia, from you!
My ear would catch your voice, my eye your eye,
my speech would catch the sweet melody of yours.
If the world were mine, all except Demetrius,
I'd give it all away if only I could be turned into you.
Oh, teach me how you look and with what charms
you have won over Demetrius' heart.

Act 1 scene 1, lines 181–194

HELENA:
Call you me fair? That 'fair' again unsay.
Demetrius loves your fair. O happy fair!
Your eyes are lodestars, and your tongue's sweet air
More tuneable than lark to shepherd's ear,
When wheat is green, when hawthorn buds appear.
Sickness is catching. O, were favour so,
Yours would I catch, fair Hermia, ere I go!
My ear should catch your voice, my eye your eye,
My tongue should catch your tongue's sweet melody.
Were the world mine, Demetrius being bated,
The rest I'd give to be to you translated.
O, teach me how you look, and with what art
You sway the motion of Demetrius' heart.

Call you me fair? That 'fair' again unsay. Demetrius loves your fair. O happy fair! Your eyes are lodestars, and your tongue's sweet air more tuneable than lark to shepherd's ear, when wheat is green, when hawthorn buds appear.

Sickness is catching. O, were favour so, yours would I catch, fair Hermia, ere I go! My ear should catch your voice, my eye your eye, my tongue should catch your tongue's sweet melody.

Were the world mine, Demetrius being bated, the rest I'd give to be to you translated. O, teach me how you look, and with what art you sway the motion of Demetrius' heart.

Act 1 scene 1 lines 226–251

HELENA:
Why are some people so much happier than others?
Throughout Athens I am thought to be as pretty as she.
But so what! Demetrius doesn't think so;
he can't see what everyone else seems to know.
And, just as he is foolishly stuck on Hermia,
so I am foolishly stuck on him.
Things that are ordinary, even awful, having no value,
love can transform into things of beauty and worth.
Love does not see with eyes, but with the mind,
that's why the winged Cupid is always shown to be blind.
Nor does Love operate using any common sense:
flying around, blind, shows great recklessness.
That's why Love is shown to be a child,
because in his choices he can be so easily deceived.
And just as playful little boys are always telling big lies,
so little Cupid can get caught creating false sighs.
Because before Demetrius looked into Hermia's eyes,
he snowed me and swore that he was only mine;
but when the snow job felt a little of Hermia's heat,
it all dissolved and he made a hasty retreat.
I will go tell him of fair Hermia's intended flight;
then he will follow her tomorrow night.
If I get any thanks for my news,
It's still a high price to pay.
But I'm willing to suffer the pain,
if only to see his face once again.

Act 1 scene 1, lines 226–251

HELENA:
How happy some o'er other some can be!
Through Athens I am thought as fair as she.
But what of that? Demetrius thinks not so;
He will not know what all but he do know.
And as he errs, doting on Hermia's eyes,
So I, admiring of his qualities.
Things base and vile, holding no quantity,
Love can transpose to form and dignity.
Love looks not with the eyes, but with the mind,
And therefore is winged Cupid painted blind.
Nor hath Love's mind of any judgment taste:
Wings, and no eyes, figure unheedy haste.
And therefore is Love said to be a child,
Because in choice he is so oft beguiled.
As waggish boys in game themselves forswear,
So the boy Love is perjured everywhere.
For ere Demetrius looked on Hermia's eyne,
He hailed down oaths that he was only mine;
And when this hail some heat from Hermia felt,
So he dissolved, and showers of oaths did melt.
I will go tell him of fair Hermia's flight.
Then to the wood will he tomorrow night
Pursue her; and for this intelligence
If I have thanks, it is a dear expense.
But herein mean I to enrich my pain,
To have his sight thither and back again.

How happy some o'er other some can be! Through Athens I am thought as fair as she. but what of that? Demetrius thinks not so; he will not know what all but he do know. And as he errs, doting on Hermia's eyes, so I, admiring of his qualities.

Things base and vile, holding no quantity, love can transpose to form and dignity. Love looks not with the eyes, but with the mind, and therefore is winged Cupid painted blind. Nor hath Love's mind of any judgment taste: wings, and no eyes, figure unheedy haste. And therefore is Love said to be a child, because in choice he is so oft beguiled. As waggish boys in game themselves forswear, so the boy Love is perjured everywhere.

For ere Demetrius looked on Hermia's eyne, he hailed down oaths that he was only mine; and when this hail some heat from Hermia felt, so he dissolved, and showers of oaths did melt.

I will go tell him of fair Hermia's flight. Then to the wood will he tomorrow night pursue her; and for this intelligence if I have thanks, it is a dear expense. But herein mean I to enrich my pain, to have his sight thither and back again.

Act 2 scene 1, lines 18–31

PUCK:
The king will be holding his festivities here tonight.
Make sure the queen stays out of his sight.
For Oberon is exceedingly full of rage,
because she has acquired as her page,
a lovely boy, stolen from the king of India.
She never had a sweeter human boy.
But jealous Oberon wants to have the child
for his entourage, to travel through the forests wild.
But she, for her part, withholds the beloved boy,
she crowns his head with flowers, and finds him a total joy,
so that now they never meet in a grove, or meadow,
by a sparkling spring, or in the glittery starlight's glow,
but they face off — so that all their elves, in fear,
creep into tiny acorn cups and hide themselves there.

Act 2 scene 1, lines 18–31

PUCK:
The king doth keep his revels here tonight.
Take heed the queen come not within his sight.
For Oberon is passing fell and wrath,
Because that she as her attendant hath
A lovely boy, stol'n from an Indian king.
She never had so sweet a changeling.
And jealous Oberon would have the child,
Knight of his train, to trace the forests wild.
But she, perforce, withholds the lovèd boy,
Crowns him with flowers, and makes him all her joy,
And now they never meet in grove, or green,
By fountain clear, or spangled starlight sheen,
But they do square — that all their elves, for fear,
Creep into acorn cups and hide them there.

The king doth keep his revels here tonight. Take heed the queen come not within his sight. For Oberon is passing fell and wrath, because that she as her attendant hath a lovely boy, stol'n from an Indian king. She never had so sweet a changeling. And jealous Oberon would have the child, knight of his train, to trace the forests wild.

But she, perforce, withholds the lovèd boy, crowns him with flowers, and makes him all her joy, and now they never meet in grove, or green, by fountain clear, or spangled starlight sheen, but they do square — that all their elves, for fear, creep into acorn cups and hide them there.

Act 2 scene 1, lines 81–117 (cut)

TITANIA:
These are lies created by your jealousy!
Not once, since the start of midsummer,
have we met on a hill, in a dale, the forest, or a meadow,
by the paved fountain, or by the overgrown stream,
or on the sandy strip of land by the sea,
(where we dance in circles to the whistling of the wind),
but, with your brawling, you have interrupted our sports.
And therefore the winds, whose music was being ignored —
as though in revenge — sucked up poisonous fogs
from the sea, which they then rained upon the land,
causing even the paltriest of rivers to puff up
so that they have overflowed their banks.
The oxen have therefore worked in vain,
the plowmen's labors were wasted, and the young corn
has rotted before developing to maturity.
And, as a consequence of this disorder, we see
the seasons altered — the spring, the summer,
the productive autumn, harsh winter, all exchange
their customary features; and the amazed world,
puzzled by the harvests of each, can't tell which is which.
And this resulting evil springs forth
from our disagreement, from our dissension:
We are its creators and originators.

Act 2 scene1, lines 81–117 (cut)

TITANIA:
These are the forgeries of jealousy!
And never, since the middle summer's spring,
Met we on hill, in dale, forest, or mead,
By pavèd fountain, or by rushy brook,
Or in the beachèd margent of the sea,
To dance our ringlets to the whistling wind,
But with thy brawls thou hast disturbed our sport.
Therefore the winds, piping to us in vain,
As in revenge, have sucked up from the sea
Contagious fogs, which falling in the land,
Hath every pelting river made so proud
That they have overborne their continents.
The ox hath therefore stretched his yoke in vain,
The ploughman lost his sweat, and the green corn
Hath rotted ere his youth attained a beard.
And thorough this distemperature we see
The seasons alter — the spring, the summer,
The childing autumn, angry winter, change
Their wonted liveries; and the mazèd world,
By their increase, now knows not which is which.
And this same progeny of evils comes
From our debate, from our dissension:
We are the parents and original.

These are the forgeries of jealousy! And never, since the middle summer's spring, — met we on hill, in dale, forest, or mead, by pavèd fountain, or by rushy brook, or in the beachèd margent of the sea, to dance our ringlets to the whistling wind, but with thy brawls thou hast disturbed our sport.

Therefore the winds, piping to us in vain, as in revenge, have sucked up from the sea contagious fogs, which falling in the land, hath every pelting river made so proud that they have overborne their continents.

The ox hath therefore stretched his yoke in vain, the ploughman lost his sweat, and the green corn hath rotted ere his youth attained a beard. And thorough this distemperature we see the seasons alter — the spring, the summer, the childing autumn, angry winter, change their wonted liveries; and the mazèd world, by their increase, now knows not which is which.

And this same progeny of evils comes from our debate, from our dissension: we are the parents and original.

Act 2 scene 1, lines 122–138

TITANIA:
                    Set your heart at rest,
nothing in fairyland could buy the child from me.
His mother was a member of my order;
and during the fragrant Indian evenings,
she often gossiped with me,
sitting beside me on the ocean's yellow beach,
as we watched the trading vessels upon the seas;
often we would laugh as we saw the sails become swelled up
like a pregnant belly when they were filled with the lusty winds;
which she, with delicate and graceful strides,
would mirror (her own womb at that time filled with my little fellow),
and imitate as she'd sail upon the land
to fetch me trinkets and then return again,
as if from a voyage, laden with treasure.
But she, being human, died in childbirth,
and for her sake I am raising her boy,
and for her sake, I will not part with him.

Act 2 scene 1, lines 122–138

TITANIA:

Set your heart at rest,
The fairyland buys not the child of me.
His mother was a vot'ress of my order;
And in the spicèd Indian air, by night,
Full often hath she gossiped by my side;
And sat with me on Neptune's yellow sands,
Marking th'embarkèd traders on the flood;
When we have laughed to see the sails conceive
And grow big-bellied with the wanton wind;
Which she, with pretty and with swimming gait
Following (her womb then rich with my young squire),
Would imitate, and sail upon the land,
To fetch me trifles, and return again,
As from a voyage, rich with merchandise.
But she, being mortal, of that boy did die;
And for her sake do I rear up her boy;
And for her sake I will not part with him.

Set your heart at rest, the fairyland buys not the child of me. His mother was a vot'ress of my order; and in the spicèd Indian air, by night, full often hath she gossiped by my side; and sat with me on Neptune's yellow sands, marking th'embarkèd traders on the flood; when we have laughed to see the sails conceive and grow big-bellied with the wanton wind; which she, with pretty and with swimming gait following (her womb then rich with my young squire), would imitate, and sail upon the land, to fetch me trifles, and return again, as from a voyage, rich with merchandise.

But she, being mortal, of that boy did die; and for her sake do I rear up her boy; and for her sake I will not part with him.

Act 2 scene 1, lines 188–237 (cut and combined)

DEMETRIUS:
I don't love you, therefore don't follow me.
Where is Lysander and beautiful Hermia?
Him, I'll murder, she murders me.
You told me they had snuck into the woods:
but here I am, going mad within the woods,
because I cannot find my Hermia.
Go, get lost, and don't follow me anymore!
Did I lure you? Did I sweet-talk you?
Or instead, didn't I tell you very plainly
that I do not nor cannot love you?
You call into question your modesty
by leaving the city and putting yourself
into the hands of someone who doesn't even love you,
by trusting the opportunities presented by darkness
and the temptations of a deserted place
with the rich jewel of your virginity.
I will not stay to debate — let me go!
Or, if you do follow me, don't doubt
that I will do some mischief to you in the woods.

Act 2 scene 1, lines 188–237 (cut and combined)

DEMETRIUS:
I love thee not, therefore pursue me not.
Where is Lysander and fair Hermia?
The one I'll slay, the other slayeth me.
Thou told'st me they were stol'n unto this wood:
And here am I, and wood within this wood,
Because I cannot meet my Hermia.
Hence, get thee gone, and follow me no more!
Do I entice you? Do I speak you fair?
Or rather do I not in plainest truth
Tell you I do not nor I cannot love you?
You do impeach your modesty too much
To leave the city and commit yourself
Into the hands of one that loves you not,
To trust the opportunity of night
And the ill counsel of a desert place
With the rich worth of your virginity.
I will not stay thy questions, let me go!
Or, if thou follow me, do not believe
But I shall do thee mischief in the wood.

I love thee not , therefore pursue me not. Where is Lysander and fair Hermia? The one I'll slay, the other slayeth me. Thou told'st me they were stol'n unto this wood: and here am I, and wood within this wood, because I cannot meet my Hermia. Hence, get thee gone, and follow me no more!

Do I entice you? Do I speak you fair? Or rather do I not in plainest truth tell you I do not nor I cannot love you? You do impeach your modesty too much to leave the city and commit yourself into the hands of one that loves you not, to trust the opportunity of night and the ill counsel of a desert place with the rich worth of your virginity.

I will not stay thy questions, let me go! Or, if thou follow me, do not believe but I shall do thee mischief in the wood.

Act 2 scene 2, lines 75–91

PUCK:
Through the forest I have gone,
but as for Athenians, I've found none
into whose eyes I might shove
the force of this flower to stir up love.
By night and silence — who is here?
Athenian clothing he does wear.
This is the one, my master said,
who despises the Athenian maid.
And here is the maiden, sleeping sound,
on the damp and dirty ground.
Pretty thing, she shouldn't lie
next to this hard-heart, this rotten heel.
Brute, into your eyes I throw
all the powers this charm can bestow.
When you awake may the torments of love never cease
and therefore keep you from ever sleeping in peace.
So awaken when I am gone;
for now I must go find Oberon.

Act 2 scene 2, lines 75–91

PUCK:
Through the forest have I gone,
But Athenian found I none
On whose eyes I might approve
This flower's force in stirring love.
Night and silence — who is here?
Weeds of Athens he doth wear.
This is he, my master said,
Despisèd the Athenian maid.
And here the maiden, sleeping sound,
On the dank and dirty ground.
Pretty soul, she durst not lie
Near this lack-love, this kill-courtesy.
Churl, upon thy eyes I throw
All the power this charm doth owe.
When thou wak'st, let love forbid
Sleep his seat on thy eyelid.
So awake when I am gone;
For I must now to Oberon.

Through the forest have I gone, but Athenian found I none on whose eyes I might approve this flower's force in stirring love.

Night and silence — who is here? Weeds of Athens he doth wear. This is he, my master said, despisèd the Athenian maid. And here the maiden, sleeping sound, on the dank and dirty ground. Pretty soul, she durst not lie near this lack-love, this kill-courtesy.

Churl, upon thy eyes I throw all the power this charm doth owe. When thou wak'st, let love forbid — sleep his seat on thy eyelid. So awake when I am gone; for I must now to Oberon.

Act 2 scene 2, 96–110

HELENA:
Oh, I am out of breath from my foolish chasing.
The more I want him, the more he wants to escape me.
Hermia is happy wherever it is that she lies,
because she has happy, attractive eyes.
How did her eyes come to be so bright? Not with salty tears.
If that were the case, my eyes cry oftener than hers.
No, no, I am as ugly as a bear,
even beasts that encounter me run away in fear.
Therefore it's no wonder that Demetrius
runs from me as though I were a monster.
What wicked and deceiving mirror of mine
made me believe that, like Hermia's, my eyes did shine?
But who is here? Lysander, on the ground?
Is he dead or asleep? I see no blood, no wound —
Lysander, if you're alive, good sir, awake.

Act 2 scene 2, lines 96–110

HELENA:
O, I am out of breath in this fond chase.
The more my prayer, the lesser is my grace.
Happy is Hermia, wheresoe'er she lies;
For she hath blessèd and attractive eyes.
How came her eyes so bright? Not with salt tears;
If so, my eyes are oft'ner washed than hers.
No, no: I am as ugly as a bear,
For beasts that meet me run away for fear.
Therefore no marvel though Demetrius
Do, as a monster, fly my presence thus.
What wicked and dissembling glass of mine
Made me compare with Hermia's sphery eyne?
But who is here? Lysander! on the ground!
Dead? or asleep? I see no blood, no wound.
Lysander, if you live, good sir, awake.

O, I am out of breath in this fond chase. The more my prayer, the lesser is my grace. Happy is Hermia, wheresoe're she lies; for she hath blessèd and attractive eyes. How came her eyes so bright? Not with salt tears; if so, my eyes are oft'ner washed than hers.

No, no: I am as ugly as a bear, for beasts that meet me run away for fear. Therefore no marvel though Demetrius do, as a monster, fly my presence thus. What wicked and dissembling glass of mine made me compare with Hermia's sphery eyne?

But who is here? Lysander! on the ground! Dead? or asleep? I see no blood, no wound. Lysander, if you live, good sir, awake.

Act 2 scene 2, lines 119–130

LYSANDER:
Content with Hermia? No. I repent
the tedious time that I have, with her, spent.
It's not Hermia, but Helena that I love.
Who would not exchange a raven for a dove?
Man's will is by his reason swayed;
and reason tells me that you are the worthier maid.
Growing things do not ripen till the right season;
so with me, being young, I wasn't mature enough to reason;
till now, having achieved the utmost of my skills,
reason has now become the guide that shapes my will,
leading me to your eyes; into which I look
and read the story of love, written in love's most precious book.

Act 2 scene 2, lines 119–130

LYSANDER:
Content with Hermia? No. I do repent
The tedious minutes I with her have spent.
Not Hermia, but Helena I love.
Who will not change a raven for a dove?
The will of man is by his reason swayed;
And reason says you are the worthier maid.
Things growing are not ripe until their season:
So I being young, till now ripe not to reason;
And touching now the point of human skill,
Reason becomes the marshal to my will,
And leads me to your eyes; where I o'erlook
Love's stories, written in Love's richest book.

Content with Hermia? No. I do repent the tedious minutes I with her have spent. Not Hermia, but Helena I love. Who will not change a raven for a dove?

The will of man is by his reason swayed; and reason says you are the worthier maid. Things growing are not ripe until their season: so I being young, till now ripe not to reason; and touching now the point of human skill, reason becomes the marshal to my will, and leads me to your eyes; where I o'erlook Love's stories, written in Love's richest book.

Act 2 scene 2, lines 131–143

HELENA:
Why was I, just to be ridiculed, ever born?
What did I do to you to deserve such scorn?
Isn't it enough, isn't it enough, young man,
that I never did, no, nor never will
ever rate a kind look from Demetrius' eyes,
but you have to make fun of my inadequacies?
Truly, you wrong me, I swear, you do,
making such fun of me by the way you woo.
But farewell to you: honestly I have to confess
I thought you possessed a true gentleness.
Oh, that a lady, by one man refused,
Should by another man, be so abused!

Act 2 scene 2, lines 131–143

HELENA:
Wherefore was I to this keen mockery born?
When at your hands did I deserve this scorn?
is't not enough, is't not enough, young man,
That I did never, no, nor never can,
Deserve a sweet look from Demetrius' eye,
Bur you must flout my insufficiency?
Good troth, you do me wrong, good sooth, you do,
In such disdainful manner me to woo.
But fare you well: perforce I must confess
I thought you lord of more true gentleness.
O, that a lady, of one man refused,
Should of another therefore be abused!

Wherefore was I to this keen mockery born? When at your hands did I deserve this scorn? is't not enough, is't not enough, young man, that I did never, no, nor never can, deserve a sweet look from Demetrius' eye, but you must flout my insufficiency?

Good troth, you do me wrong, good sooth, you do, in such disdainful manner me to woo. But fare you well: perforce I must confess I thought you lord of more true gentleness.

O, that a lady, of one man refused, should of another therefore be abused!

Act 2 scene 2, lines 153–165

HERMIA:
Help me, Lysander, help me; do your best
to pluck this crawling snake from off my breast.
Oh my, for pity's sake! what was I dreaming here?
Lysander, look how I am quaking with fear.
I thought that a serpent was eating my heart away,
and that you sat smiling while he continued to prey.
Lysander! what, departed? Lysander! lord!
What, out of earshot? not a sound, not a word?
Yahoo, where are you? speak, if you can hear;
Speak, in the name of love! I'm almost fainting with fear.
Nothing? then I am sure you are no longer near.
Either my death or you I'll find immediately.

Act 2 scene 2, lines 153–165

HERMIA:
Help me, Lysander, help me; do thy best
To pluck this crawling serpent from my breast.
Ay me, for pity! what a dream was here?
Lysander, look how I do quake with fear.
Methought a serpent eat my heart away,
And you sat smiling at his cruel prey.
Lysander! what, removed? Lysander! lord!
What, out of hearing gone? no sound, no word?
Alack, where are you? speak, an if you hear;
Speak, of all loves! I swoon almost with fear.
No? then I well perceive you are not nigh.
Either death or you I'll find immediately.

Help me, Lysander, help me; do thy best to pluck this crawling serpent from my breast.
Ay me, for pity! what a dream was here? Lysander, look how I do quake with fear.
Methought a serpent eat my heart away, and you sat smiling at his cruel prey.
Lysander! what, removed? Lysander! lord! What, out of hearing gone? no sound, no word?
Alack, where are you? speak, an if you hear; speak, of all loves! I swoon almost with fear. No?
then I well perceive you are not nigh. Either death or you I'll find immediately.

Act 3 scene 1, lines 25–42 (cut)

BOTTOM:
Fellows, you've got to sincerely ask yourself —
to bring in (God protect us!) a lion in the midst of ladies is
a really dreadful thing. For there is not a scarier
wildfowl than your lion living; and we ought to think about this.
[So,] you must say his name, and half his
face must show through the lion's neck, and he himself
must speak through the neck, saying thus, or something to this defect:
'Ladies,' or 'Fair ladies — I would wish you,' or 'I would
request you,' or 'I would entreat you, not to fear, not to
tremble. I stake my life on it. If you think I come here
as a lion, I'd be risking my own life. No, I am no such
thing, I am a man just like any other man.' And at this point
let him name his name, and tell them simply that he is Snug
the furniture maker.

Act 3 scene 1, lines 25–42 (cut)

BOTTOM:
Masters, you ought to consider with yourselves —
to bring in (God shield us!) a lion among ladies is
a most dreadful thing. For there is not a more fearful
wildfowl than your lion living; and we ought to look to't.
[So,] you must name his name, and half his
face must be seen through the lion's neck, and he himself
must speak through, saying thus, or to the same defect:
'Ladies,' or 'Fair ladies — I would wish you,' or 'I would
request you,' or 'I would entreat you, not to fear, not to
tremble. My life for yours. If you think I come hither
as a lion, it were pity of my life. No, I am no such
thing, I am a man as other men are.' And there indeed
let him name his name, and tell them plainly he is Snug
the joiner.

Act 3 scene 1, lines 143–165 (cut and combined)

TITANIA:
Out of these woods, do not wish to go,
you will remain here whether you want to or no.
I am not a spirit with only ordinary skill.
Even the summer obeys my will,
and I'm in love with you — therefore come with me.
I'll give you fairies to wait on you,
and they shall fetch you jewels from the deep,
and sing while you, on a bed of crushed flowers, sleep.
And I will alter your physical body so
that you may, like a ethereal spirit, go.
Peaseblossom, Cobweb, Moth, and Mustardseed!
Be kind and courteous to this gentleman.
Remain with him where he goes and stay in his sight;
supply him with apricots and blackberries,
with purple grapes, green figs, and mulberries;
steal the honey from the bumble bees,
and for night lights, cut off their waxy thighs
and light them by the fire in the glowworms' eyes
for my love to use as he goes to bed and as he arises.
And pluck the wings from colorful butterflies
to help fan away the moonbeams from his sleepy eyes.
Bow to him, elves, and pay him your courtesy.

Act 3 scene 1, lines 143–165 (cut and combined)

TITANIA:
Out of this wood do not desire to go.
Thou shalt remain here whether thou wilt or no.
I am a spirit of no common rate.
The summer still doth tend upon my state,
And I do love thee. Therefore go with me.
I'll give thee fairies to attend on thee,
And they shall fetch thee jewels from the deep
And sing while thou on pressèd flowers dost sleep,
And I will purge thy mortal grossness so
That thou shalt like an airy spirit go.
Peaseblossom, Cobweb, Moth, and Mustardseed!
Be kind and courteous to this gentleman.
Hop in his walks and gambol in his eyes;
Feed him with apricocks and dewberries,
With purple grapes, green figs, and mulberries;
The honey bags steal from the humblebees,
And for night tapers crop their waxen thighs
And light them at the fiery glowworms' eyes
to have my love to bed and to arise;
And pluck the wings form painted butterflies
To fan the moonbeams from his sleeping eyes.
Nod to him, elves, and do him courtesies.

Out of this wood do not desire to go. Thou shalt remain here whether thou wilt or no. I am a spirit of no common rate. The summer still doth tend upon my state, and I do love thee. Therefore go with me. I'll give thee fairies to attend on thee, and they shall fetch thee jewels from the deep and sing while thou on pressèd flowers dost sleep, and I will purge thy mortal grossness so that thou shalt like an airy spirit go.

Peaseblossom, Cobweb, Moth, and Mustardseed! be kind and courteous to this gentleman. Hop in his walks and gambol in his eyes; feed him with apricocks and dewberries, with purple grapes, green figs, and mulberries; the honey bags steal from the humblebees, and for night tapers crop their waxen thighs and light them at the fiery glowworms' eyes to have my love to bed and to arise; and pluck the wings from painted butterflies to fan the moonbeams from his sleeping eyes. Nod to him, elves, and do him courtesies.

Act 3 scene 2, lines 48–75 (cut and combined)

HERMIA:
Now I'm merely scolding, but I should be doing much worse,
for you, I'm afraid, have given me just cause to curse.
If you have slain Lysander in his sleep,
and are therefore up to your ankles in blood, go all the way
and kill me too.
The sun is not as faithful to the day
as he is to me. Would be have crept away
from his sleeping Hermia? I'd as soon believe
that the whole earth could be drilled through its center, and that
    the moon
could slip through and disrupt noontime on the opposite side of
    the world!
The only conclusion is that you have murdered him.
You look like a murderer looks, just as deadly, just as grim.
Get lost, you dog! Get lost, you mongrel! I am the end
of my maidenly rope. Have you killed him, then?
From here on never count yourself among men.
Oh, just tell me the truth! Tell the truth for my sake.
Could you have faced him if he were awake?
And have you killed him in his sleep? Oh bravely done!
Could a serpent, a snake in the grass, do the same?
A snake in the grass did it, for with a more deceitful tongue
than yours, you snake, no serpent ever stung.

Act 3 scene 2, lines 48–75 (cut and combined)

HERMIA:
Now I but chide, but I should use thee worse,
For thou, I fear, hast given me cause to curse.
If thou hast slain Lysander in his sleep,
Being o'er shoes in blood, plunge in the deep
And kill me too.
The sun was not so true unto the day
As he to me. Would he have stolen away
From sleeping Hermia? I'll believe as soon
This whole earth may be bored, and that the moon
May through the center creep and so displease
Her brother's noontide with th'Antipodes.
It cannot be but thou hast murdered him.
So should a murderer look, so dead, so grim.
Out, dog! Out, cur! Thou driv'st me past the bounds
Of maiden's patience. Hast thou slain him, then?
Henceforth be never numbered among men.
O, once tell true! Tell true, even for my sake!
Durst thou have looked upon him, being awake?
And hast thou killed him sleeping? O brave touch!
Could not a worm, an adder, do so much?
An adder did it, for with doubler tongue
Than thine, thou serpent, never adder stung.

Now I but chide, but I should use thee worse, for thou, I fear, hast given me cause to
curse. If thou hast slain Lysander in his sleep, being o'er shoes in blood, plunge in the deep and
kill me too.

The sun was not so true unto the day as he to me. Would he have stolen away from sleeping Hermia? I'll believe as soon this whole earth may be bored, and that the moon may through
the center creep and so displease her brother's noontide with th'Antipodes. It cannot be but thou
hast murdered him. So should a murderer look, so dead, so grim. Out, dog! Out, cur! Thou dri-
v'st me past the bounds of maiden's patience.

Hast thou slain him, then? Henceforth be never numbered among men. O, once tell true!
Tell true, even for my sake! Durst thou have looked upon him, being awake? And hast thou
killed him sleeping? O brave touch! Could not a worm, an adder, do so much? An adder did it,
for with doubler tongue than thine, thou serpent, never adder stung.

Act 3 scene 2, lines 148–164

HELENA:
Oh, how spiteful! Oh, what hell! You're all
making fun of me, I can tell.
If you were decent and knew courtesy,
you would not do me such an injury.
Can't you just hate me, as I know you all do,
without joining forces to make fun of me too?
If you were gentlemen, as you appear to be,
you would not be so cruel to me,
to make vows and swear love and overpraise my parts,
when I am sure, you hate me with all your hearts.
You are both rivals for the love of Hermia,
and now both rivals to make fun of Helena.
A mighty fine deed, such a manly enterprise,
to force up tears in a poor maiden's eyes
with your contempt! No one of a noble temperament
would so offend a virgin and torture
a poor soul's patience, for their own amusement.

Act 3 scene 2, lines 148–164

HELENA:
O, spite! O, hell! I see you all are bent
To set against me for your merriment.
If you were civil and knew courtesy,
You would not do me thus much injury.
Can you not hate me, as I know you do,
But you must join in souls to mock me too?
If you were men, as men you are in show,
You would not use a gentle lady so,
To vow and swear and superpraise my parts,
When, I am sure, you hate me with your hearts.
You both are rivals and love Hermia,
And now both rivals to mock Helena.
A trim exploit, a manly enterprise,
To conjure tears up in a poor maid's eyes
With your derision! None of noble sort
Would so offend a virgin and extort
A poor soul's patience, all to make you sport.

O, spite! O, hell! I see you all are bent to set against me for your merriment. If you were civil and knew courtesy, you would not do me thus much injury.

Can you not hate me, as I know you do, but you must join in souls to mock me too? If you were men, as men you are in show, you would not use a gentle lady so, to vow and swear and superpraise my parts, when, I am sure, you hate me with your hearts.

You both are rivals and love Hermia, and now both rivals to mock Helena. A trim exploit, a manly enterprise, to conjure tears up in a poor maid's eyes with your derision! None of noble sort would so offend a virgin and extort a poor soul's patience, all to make you sport.

Act 3 scene 2, lines 195–224 (cut)

HELENA:
Oh, she is part of the confederacy!
Now I see, they have all joined forces,
all three, in order to make fun of me.
Cruel Hermia, most ungrateful maiden,
have you conspired, have you, with them, contrived,
to torment me with this loathsome contempt?
Are all the secrets that we have shared,
our sisterly vows, the hours that we've spent together,
when we scolded the speeding moments of time
for parting us — Oh, is it all forgotten?
Our schooldays friendship, our childhood innocence?
We, Hermia, like two very skillful gods,
have both embroidered the very same flower
upon the very same sampler, sitting on the very same cushion,
singing the same tune, in the same key,
as if our hands, our sides, our voices, and minds
had been one. In this way we grew together
like a conjoined cherry, appearing separated,
but still united in that separateness,
like two lovely berries hanging from a single stem;
thus, with two apparent bodies but with a single heart.
And will you tear our lifelong love apart,
And side with men to scorn your poor friend?
It is not friendly; it is not ladylike,
All women, along with me, will scold you for this,
though I alone do suffer for it.

Act 3 scene 2, lines 195–224 (cut)

HELENA:
Lo, she is one of this confederacy!
Now I perceive they have conjoined all three
To fashion this false sport in spite of me.
Injurious Hermia, most ungrateful maid,
Have you conspired, have you with these contrived,
To bait me with this foul derision?
Is all the counsel that we two have shared,
The sisters' vows, the hours that we have spent
When we have chid the hasty-footed time
For parting us — O, is all forgot?
All school days' friendship, childhood innocence?
We, Hermia, like two artificial gods,
Have with our needles created both one flower,
Both on one sampler, sitting on one cushion,
Both warbling of one song, both in one key,
As if our hands, our sides, voices, and minds
had been incorporate. So we grew together
Like to a double cherry, seeming parted,
But yet an union in partition,
Two lovely berries molded on one stem;
So with two seeming bodies but one heart.
And will you rend our ancient love asunder,
To join with men in scorning your poor friend?
It is not friendly; 'tis not maidenly.
Our sex, as well as I, may chide you for it,
Though I alone do feel the injury.

Lo, she is one of this confederacy! Now I perceive they have conjoined all three to fashion this false sport in spite of me. — Injurious Hermia, most ungrateful maid, have you conspired, have you with these contrived, to bait me with this foul derision? Is all the counsel that we two have shared, — the sisters' vows, the hours that we have spent when we have chid the hasty-footed time for parting us — O, is all forgot? All school days' friendship, childhood innocence?

We, Hermia, like two artificial gods, have with our needles created both one flower, both on one sampler, sitting on one cushion, both warbling of one song, both in one key, as if our hands, our sides, voices, and minds had been incorporate. So we grew together, like to a double cherry, seeming parted, but yet an union in partition, two lovely berries molded on one stem; so with two seeming bodies but one heart.

And will you rend our ancient love asunder, to join with men in scorning your poor friend? It is not friendly; 'tis not maidenly. Our sex, as well as I, may chide you for it, though I alone do feel the injury.

Act 3 scene 2, lines 354–377

OBERON:
You can see these lovers are searching for a place to fight,
therefore hurry, Robin, blot out the moonlight;
the starry sky you must cover immediately
with a curtain of fog as black as hell,
and lead these testy rivals so astray
that neither comes in the other's way.
At times you must imitate Lysander's voice;
and thus stir Demetrius to a rage.
Then you must rant like Demetrius would.
And in this way you must keep them apart,
till their eyes become dead tired with sleep
and their legs get so heavy they drop off their feet.
Then squeeze this flower into Lysander's eye,
whose juice has this virtuous property,
to remove all errors with its powers
and make his eyes see as they normally would.
When they next awaken, all this contemptuous behavior
shall seem like a dream — an idle vision.
Then back to Athens will the lovers wend,
joined in eternal friendship that will never end.
While you perform this in my employ,
I will go to my queen and beg for her Indian boy;
and then I will release her eye from the charm
that makes her love the monster, and there shall be no more harm.
And back to Athens shall the lovers wend, with league whose date
till death shall never end.
Whiles I in this affair do thee employ, I'll to my queen and beg her
Indian boy; and then I will her charmèd eye release from monster's
view, and all things shall be peace.

Act 3 scene 2, lines 354–377

OBERON:
Thou seest these lovers seek a place to fight,
Hie, therefore, Robin, overcast the night;
The starry welkin cover thou anon
With drooping fog as black as Acheron,
And lead these testy rivals so astray
As one come not within another's way.
Like to Lysander sometime frame thy tongue;
Then stir Demetrius up with bitter wrong.
And sometime rail thou like Demetrius.
And from each other look thou lead them thus,
Till o'er their brows death-counterfeiting sleep
With leaden legs and batty wings doth creep.
Then crush this herb into Lysander's eye,
Whose liquor hath this virtuous property,
To take from thence all error with his might
And make his eyeballs roll with wonted sight.
When they next wake, all this derision
Shall seem a dream and fruitless vision.
And back to Athens shall the lovers wend,
With league whose date till death shall never end.
Whiles I in this affair do thee employ,
I'll to my queen and beg her Indian boy;
And then I will her charmèd eye release
From monster's view, and all things shall be peace.

Thou seest these lovers seek a place to fight, hie, therefore, Robin, overcast the night; the starry welkin cover thou anon with drooping fog as black as Acheron, and lead these testy rivals so astray as one come not within another's way.

Like to Lysander sometime frame thy tongue; then stir Demetrius up with bitter wrong. And sometime rail thou like Demetrius. And from each other look thou lead them thus, till o'er their brows death-counterfeiting sleep with leaden legs and batty wings doth creep.

Then crush this herb into Lysander's eye, whose liquor hath this virtuous property, to take from thence all error with his might and make his eyeballs roll with wonted sight. When they next wake, all this derision shall seem a dream and fruitless vision.

Act 4 scene 1, lines 166–184

DEMETRIUS:
My lord, fair Helena told me of their running away,
of their intention to come here to this wood,
and I, in a fury, followed them here;
fair Helena, out of love, followed me.
But, my good lord, I don't know what caused it
(but something surely did) the love I felt for Hermia,
melted just like the snow, and seems to me now
as a faint memory of some silly plaything
which, in my childhood, I once adored.
But now, all the true love, the very essence of my heart,
the most pleasing thing for me to see,
is only Helena. I was engaged to her,
my lord, before I ever saw Hermia.
But, as though sick, I could not accept her love,
but, now healthy again, my natural appetite has returned,
and now I wish for her love, love her love, long for her love,
and will forevermore be true to her love.

Act 4 scene 1, lines 166–184

DEMETRIUS:
My lord, fair Helen told me of their stealth,
Of this their purpose hither to this wood,
And I in fury hither followed them;
Fair Helena in fancy following me.
But, my good lord, I wot not by what power
(But by some power it is), my love to Hermia,
Melted as the snow, seems to me now
As the remembrance of an idle gaud
Which in my childhood I did dote upon.
And all the faith, the virtue of my heart,
The object and pleasure of mine eye,
Is only Helena. To her, my lord,
Was I betrothed ere I saw Hermia.
But like a sickness did I loathe this food,
But, as in health, come to my natural taste,
Now I do wish it, love it, long for it,
And will forevermore be true to it.

My lord, fair Helen told me of their stealth, of this their purpose hither to this wood, and I in fury hither followed them; — fair Helena in fancy following me.

But, my good lord, I wot not by what power (but by some power it is), my love to Hermia, melted as the snow — seems to me now as the remembrance of an idle gaud which in my childhood I did dote upon. And all the faith, the virtue of my heart, the object and pleasure of mine eye, is only Helena. To her, my lord, was I betrothed ere I saw Hermia. But like a sickness did I loathe this food, — but, as in health, come to my natural taste, now I do wish it, love it, long for it, and will forevermore be true to it.

Act 1 scene 3, lines 10–34 (combined)

DON JOHN:
I wonder that you — being, as you say you were, born under such an evil sign — always strive to apply morality to misfortunes of life-and-death proportions. I cannot hide what I am: I must be sad when I have cause, and not laugh at someone's stupid jokes; eat when I am hungry, and not wait for everyone to be seated at the table; sleep when I am drowsy, and not be kept waiting by anyone; laugh when I feel merry, and not just to flatter someone's ego. I'd rather be an ugly weed in a hedge than a rose that he's fond of, and it suits me better to be despised by everyone than to put on a front to garner anyone's approval. Therefore, though no one may call me a phony yes-man, it cannot be denied that I am a straight-forward villain. I have been muzzled and weighed down with restrictions; therefore I have decided not to pretend to be happy. If I were not so restricted, I would do harm; if I were free to act, I'd do as I please. In the meantime, let me be as I am, and don't try to alter me.

Act 1 scene 3, lines 10–34 (combined)

DON JOHN:
I wonder that thou — being, as thou say'st thou art, born under Saturn —
goest about to apply a moral medicine to a mortifying mischief. I cannot
hide what I am: I must be sad when I have cause, and smile at no man's
jests; eat when I have stomach, and wait for no man's leisure; sleep when
I am drowsy, and tend on no man's business; laugh when I am merry, and
claw no man in his humor. I had rather be a canker in a hedge than a rose
in his grace, and it better fits my blood to be disdained of all than to
fashion a carriage to rob love from any. In this, though I cannot be said to
be a flattering honest man, it must not be denied but I am a plain-dealing
villain. I am trusted with a muzzle and enfranchised with a clog; therefore
I have decreed not to sing in my cage. If I had my mouth I would bite; if I
had my liberty I would do my liking. In the meantime, let me be that I am,
and seek not to alter me.

Act 2 scene 1, lines 26–45 (cut and combined)

BEATRICE:
Lord, I could not bear to have a husband with a beard on his face!
I'd rather sleep on itchy bed sheets! [And as for one with no
beard?] What would I do with him? Dress him up in my clothing
and employ him as my chambermaid? He that has a beard is older
than a youth, and he that has no beard is not yet a man; and he
that isn't youthful — isn't right for me, and he that isn't a man —
I want no part of him. Therefore I will accept the fate of old maids,
and for a small fee from the bear keeper, lead his apes into hell.
[And at] the gate, the Devil will meet me — looking like an old
cuckold with horns on his head — and say, 'Get yourself up to
heaven, Beatrice, get yourself up to heaven, this is no place for
maidens such as you.' So I deliver the apes to him and I'm off to
Saint Peter, to heaven; he shows me where the bachelors congre-
gate, and we all live there as merry as the day is long.

Act 2 scene 1, lines 26–45 (cut and combined)

BEATRICE:
Lord, I could not endure a husband with a beard on his face! I had rather
lie in the woollen! [And one that hath no beard?] What should I do with
him? Dress him in my apparel and make him my waiting gentlewoman?
He that hath a beard is more than a youth, and he that hath no beard is
less than a man; and he that is more than a youth is not for me; and he
that is less than a man, I am not for him. Therefore I will even take
sixpence in earnest of the bearward and lead his apes into hell. [And at]
the gate, there will the Devil meet me like an old cuckold with horns on
his head, and say, 'Get you to heaven, Beatrice, get you to heaven, here's
no place for you maids.' So deliver I up my apes, and away to Saint Peter,
for the heavens; he shows me where the bachelors sit, and there live we as
merry as the day is long.

Act 2 scene 3, lines 7–35

BENEDICK:

It puzzles me greatly that one man, seeing what a fool another man becomes when he commits himself to love, will, after having laughed at such foolishness in others, become the object of his own derision by falling in love: and such a man is Claudio. I have known when the only music he cared to hear was the pounding of a drum and the fife, and now he'd rather hear the tapping of a tabor and the piccolo. I have known when he would have walked ten miles on foot to go see a good suit of armor, and now he'll lie awake for ten nights fashioning the lines of a new suit. He used to speak plainly and to the point, like an honest man and a soldier, and now he's become all flowery — his words are like an exotic banquet, just one strange dish after another. Could I be changed and see things so differently? I can't be sure; I don't think so. I won't swear to it because love may shut me up like a clam, but I will swear that, till he has shut me up, he shall never turn me into such a fool. One woman may be pretty, yet I'm just fine; another may be wise, yet I'm still okay; another is virtuous, yet I am well; but till all graces can be found in one woman, one woman shall not find herself in my good graces. Rich she shall be, that's certain; wise, or I'll have none of her; virtuous, or I'll never cheapen her; fair, or I'll never look at her; mild-mannered, or don't come near me; well-born, or I wouldn't give a penny for her; a good conversationalist, an excellent musician, and her hair shall be — whatever color God pleases.

Act 2 scene 3, lines 7–35

BENEDICK:

I do much wonder that one man, seeing how much another man is a fool
when he dedicates his behaviors to love, will, after he hath laughed at such
shallow follies in others, become the argument of his own scorn by falling
in love: and such a man is Claudio. I have known when there was no music
with him but the drum and the fife, and now had he rather hear the tabor
and the pipe. I have known when he would have walked ten mile afoot to
see a good armor, and now well he lie ten nights awake carving the fashion
of a new doublet. He was wont to speak plain and to the purpose, like an
honest man and a soldier, and now is he turned orthography; his words are
a very fantastical banquet, just so many strange dishes. May I be so converted and see with these eyes? I cannot tell; I think not. I will not be
sworn but love may transform me to an oyster, but I'll take my oath on it,
till he have made an oyster of me, he shall never make me such a fool. One
woman is fair, yet I am well; another is wise, yet I am well; another virtuous, yet I am well; but till all graces be in one woman, one woman shall
not come in my grace. Rich she shall be, that's certain; wise, or I'll none;
virtuous, or I'll never cheapen her; fair, or I'll never look on her; mild, or
come not near me; noble, or not I for an angel; of good discourse, an excellent musician, and her hair shall be — of what color it please God.

Act 2 scene 3, lines 211–235

BENEDICK:
This can't be a trick: they bore themselves so seriously; they've learned the truth of this from Hero. They seem to pity the lady. It appears her love is full blown. Love me? Why, it must be requited! I heard what they think of me: they say I'll become too conceited if I know she loves me. They also say she'd rather die than show any signs that she loves me. I never thought to marry. But I mustn't be selfish. Happy is he who takes note of his faults and corrects them. They say the lady is fair — it's true, I can attest to that; and virtuous — that's so, I can't disprove it; and wise, except for loving me — for truly it's no proof of her wit, nor any great evidence she's a fool, for I will be dreadfully in love with her. I may perhaps be the butt of some jokes and some witty attacks because I have so long spoken against marriage. But doesn't the appetite alter? A man may love certain foods in his youth that he cannot endure in old age. Shall sarcasm and snide cracks and harmless jibes deter a man's course of action? No, the world must be peopled. When I said I would die a bachelor, I did not think I would live long enough to be married.

Act 2 scene 3, lines 211–235

BENEDICK:
This can be no trick: the conference was sadly borne; they have the truth of this from Hero. They seem to pity the lady: it seems her affections have their full bent. Love me? Why, it must be requited. I hear how I am censured: they say I will bear myself proudly, if I perceive the love come from her. They say too that she will rather die than give any sign of affection. I did never think to marry. I must not seem proud. Happy are they that hear their detractions and can put them to mending. They say the lady is fair — 'tis a truth, I can bear them witness; and virtuous — 'tis so, I cannot reprove it; and wise, but for loving me — by my troth, it is no addition to her wit, nor no great argument of her folly, for I will be horribly in love with her. I may chance have some odd quirks and remnants of wit broken on me because I have railed so long against marriage: but doth not the appetite alter? A man loves the meat in his youth that he cannot endure in his age. Shall quips and sentences and these paper bullets of the brain awe a man from the career of his humor? No, the world must be peopled. When I said I would die a bachelor, I did not think I should live till I were married.

Act 3 scene 1, lines 48–80 (cut and combined)

HERO:

    Nature never created a woman's heart
as conceited as that of Beatrice.
Her eyes sparkle with disdain and scorn,
undervaluing all they see, and she thinks
so much of her own wittiness that
no other subject interests her. She cannot love,
nor even appear to comprehend the concept of affection,
she is so self-centered. I've never seen a man,
no matter how wise, how noble, how young, how good-looking,
but she would put the worst face on him: if pale-skinned,
she would swear the gentleman were a woman;
if tanned, why then, Nature, trying to be funny,
botched it; if tall, he was a spear with an odd-shaped head;
if short, he was a funny-looking little shrimp;
if speaking, a windbag full of hot air;
if quiet, why then, a blockhead without a brain.
In this way she turns every man's favors into faults.
Therefore let Benedick, like a smoldering fire,
burn slowly out, consuming himself from within.
It'd be better to die like that than to be ridiculed to death,
which is as bad as being tickled to death.

Act 3 scene 1, lines 48–80 (cut and combined)

HERO:

         Nature never framed a woman's heart
Of prouder stuff than that of Beatrice.
Disdain and scorn ride sparkling in her eyes,
Misprising what they look on, and her wit
Values itself so highly that to her
All matter else seems weak. She cannot love,
Nor take no shape nor project of affection,
She is so self-endeared. I never yet saw man,
How wise, how noble, young, how rarely featured,
But she would spell him backward: if fair-faced,
She would swear the gentleman should be her sister;
If black, why, Nature, drawing of an antic,
Made a foul blot; if tall, a lance ill-headed;
If low, an agate very vilely cut;
If speaking, why a vane blown with all winds;
If silent, why, a block moved with none.
So turns she every man the wrong side out.
Therefore let Benedick, like covered fire,
Consume away in sighs, waste inwardly.
It were a better death than die with mocks,
Which is as bad as die with tickling.

Nature never framed a woman's heart of prouder stuff than that of Beatrice. Disdain and scorn ride sparkling in her eyes, misprising what they look on, and her wit values itself so highly that to her all matter else seems weak. She cannot love, nor take no shape nor project of affection, she is so self-endeared.

I never yet saw man, how wise, how noble, young, how rarely featured, but she would spell him backward: if fair-faced, she would swear the gentleman should be her sister; if black, why, Nature, drawing of an antic, made a foul blot; if tall, a lance ill-headed; if low, an agate very vilely cut; if speaking, why a vane blown with all winds; if silent, why, a block moved with none.

So turns she every man the wrong side out. Therefore let Benedick, like covered fire, consume away in sighs, waste inwardly. It were a better death than die with mocks, which is as bad as die with tickling.

Act 4 scene 1, lines 297–323 (cut and combined)

BEATRICE:
You dare to call yourself my friend but you won't take on my enemies. Isn't he proven an absolute villain, who has slandered, scorned, dishonored my cousin? Oh, if only I were a man! What, lead her on until they come to be married, and then with public accusations, barefaced slander, unmitigated rancor — oh, God if only I were a man! I would eat his heart in the town square. Talk with a man out of a window! What a thing to say! Sweet Hero! She is wronged, she is slandered, she is ruined. Princes and counts! Surely a princely thing to say, a fine count, a real candy-ass, a sweet fellow surely! Oh if only I could be a man for his sake, or if I had any friend willing to be a man for my sake! But manhood is dissolved into mincing manners, valor into flattery, and men are all talk, just fancy talk: today the biggest liar in the world is considered as valiant as Hercules as long as he swears he's telling the truth. I cannot become a man by wishing, therefore I will die a woman with grieving.

Act 4 scene 1, lines 297–323 (cut and combined)

BEATRICE:
You dare easier be friends with me than fight with mine enemy. Is he not approved in the height a villain, that hath slandered, scorned, dishonored my kinswoman? O, that I were a man! What, bear her in hand until they come to take hands, and then with public accusation, uncovered slander, unmitigated rancour. O, God that I were a man! I would eat his heart in the market place. Talk with a man out a window! A proper saying! Sweet Hero! She is wronged, she is slandered, she is undone. Princes and counties! Surely a princely testimony, a goodly count, Count Comfect, a sweet gallant surely! O, that I were a man for his sake, or that I had any friend would be a man for my sake! But manhood is melted into curtsies, valour into compliment, and men are only turned into tongue, and trim ones too: he is now as valiant as Hercules that only tells a lie and swears it. I cannot be a man with wishing, therefore I will die a woman with grieving.

Act 1 scene 1, lines 35–65 (cut and combined)

IAGO:
               It's the bane of the enlisted man.
Promotions are now gotten by recommendations and favoritism,
and not, as traditionally, by advancement through the ranks, where
    you moved
up into the place of your superior. Now, sir, judge for yourself,
whether there's any just basis for me to be obliged
to love the Moor. Let it satisfy you to know;
I serve him now to use him later.
We can't all be masters, nor are all masters
worthy of being followed. You can see
many a dutiful, kowtowing fellow
who, content with his own devoted servitude
lives out his days, just like his master's mule,
getting nothing in the end but his food; and when he's too old to
    work, he's tossed out.
Just beat such honest fools! But there are others
who, while looking to be the picture of the perfect servant,
are still keeping their hearts and souls to themselves;
and, while appearing to serve their masters,
they're actually serving themselves, and when they have lined their
    own pockets,
they're able to take care of themselves. These fellows have some
    character,
and I profess to be one of these. For sir,
as surely as you are Roderigo,
if I were the moor, I wouldn't have me as a follower.
In appearing to follow him, I am really serving myself.
Let heaven be my judge, I am not what I appear.

Act 1 scene 1, lines 35–65 (cut and combined)

IAGO:

'Tis the curse of service.
Preferment goes by letter and affection,
And not by old gradation, where each second
Stood heir to th'first. Now, sir, be judge yourself,
Whether I in any just term am affined
To love the Moor. O, sir, content you;
I follow him to serve my turn upon him.
We cannot all be masters, nor all masters
Cannot be truly followed. You shall mark
Many a duteous and knee-crooking knave
That, doting on his own obsequious bondage,
Wears out his time, much like his master's ass,
For naught but provender; and when he's old, cashiered.
Whip me such honest knaves! Others there are
Who, trimmed in forms and visages of duty,
Keep yet their hearts attending on themselves;
And, throwing but shows of service on their lords,
Do well thrive by them, and when they have lined their coats,
Do themselves homage. These fellows have some soul;
And such a one do I profess myself. For, sir,
It is as sure as you are Roderigo,
Were I the Moor, I would not be Iago.
In following him, I follow but myself;
Heaven is my judge, I am not what I am.

'Tis the curse of service. Preferment goes by letter and affection, and not by old gradation, where each second stood heir to th'first. Now, sir, be judge yourself, whether I in any just term am affined to love the Moor. O, sir, content you; I follow him to serve my turn upon him. We cannot all be masters, nor all masters cannot be truly followed. You shall mark many a duteous and knee-crooking knave that, doting on his own obsequious bondage, wears out his time, much like his master's ass, for naught but provender; and when he's old, cashiered. Whip me such honest knaves!

Others there are who, trimmed in forms and visages of duty, keep yet their hearts attending on themselves; and, throwing but shows of service on their lords, do well thrive by them, and when they have lined their coats, do themselves homage. These fellows have some soul; and such a one do I profess myself. For, sir, it is as sure as you are Roderigo, — were I the Moor, I would not be Iago. In following him, I follow but myself; heaven is my judge, I am not what I am.

Act 1 scene 3, lines 243–259 (combined)

DESDEMONA:
                    Most gracious Duke,
lend a favorable ear to my story,
and give me the benefit of your support,
to assist me where I am so naive.
The fact that I loved the Moor enough to become his wife,
my rebelliousness, and the rejection of what was expected of me,
proves to the world. My heart's been conquered
by the very essence of my lord.
I came to know Othello through his mind,
and it was to his honor and bravery
to which I tied my soul and future.
So that, dear lords, if I be left here,
to live in peace, while he goes off to war,
the marital rites for which I love him are taken from me,
and I will suffer greatly
by his deeply-felt absence. Let me go with him.

Act 1 scene 3, lines 243–259 (combined)

DESDEMONA:

               Most gracious Duke,
To my unfolding lend your prosperous ear,
And let me find a charter in your voice,
T'assist my simpleness.
That I did love the Moor to live with him,
My downright violence, and storm of fortunes,
May trumpet to the world. My heart's subdued
Even to the very quality of my lord.
I saw Othello's visage in his mind,
And to his honors and his valiant parts
Did I my soul and fortunes consecrate.
So that, dear lords, if I be left behind,
A moth of peace, and he go to the war,
The rites for which I love him are bereft me,
And I a heavy interim shall support
By his dear absence. Let me go with him.

Most gracious Duke, to my unfolding lend your prosperous ear, and let me find a charter in your voice, t'assist my simpleness. That I did love the Moor to live with him, my downright violence, and storm of fortunes, may trumpet to the world. My heart's subdued even to the very quality of my lord. I saw Othello's visage in his mind, and to his honors and his valiant parts did I my soul and fortunes consecrate. So that, dear lords, if I be left behind, a moth of peace, and he go to the war, the rites for which I love him are bereft me, and I a heavy interim shall support by his dear absence. Let me go with him.

Act 2 scene 3, lines 268–295 (cut and combined, starts midspeech)

CASSIO:

Drunk! And babble! And quarrel! Rant! Curse! Speak overblown nonsense to my own shadow! Oh, you invisible spirit of drink, if you have no other name to be known by, we'll call you the devil! I remember a whole jumble of things, but nothing distinctly; some sort of quarrel, but I can't remember what it was about. Oh, God, that men should put such a lethal adversary into their mouths to take their brains captive! that we should with joy, gaiety, merry-making, and the need to impress transform ourselves into beasts! To be one moment a sensible person, and in the next moment a fool, and in no time at all a beast! Oh, how strange! Every immoderate glass of it is cursed, and it contains the devil!

Act 2 scene 3, lines 268–295 (cut and combined. starts midspeech)

CASSIO:
Drunk! And speak parrot! And squabble! Swagger! Swear! And discourse fustian with one's own shadow! O thou invisible spirit of wine, if thou hast no name to be known by, let us call thee devil! I remember a mass of things, but nothing distinctly; a quarrel, but nothing wherefore. O God, that men should put an enemy in their mouths to steal away their brains! That we should with joy, pleasance, revel, and applause transform ourselves into beasts! To be now a sensible man, by and by a fool, and presently a beast! O strange! Every inordinate cup is unblest, and the ingredient is a devil!

Act 3 scene 3, lines 45–74 (cut and combined)

DESDEMONA:

My good lord,
if I have any charms or power to influence you,
make peace with him immediately;
because if he's not someone that truly loves you,
whose mistakes come out of ignorance, and are in no way intentional,
I'm no judge of honesty.
I beg you to call him back. Truly, he's sorry;
even though his error, as we all know
(except of course that, it's the rule, that in wartime we must make
    examples
of our finest soldiers), is certainly only a fault
that would require a private reprimand. When shall he come here?
Tell me, Othello. With all my heart I wonder
what you could ask of me that I would say no to
or be so indecisive about. What? Michael Cassio,
who came with you when you were wooing me, and so often,
when I spoke negatively of you,
has taken your side — do I have to work so hard
to make peace between you?

Act 3 scene 3, lines 45–74 (cut and combined)

DESDEMONA:

Good my lord,
If I have any grace or power to move you,
His present reconciliation take;
For if he be not one that truly loves you,
That errs in ignorance, and not in cunning,
I have no judgment in an honest face.
I prithee call him back. In faith, he's penitent;
And yet his trespass, in our common reason
(Save that, they say, the wars must make examples
Out of their best), is not almost a fault
T'incur a private check. When shall he come?
Tell me, Othello. I wonder in my soul
What you could ask me that I should deny
Or stand so mamm'ring on. What? Michael Cassio,
That came a-wooing with you, and so many a time,
When I have spoke of you dispraisingly,
Hath ta'en your part — to have so much to do
To bring him in?

    Good my lord, if I have any grace or power to move you, his present reconciliation take; for if he be not one that truly loves you, that errs in ignorance, and not in cunning, I have no judgment in an honest face.

    I prithee call him back. In faith, he's penitent; and yet his trespass, in our common reason (save that, they say, the wars must make examples out of their best), is not almost a fault t'incur a private check. When shall he come?

    Tell me, Othello. I wonder in my soul what you could ask me that I should deny or stand so mamm'ring on. What? Michael Cassio, that came a-wooing with you, and so many a time, when I have spoke of you dispraisingly, hath ta'en your part — to have so much to do to bring him in?

Act 3 scene 3, lines 334–362 (cut and combined)

OTHELLO:
                    What! What! untrue to me?
Go! get out! you're torturing me.
I swear it's better to be beaten to a pulp
than to be tortured with a *glimmer* of suspicion.
What knowledge did I have of her secret affairs?
I didn't see them, didn't think of them, they didn't bother me;
I could sleep well at night, eat well, was easygoing and happy;
I never felt Cassio's kisses on her lips.
Someone who is robbed, and doesn't miss what's been stolen,
if he never realizes it, he isn't really robbed at all.
You wretch, make sure you prove that my love is a whore!
Make certain of it; give me visible proof;
if not, I swear on my very soul,
you'd have been better off born a dog
than have to answer to the rage you've awakened in me!
Let me see it; if not, you'll wish you were dead!

Act 3 scene 3, lines 334–364 (cut and combined)

OTHELLO:

Ha! ha! false to me?
Avaunt! Be gone! Thou hast set me on the rack.
I swear 'tis better to be abused
Than but to know't a little.
What sense had I of her stol'n hours of lust?
I saw't not, thought it not, it harmed not me;
I slept the next night well, fed well, was free and merry;
I found not Cassio's kisses on her lips.
He that is robbed, not wanting what is stol'n,
Let him not know't, and he's not robbed at all.
Villain, be sure thou prove my love a whore!
Be sure of it; give me the ocular proof;
Or, by the worth of mine eternal soul,
Thou hadst been better have been born a dog
Than answer my waked wrath!
Make me to see't, or woe upon thy life!

Ha! ha! false to me? Avaunt! Be gone! Thou hast set me on the rack. I swear 'tis better to be abused than but to know't a little. What sense had I of her stol'n hours of lust? I saw't not, thought it not, it harmed not me; I slept the next night well, fed well, was free and merry; I found not Cassio's kisses on her lips. He that is robbed, not wanting what is stol'n, let him not know't, and he's not robbed at all.

Villain, be sure thou prove my love a whore! Be sure of it; give me the ocular proof; or, by the worth of mine eternal soul, thou hadst been better have been born a dog than answer my waked wrath! Make me to see't, or woe upon thy life!

Act 4 scene 2, lines 149–165

DESDEMONA:
                    Oh, Iago,
what do I have to do to win back my lord?
Dear friend, go to him; for, I swear by this heavenly light,
that I don't know how I lost him. On my knees I swear:
if I ever cheated on his love
either in my thoughts or in reality,
or that I ever saw, heard, or in any way
found myself enchanted by anyone else,
or that I do not now, always did,
and ever will (even if he were to abandon me
and divorce me); love him totally,
let me suffer everlastingly! Unkindness is a powerful thing;
and his unkindness may kill me in the end,
but never ruin my love. I cannot say 'whore.'
It sickens me now even to speak the word;
to do that deed which would brand me one —
nothing in the world could make me.

Act 4 scene 2, lines 149–165

DESDEMONA:
               Alas, Iago,
What shall I do to win my lord again?
Good friend, go to him; for, by this light of heaven,
I know not how I lost him. Here I kneel:
If e'er my will did trespass 'gainst his love
Either in discourse of thought or actual deed,
Or that mine eyes, mine ears, or any sense
Delighted them in any other form,
Or that I do not yet, and ever did,
And ever will (though he do shake me off
To beggarly divorcement); love him dearly,
Comfort forswear me! Unkindness may do much;
And his unkindness may defeat my life,
But never taint my love. I cannot say 'whore.'
It does abhor me now I speak the word;
To do the act that might the addition earn
Not the world's mass of vanity could make me.

Alas, Iago, what shall I do to win my lord again? Good friend, go to him; for, by this light of heaven, I know not how I lost him. Here I kneel: if e'er my will did trespass 'gainst his love either in discourse of thought or actual deed, or that mine eyes, mine ears, or any sense delighted them in any other form, or that I do not yet, and ever did, and ever will (though he do shake me off to beggarly divorcement); love him dearly, comfort forswear me!

Unkindness may do much; and his unkindness may defeat my life, but never taint my love. I cannot say 'whore.' It does abhor me now I speak the word; to do the act that might the addition earn — not the world's mass of vanity could make me.

Act 4 scene 3, lines 85–102

EMILIA:
          I think it is the fault of their husbands
if wives stray. Say that men lose interest
and make love to other women;
or else become overly jealous
and restrain us with rules; or say they beat us,
or neglect us out of spite.
Why, we can feel resentment; and though we have womanly grace,
still we are capable of revenge. Let husbands realize
that their wives can feel as they do. They see and smell
and have a taste for both sweet and sour things,
as their husbands have. What do they think they're doing
when they swap us for another? Is it for amusement?
I think it is. And does it spring from their natural instincts?
I think it does. Is it their weakness that causes it?
I think it's so. But haven't we natural instincts,
desires for amusement, and our own weakness, just as men have?
Then let them treat us well; else let them realize,
that the wicked things we do, we've learned from their example.

Act 4 scene 3, lines 85–102

EMILIA:
        I do think it is their husbands' faults
If wives do fall. Say that they slack their duties
And pour our treasures into foreign laps;
Or else break out in peevish jealousies,
Throwing restraint upon us; or say they strike us,
Or scant our former having in despite:
Why, we have galls; and though we have some grace,
Yet have we some revenge. Let husbands know
Their wives have sense like them. They see and smell
And have their palates both for sweet and sour,
As husbands have. What is it that they do
When they change us for others? Is it sport?
I think it is. And doth affection breed it?
I think it doth. Is't frailty that thus errs?
It is so too. And have not we affections,
Desires for sport, and frailty, as men have?
Then let them use us well; else let them know,
The ills we do, their ills instruct us so.

I do think it is their husbands' faults if wives do fall. Say that they slack their duties and pour our treasures into foreign laps; or else break out in peevish jealousies, throwing restraint upon us; or say they strike us, or scant our former having in despite: Why, we have galls; and though we have some grace, yet have we some revenge. Let husbands know their wives have sense like them. They see and smell and have their palates both for sweet and sour, as husbands have.

What is it that they do when they change us for others? Is it sport? I think it is. And doth affection breed it? I think it doth. Is't frailty that thus errs? It is so too. And have not we affections, desires for sport, and frailty, as men have?

Then let them use us well; else let them know, the ills we do, their ills instruct us so.

Act 1 scene 1, lines 165–185 (cut and combined)

MOWBRAY:
I throw myself, mighty king, at your feet.
You may have power over my life, but my honor is my own;
I owe you my life, but as for my good name,
I will not act dishonorably even for your sake.
I've been disgraced, accused, and treated with contempt,
cut to my very soul with the poisonous spear of slander,
which no medicine can cure, except the blood
of him who uttered this poison. My dear, dear lord,
the most treasured thing we possess in this life
is a spotless reputation; without that,
men are merely glorified lumps of clay.
As valuable as is a jewel that is stored at Fort Knox
is an honorable spirit beating in a loyal breast.
My honor is my life, one cannot exist without the other,
take honor from me, and my life is over,
then, my dear lord, allow me to fight so I may prove my honor;
only then can I live, and I would risk my life to attempt it.

Act 1 scene 1, lines 165–185 (cut and combined)

MOWBRAY:
Myself I throw, dread sovereign, at thy foot.
My life thou shalt command, but not my shame;
The one my duty owes, but my fair name,
To dark dishonour's use thou shalt not have.
I am disgraced, impeached, and baffled here,
Pierced to the soul with slander's venomed spear,
The which no balm can cure, but his heart-blood
Which breathed this poison. My dear dear lord,
The purest treasure mortal times afford
Is spotless reputation; that away,
Men are but gilded loam or painted clay.
A jewel in a ten times barred-up chest
Is a bold spirit in a loyal breast.
Mine honour is my life, both grow in one,
Take honour from me, and my life is done,
Then, dear my liege, mine honour let me try;
In that I live, and for that will I die.

Myself I throw, dread sovereign, at thy foot. My life thou shalt command, but not my shame; the one my duty owes, but my fair name, to dark dishonour's use thou shalt not have. I am disgraced, impeached, and baffled here, pierced to the soul with slander's venomed spear, the which no balm can cure, but his heart-blood which breathed this poison.

My dear dear lord, the purest treasure mortal times afford is spotless reputation; that away, men are but gilded loam or painted clay. A jewel in a ten times barred-up chest is a bold spirit in a loyal breast. Mine honour is my life, both grow in one, take honour from me, and my life is done, then, dear my liege, mine honour let me try; in that I live, and for that will I die.

Act 3 scene 2, lines 155–177 (cut)

RICHARD:
For God's sake let's sit here on the ground,
and recount the sad tales of the deaths of kings —
how some have been deposed, some slain in war,
some poisoned by their wives, some killed while sleeping,
all murdered. For inside the hollow crown
that circles the living head of a king
Death is holding court; and there that grotesque figure sits,
ridiculing the king's power and being scornful of his splendor,
allowing him his moments, his little scenes,
to act kingly, instill fear, and kill with a look,
making him conceited and self-confident,
till he comes to believe that his very flesh
is as impregnable as brass; and having convinced him of this,
Death comes in the end, and with a little pin
pokes through his mortal flesh, and good-bye, king!
Put your hats back on your heads, and don't mock a flesh and
    blood man
with such reverence; stop all this deference,
customs, rituals, and ceremonial duty,
for you have mistaken me all this while,
I need to eat as you do, have yearnings,
feel grief, need friends; subject as I am to all this,
how can you tell me that I am a king?

Act 3 scene 2, lines155–177 (cut)

RICHARD:
For God's sake let us sit upon the ground,
And tell sad stories of the death of kings,
How some have been deposed,
Some poisoned by their wives, some sleeping killed,
All murdered. For within the hollow crown
That rounds the mortal temples of a king
Keeps Death his court, and there the antic sits,
Scoffing his state and grinning at his pomp,
Allowing him a breath, a little scene,
To monarchize, be feared, and kill with looks,
Infusing him with self and vain conceit,
As if this flesh which walls about our life,
Were brass impregnable; and humoured thus,
Comes at the last, and with a little pin
Bores through his castle wall, and farewell king!
Cover your heads, and mock not flesh and blood,
With solemn reverence; throw away respect,
Tradition, form, and ceremonious duty,
For you have but mistook me all this while,
I live with bread like you, feel want,
Taste grief, need friends; subjected thus,
How can you say to me, I am a King?

For God's sake let us sit upon the ground, and tell sad stories of the death of kings, how some have been deposed, some poisoned by their wives, some sleeping killed, all murdered. For within the hollow crown that rounds the mortal temples of a king keeps Death his court, and there the antic sits, scoffing his state and grinning at his pomp, allowing him a breath, a little scene, to monarchize, be feared, and kill with looks, infusing him with self and vain conceit, as if this flesh which walls about our life, were brass impregnable; and humoured thus, comes at the last, and with a little pin bores through his castle wall, and farewell king!

Cover your heads, and mock not flesh and blood, with solemn reverence; throw away respect, tradition, form, and ceremonious duty, for you have but mistook me all this while, I live with bread like you, feel want, taste grief, need friends; subjected thus, how can you say to me, I am a King?

Act 3 scene 3, lines 143–159

RICHARD:
What must the King do now? Must he give in?
The King will do it: must he be deposed?
The King accepts this: must he give up
the title of King? In the name of God, I give it up.
I'll trade my jewels for a rosary;
my gorgeous palace for a monastery;
my fine apparel for a beggars' rags;
my carved goblets for a wooden plate;
my scepter for a wanderer's walking stick;
my subjects for a pair of carved saints,
and my large kingdom for a little grave,
a little tiny grave, an obscure grave;
or I'll be buried on the King's highway,
where ordinary people walk, where my subjects' feet
may every hour walk on their king's head;
for they are treading on my heart while I'm alive;
and once I'm buried, why not upon my head?

Act 3 scene 3, lines 143–159

RICHARD:
What must the King do now? Must he submit?
The King shall do it: must he be deposed?
The King shall be contented: must he lose
The name of King? A God's name, let it go.
I'll give my jewels for a set of beads;
My gorgeous palace for a hermitage;
My gay apparel for an almsman's gown;
My figured goblets for a dish of wood;
My sceptre for a palmer's walking staff;
My subjects for a pair of carvèd saints,
And my large kingdom for a little grave,
A little little grave, an obscure grave;
Or I'll be buried in the King's highway,
Some way of common trade, where subjects' feet
May hourly trample on their sovereign's head;
For on my heart they tread now whilst I live;
And buried once, why not upon my head?

What must the King do now? Must he submit? The King shall do it: must he be deposed? The King shall be contented: must he lose the name of King? A God's name, let it go. I'll give my jewels for a set of beads; my gorgeous palace for a hermitage; my gay apparel for an alms-man's gown; my figured goblets for a dish of wood; my sceptre for a palmer's walking staff; my subjects for a pair of carvèd saints; and my large kingdom for a little grave, a little little grave, an obscure grave; or I'll be buried in the King's highway.

Some way of common trade, where subjects' feet may hourly trample on their sovereign's head; for on my heart they tread now whilst I live; and buried once, why not upon my head?

Act 5 scene 1, lines 55–68

RICHARD:
Northumberland — you stepping stone whereby
that ambitious Bolingbroke means to ascend my throne —
it will not be too long
into the future, before the evils which are gathering forces
shall break out into pure corruption. You will then think,
even if he were to divide the realm and give you half,
that it isn't enough, since you have helped him to get it all.
He will think that you, who knows the methods
to put unlawful kings upon the throne, will do it again,
if you are urged to by someone else,
and that you will throw him headfirst from his usurped throne.
The attachments between evil men converts to fear,
that fear to hatred, and that hatred will subject one or both of them
to well-deserved danger and death.

Act 5 scene 1, lines 55–68

RICHARD:
Northumberland, thou ladder wherewithal
The mounting Bolingbroke ascends my throne,
The time shall not be many hours of age
More than it is, ere foul sin gathering head
Shall break into corruption. Thou shalt think,
Though he divide the realm and give thee half,
It is too little, helping him to all.
He shall think that thou, which know'st the way
To plant unrightful kings, wilt know again,
Being ne'er so little urged another way,
To pluck him headlong from the usurped throne.
The love of wicked men converts to fear,
That fear to hate, and hate turns one or both
To worthy danger and deservèd death.

Northumberland, thou ladder wherewithal the mounting Bolingbroke ascends my throne, the time shall not be many hours of age more than it is, ere foul sin gathering head shall break into corruption. Thou shalt think, though he divide the realm and give thee half, it is too little, helping him to all. He shall think that thou, which know'st the way to plant unrightful kings, wilt know again, being ne'er so little urged, another way to pluck him headlong from the usurped throne.

The love of wicked men converts to fear, that fear to hate, and hate turns one or both to worthy danger and deservèd death.

Act 5 scene 2, lines 23–40

YORK:
It's like being in a theater after you've just seen
a particularly wonderful actor exit the stage,
and you have little expectation for the actor who enters next,
and regard whatever he utters as totally boring;
in this same manner, or with even more contempt, people
glared at gentle Richard. No man yelled out 'God save him!'
Nor was he welcomed home with any joyful greetings,
instead dust was thrown on his royal head;
which he shook off with such a look of gentle sorrow,
his expression wavering between tears and smiles,
(the outward signs of his grief and patience),
so that if God had not, for some good reason, hardened
men's hearts, they would have surely melted,
and even the most barbaric would have pitied him.
But heaven must have some reason for this,
and therefore we must calmly acquiesce to it.
We are sworn subjects of Bolingbroke now,
whose greatness and renown we must forever acknowledge.

Act 5 scene 2, lines 23–40

YORK:

As in a theatre the eyes of men,
After a well-graced actor leaves the stage,
Are idly bent on him that enters next,
Thinking his prattle to be tedious;
Even so, or with much more contempt, men's eyes
Did scowl on gentle Richard. No man cried 'God save him,'
No joyful tongue gave him his welcome home,
But dust was thrown upon his sacred head;
Which with such gentle sorrow he shook off,
His face still combating with tears and smiles,
The badges of his grief and patience,
That had not God for some strong purpose steeled
The hearts of men, they must perforce have melted,
And barbarism itself have pitied him.
But heaven hath a hand in these events,
To whose high will we bound our calm contents.
To Bolingbroke are we sworn subjects now,
Whose state and honour I for aye allow.

As in a theatre the eyes of men, after a well-graced actor leaves the stage, are idly bent on him that enters next, thinking his prattle to be tedious; even so, — or with much more contempt, men's eyes did scowl on gentle Richard. No man cried 'God save him,' no joyful tongue gave him his welcome home, but dust was thrown upon his sacred head; which with such gentle sorrow he shook off — his face still combating with tears and smiles, the badges of his grief and patience — that had not God for some strong purpose steeled the hearts of men, they must perforce have melted, and barbarism itself have pitied him. But heaven hath a hand in these events, to whose high will we bound our calm contents. To Bolingbroke are we sworn subjects now, whose state and honour I for aye allow.

Act 1 scene 2, lines 1–28 (cut)

ANNE:
Set down, set down the honorable burden you're bearing,
if it can be said that honor can be contained in a coffin,
while I for a while mourn for
the premature death of virtuous Lancaster.
Poor ice-cold body of a holy king,
pale ashes of the line of Lancaster,
you bloodless remains of the royal blood,
let it be permitted for me to call upon your ghost
to hear the grief expressed by poor Anne,
wife to your Edward, your murdered son,
who was stabbed by the very same hand that caused your wounds!
I curse the hand that made these holes!
I curse the heart that had the heart to do it!
I curse the blood that let this blood pour forth!
Let more horrible things happen to that wretched being
than I could wish to wolves, to spiders, toads,
or any creeping vermin that lives on earth!
If ever he has a child, let it be premature,
ill-fated, born before its time,
whose ugly and monstrous appearance
frightens the expectant mother when she sees it.
If ever he have a wife, let her be made
more miserable by his death
than I am made by my young lord's and yours!

Act 1 scene 2, lines 1–28 (cut)

ANNE:
Set down, set down your honorable load —
If honor may be shrouded in a hearse —
Whilst I awhile obsequiously lament
The untimely fall of virtuous Lancaster.
Poor key-cold figure of a holy king,
Pale ashes of the house of Lancaster,
Thou bloodless remnant of that royal blood,
Be it lawful that I invocate thy ghost
To hear the lamentations of poor Anne,
Wife to thy Edward, to thy slaughtered son,
Stabbed by the selfsame hand that made these wounds!
O cursèd be the hand that made these holes!
Cursèd the heart that had the heart to do it!
Cursèd the blood that let this blood from hence!
More direful hap betide that hated wretch
Than I can wish to wolves, to spiders, toads,
Or any creeping venomed thing that lives!
If ever he have child, abortive be it,
Prodigious, and untimely brought to light,
Whose ugly and unnatural aspect
May fright the hopeful mother at the view,
If ever he have wife, let her be made
More miserable by the death of him
Than I am made by my young lord and thee!

Set down, set down your honorable load — if honor may be shrouded in a hearse — whilst I awhile obsequiously lament the untimely fall of virtuous Lancaster. Poor key-cold figure of a holy king, pale ashes of the house of Lancaster, thou bloodless remnant of that royal blood, be it lawful that I invocate thy ghost to hear the lamentations of poor Anne, wife to thy Edward, to thy slaughtered son, stabbed by the selfsame hand that made these wounds!

O cursèd be the hand that made these holes! Cursèd the heart that had the heart to do it! Cursèd the blood that let this blood from hence! More direful hap betide that hated wretch than I can wish to wolves, to spiders, toads, or any creeping venomed thing that lives! If ever he have child, abortive be it, prodigious, and untimely brought to light, whose ugly and unnatural aspect may fright the hopeful mother at the view. If ever he have wife, let her be made more miserable by the death of him than I am made by my young lord and thee!

Act 1 scene 3, lines 52–73 (cut and combined)

RICHARD:
They're doing me wrong, and I won't take it!
Which of you has complained to the King
that I — blast it — am hard-hearted and don't like them?
I swear by St. Paul, they obviously don't care much for the King
if they fill his ears with such seditious rumors.
Just because I don't flatter and appear kindly,
smile all the time, humor, deceive, and cheat,
I'm thought to be a bitter enemy.
Can't a plain man just live and do no harm,
without having his simple honesty perverted
by effeminate, sly, ingratiating brown noses?
When have I injured you? When done you any wrong?
Or you? Or you? Or any of your cohorts?
A curse on all of you! His royal Highness,
whom I hope God blesses more than you wish he would,
can't get a moment's peace
without you troubling him with vicious complaints.

Act 1 scene 3, lines 52–73 (cut and combined)

RICHARD:
They do me wrong, and I will not endure it!
Who is it that complains unto the King
That I, forsooth, am stern, and love them not?
By holy Paul, they love his Grace but lightly
That fill his ears with such dissentious rumors.
Because I cannot flatter and look fair,
Smile in men's faces, smooth, deceive, and cog,
I must be held a rancorous enemy.
Cannot a plain man live and think no harm,
But thus his simple truth must be abused
With silken, sly, insinuating Jacks?
When have I injured thee? When done thee wrong?
Or thee? Or thee? Or any of your faction?
A plague upon you all! His royal Grace —
Whom God preserve better than you would wish —
Cannot be quiet scarce a breathing-while
But you must trouble him with lewd complaints.

They do me wrong, and I will not endure it! Who is it that complains unto the King that I, forsooth, am stern, and love them not? By holy Paul, they love his Grace but lightly that fill his ears with such dissentious rumors.

Because I cannot flatter and look fair, smile in men's faces, smooth, deceive, and cog, I must be held a rancorous enemy. Cannot a plain man live and think no harm, but thus his simple truth must be abused with silken, sly, insinuating Jacks?

When have I injured thee? When done thee wrong? Or thee? Or thee? Or any of your faction? A plague upon you all! His royal Grace — whom God preserve better than you would wish — cannot be quiet scarce a breathing-while but you must trouble him with lewd complaints.

Act 1 scene 4, lines 2–35 (cut and combined)

CLARENCE:
Oh, I have spent such a miserable night,
so filled with horrible dreams, and of hideous visions,
that, as I'm a good Christian,
I would not spend another night like that
even if it would ensure me of a lifetime of happiness.
I thought that I had broken out of the Tower,
and was in a ship crossing over to Burgundy,
accompanied by my brother, Gloucester,
who invited me to leave my cabin and walk
on the decks. As we marched along
I thought that Gloucester stumbled, and as he fell down
he knocked me — while I was trying to steady him — overboard
into the crashing waves of the sea.
Oh Lord! I thought how painful it was to drown!
What a dreadful rush of water was in my ears!
What visions of ugly death in my eyes!
I thought I saw the remains of a thousand dreadful shipwrecks;
a thousand bodies that had been gnawed by fish;
bars of gold, piles of pearls, priceless jewels,
all scattered at the bottom of the sea.
Some lay in dead men's skulls, and in the holes
where the eyes once were, were hiding,
as if in place of eyes, shiny gems,
appearing to flirt with the slimy bottom of the ocean,
and taunting the dead bones that lay scattered about.

Act 1 scene 4, lines 2–35 (cut and combined)

CLARENCE:
O, I have passed a miserable night,
So full of fearful dreams, of ugly sights,
That, as I am a Christian faithful man,
I would not spend another such a night
Though 'twere to buy a world of happy days.
Methought that I had broken from the Tower,
And was embarked to cross to Burgundy,
And in my company my brother Gloucester,
Who from my cabin tempted me to walk
Upon the hatches. As we paced along
Methought that Gloucester stumbled, and in falling
Struck me — that thought to stay him — overboard
Into the tumbling billows of the main.
O Lord! Methought what pain it was to drown!
What dreadful noise of waters in mine ears!
What sights of ugly death within mine eyes!
Methought I saw a thousand fearful wracks;
A thousand men that fishes gnawed upon;
Wedges of gold, heaps of pearl, unvalued jewels,
All scattered in the bottom of the sea.
Some lay in dead men's skulls, and in the holes
Where eyes did once inhabit, there were crept,
As 'twere in scorn of eyes, reflecting gems,
That wooed the slimy bottom of the deep,
And mocked the dead bones that lay scattered by.

O, I have passed a miserable night, so full of fearful dreams, of ugly sights, that, as I am a Christian faithful man, I would not spend another such a night though 'twere to buy a world of happy days. Methought that I had broken from the Tower, and was embarked to cross to Burgundy, and in my company my brother Gloucester, who from my cabin tempted me to walk upon the hatches. As we paced along methought that Gloucester stumbled, and in falling struck me — that thought to stay him – overboard into the tumbling billows of the main. O Lord! Methought what pain it was to drown! What dreadful noise of waters in mine ears! What sights of ugly death within mine eyes! Methought I saw a thousand fearful wracks; a thousand men that fishes gnawed upon; wedges of gold, heaps of pearl, unvalued jewels, all scattered in the bottom of the sea. Some lay in dead men's skulls, and in the holes where eyes did once inhabit, there were crept, as 'twere in scorn of eyes, reflecting gems, that wooed the slimy bottom of the deep, and mocked the dead bones that lay scattered by.

Act 1 scene 4, lines 137–147

SECOND MURDERER:
[Conscience!] I want no part of it; it turns a man into a coward.
A man can't steal anything, without it pointing the finger at him;
aman can't swear, without it scolding him; a man can't sleep with
his neighbor's wife, without it finding him out. It's a humiliating
shamefaced emotion that rebels in a man's heart. It doesn't allow a
man to act freely. It once made me return a purse filled with gold
that I had found by accident.It reduces a man to have to beg for his
living. It is thrown out of cities and towns because it's a dangerous
thing and every man that intends to live well must attempt to put
his trust in himself and live without it.

Act 1 scene 4, lines 137–147

SECOND MURDERER:
[Conscience!] I'll not meddle with it; it makes a man a coward. A man cannot steal, but it accuseth him; a man cannot swear, but it checks him; a man cannot lie with his neighbor's wife, but it detects him. 'Tis a blushing shamefaced spirit that mutinies in a man's bosom, It fills a man full of obstacles. It made me once restore a purse of gold that by chance I found. It beggars any man that keeps it. It is turned out of towns and cities for a dangerous thing and every man that means to live well endeavors to trust to himself and live without it.

Act 4 scene 4, 329–348 (cut)

RICHARD:
Look, what's been done cannot be changed.
Men make mistakes sometimes,
which afterwards they may be sorry for.
If I did take the kingdom away from your sons,
to make up for it I'll give it to your daughter.
If I have killed some of your children,
to revitalize your offspring I will father
children of your line with your daughter.
The grandma is only a bit less loved
than is the one with the tender title 'mother';
they are like children one step removed,
still with your genes, of your blood.
Your children were nothing but trouble when you were young,
but mine shall be a comfort to you in your old age.
What you lack is a son to be King,
but by that loss, your daughter will be made Queen.
I cannot atone as I wish I could;
therefore accept the kindness which I am able to give.

Act 4 scene 4, lines 329–348 (cut)

RICHARD:
Look, what is done cannot be now amended.
Men shall deal unadvisedly sometimes,
Which afterhours gives leisure to repent.
If I did take the kingdom from your sons,
To make amends I'll give it to your daughter.
If I have killed the issue of your womb,
To quicken your increase I will beget
Mine issue of your blood upon your daughter.
A grandam's name is little less in love
Than is the doting title of a mother;
They are as children but one step below,
Even of your metal, of your very blood.
Your children were vexation to your youth,
But mine shall be a comfort to your age.
The loss you have is but a son being King,
And by that loss your daughter is made Queen.
I cannot make you what amends I would;
Therefore accept such kindness as I can.

Look, what is done cannot be now amended. Men shall deal unadvisedly sometimes, which afterhours gives leisure to repent. If I did take the kingdom from your sons, to make amends I'll give it to your daughter. If I have killed the issue of your womb, to quicken your increase I will beget mine issue of your blood upon your daughter. A grandam's name is little less in love than is the doting title of a mother; they are as children but one step below, even of your metal, of your very blood. Your children were vexation to your youth, but mine shall be a comfort to your age.

The loss you have is but a son being King, and by that loss your daughter is made Queen. I cannot make you what amends I would; therefore accept such kindness as I can.

Act 5 scene 3, lines 269–304 (in some editions, act 5, scene 6, lines 190–225) (cut)

RICHMOND:
Any more than I have said, loving countrymen,
the lack of, and the constraints upon our time
don't allow me to dwell upon. Still remember this:
God and our just cause will fight upon our side.
Except for Richard himself, those whom we're fighting against
would rather have us win than him who they follow.
For what is he they follow? Truly, gentlemen,
a bloody tyrant and a murderer;
one who got where he is and maintained that position through
    bloody deeds;
one who manipulated things to achieve his ends,
and murdered whomever he needed to, to help him on his way;
one who has always been God's enemy.
Then if you fight against God's enemy,
God will justly reward you as his soldiers;
if you labor to put a tyrant down,
you'll be able to sleep peacefully, once the tyrant's slain;
if you fight against your country's foes,
your country will reward you with the fat of the land;
if you fight to safeguard your wives,
your wives shall welcome you home as conquerors;
if you free your children from strife,
your children's children will give you thanks in your old age.
Then in the name of God and all that is just,
raise up your banners, draw your ready swords.
Sound the drums and trumpets courageously and with good spirits:
God and Saint George! Richmond and victory!

Act 5 scene 3, lines 269–304 (cut)

RICHMOND:
More than I have said, loving countrymen,
The leisure and enforcement of the time
Forbids to dwell upon. Yet remember this:
God and our good cause fight upon our side.
Richard except, those whom we fight against
Had rather have us win than him they follow.
For what is he they follow? Truly, gentlemen,
A bloody tyrant and a homicide;
One raised in blood and one in blood established;
One that made means to come by what he hath,
And slaughtered those that were the means to help him;
One that hath ever been God's enemy.
Then if you fight against God's enemy,
God will in justice ward you as his soldiers;
If you do sweat to put a tyrant down,
You sleep in peace, the tyrant being slain;
If you do fight against your country's foes,
Your country's fat shall pay your pains the hire;
 If you do fight in safeguard of your wives,
Your wives shall welcome home the conquerors;
If you do free your children from the sword,
Your children's children quits it in your age.
Then in the name of God and all these rights,
Advance your standards, draw your willing swords.
Sound drums and trumpets boldly and cheerfully:
God and Saint George! Richmond and victory!

More than I have said, loving countrymen, the leisure and enforcement of the time forbids to dwell upon Yet remember this: God and our good cause fight upon our side. Richard except, those whom we fight against had rather have us win than him they follow. For what is he they follow? Truly, gentlemen, a bloody tyrant and a homicide; one raised in blood and one in blood established; one that made means to come by what he hath, and slaughtered those that were the means to help him; one that hath ever been God's enemy.

Then if you fight against God's enemy, God will in justice ward you as his soldiers; if you do sweat to put a tyrant down, you sleep in peace, the tyrant being slain; if you do fight against your country's foes, your country's fat shall pay your pains the hire; if you do fight in safeguard of your wives, your wives shall welcome home the conquerors; if you do free your children from the sword, your children's children quits it in your age.

Then in the name of God and all these rights, advance your standards, draw your willing swords. Sound drums and trumpets boldly and cheerfully: God and Saint George! Richmond and victory!

Prologue, lines 1–14

CHORUS:
Two families, of equal stature,
living in lovely Verona, where this play is set,
fan again the flames of their past hatred,
so that the blood of one faction will cover the hands of the other.
From the ill-fated loins of these feuding clans
a pair of doomed lovers will be brought to life;
whose unfortunate and pitiable downfalls
will, with their deaths, bury their parents' discord.
The dreadful course of their tragic love,
and the continuation of their parents' fury
(which nothing but their children's deaths could end).
is now the story we're about to tell,
which, if you will patiently listen to,
whatever hasn't been covered here, our work shall strive to clarify.

Prologue, lines 1–14

CHORUS:
Two households, both alike in dignity,
In fair Verona, where we lay our scene,
From ancient grudge break to new mutiny,
Where civil blood makes civil hands unclean.
From forth the fatal loins of these two foes
A pair of star-crossed lovers take their life;
Whose misadventured piteous overthrows
Doth with their death bury their parents' strife.
The fearful passage of their death-marked love,
And the continuance of their parents' rage,
Which, but their children's end, nought could remove,
Is now the two hours' traffic of our stage;
The which if you with patient ears attend,
What here shall miss, our toil shall strive to mend.

Two households, both alike in dignity, in fair Verona, where we lay our scene, from ancient grudge break to new mutiny, where civil blood makes civil hands unclean.

From forth the fatal loins of these two foes a pair of star-crossed lovers take their life; whose misadventured piteous overthrows doth with their death bury their parents' strife.

The fearful passage of their death-marked love, and the continuance of their parents' rage, which, but their children's end, nought could remove, is now the two hours' traffic of our stage; the which if you with patient ears attend, what here shall miss, our toil shall strive to mend.

Act 1 scene 5, lines 41–53 (combined)

ROMEO:
Who is that lady, who brings such honor to that
knight by just touching his hand?
Oh, she could teach torches how to burn bright!
She stands out against the backdrop of the night
as a sparkling jewel would in an Ethiopian's ear —
She's too beautiful to ever touch, too perfect to exist on earth!
As a snow white dove would in the midst of crows
so this lady overshadows all her peers.
When the dance is done, I'll note where she goes
and, by touching her hand, will make my hand blessed.
Was I ever really in love till now? If so, renounce it!
For I've never seen true beauty until tonight.

Act 1 scene 5, lines 41–53 (combined)

ROMEO:
What lady's that, which doth enrich the hand
Of yonder knight?
O, she doth teach the torches to burn bright!
It seems she hangs upon the cheek of night
As a rich jewel in an Ethiop's ear —
Beauty too rich for use, for earth too dear!
So shows a snowy dove trooping with crows
As yonder lady o'er her fellows shows.
The measure done, I'll watch her place of stand
And, touching hers, make blessèd my rude hand.
Did my heart love till now? Forswear it, sight!
For I ne'er saw true beauty till this night.

What lady's that, which doth enrich the hand of yonder knight? O, she doth teach the torches to burn bright! It seems she hangs upon the cheek of night as a rich jewel in an Ethiop's ear — beauty too rich for use, for earth too dear! So shows a snowy dove trooping with crows as yonder lady o'er her fellows shows.

The measure done, I'll watch her place of stand and, touching hers, make blessèd my rude hand. Did my heart love till now? Forswear it, sight! For I ne'er saw true beauty till this night.

Act 2 scene 2, lines 2–25

ROMEO:
Hush! What is that light in that window there?
It is the dawn and Juliet is the sun!
Rise up, beautiful sun, and wipe out the envious moon,
who is already so pale and green with envy
because you (her servant) are so much more lovely than she.
Don't serve her any longer, since she is so envious.
Her virginal garments are too sickly and green,
and no one but a fool would wear them. Throw them off.
It is my lady; oh, it is my love!
Oh if only she knew she was!
She's speaking, but I can't hear what she's saying. So what!
Her eyes speak volumes; I will answer them.
I am too brazen; it's not to me they are speaking.
Two of the loveliest stars in all the heavens,
have to go on an errand, and they are begging her eyes
to twinkle in their orbits until they can return.
What if her eyes were shining in the heavens, and those stars were
	in her head?
The brightness of her complexion would overshadow those stars
as sunlight overshadows lamplight; her eyes up in the heavens
would shine so brightly through the atmosphere
that the birds would be singing because they wouldn't realize
	it was night.
Look how she leans her cheek on her hand!
I wish I could be a glove on that hand,
so that I might touch her cheek!

Act 2 scene 2, lines 2–25

ROMEO:
But soft! What light through yonder window breaks?
It is the East, and Juliet is the sun!
Arise, fair sun, and kill the envious moon,
Who is already sick and pale with grief
That thou her maid art far more fair than she.
Be not her maid, since she is envious.
Her vestal livery is but sick and green,
And none but fools do wear it. Cast it off.
It is my lady; O, it is my love!
O, that she knew she were!
She speaks, yet she says nothing. What of that?
Her eye discourses; I will answer it.
I am too bold; 'tis not to me she speaks.
Two of the fairest stars in all the heaven,
Having some business, do entreat her eyes
To twinkle in their spheres till they return.
What if her eyes were there, they in her head?
The brightness of her cheek would shame those stars
As daylight doth a lamp; her eyes in heaven
Would through the airy region stream so bright
That birds would sing and think it were not night.
See how she leans her cheek upon her hand!
O that I were a glove upon that hand,
That I might touch that cheek!

But soft! What light through yonder window breaks? It is the East, and Juliet is the sun! Arise, fair sun, and kill the envious moon, who is already sick and pale with grief that thou her maid art far more fair than she. Be not her maid, since she is envious. Her vestal livery is but sick and green, and none but fools do wear it. Cast it off. It is my lady; O, it is my love! O, that she knew she were!

She speaks, yet she says nothing. What of that? Her eye discourses; I will answer it. I am too bold; 'tis not to me she speaks. Two of the fairest stars in all the heaven, having some business, do entreat her eyes to twinkle in their spheres till they return. What if her eyes were there, they in her head? The brightness of her cheek would shame those stars as daylight doth a lamp; her eyes in heaven would through the airy region stream so bright that birds would sing and think it were not night.

See how she leans her cheek upon her hand! O that I were a glove upon that hand, that I might touch that cheek!

Act 2 scene 2, lines 33–48 (cut and combined)

JULIET:
Oh Romeo, Romeo! Why do you have to be Romeo?
Disown your family and give up your name;
or, if you won't do that, swear that you love me,
and I'll stop being a Capulet.
It is your name that my family hates.
You are yourself though, not a Montague.
What's Montague? It is not a hand, nor a foot,
nor an arm, nor a face, nor any other part
which makes up a man. Oh, be another name!
What is a name? The thing we call a rose,
called by another name would still smell as sweet.
So would Romeo, if he weren't called Romeo,
be just as perfect as he is now
without that name. Romeo, give up your name;
and in exchange for it, which is no part of you,
take me.

Act 2 scene 2, lines 33–48 (cut and combined)

JULIET:
O Romeo, Romeo! wherefore art thou Romeo?
Deny thy father and refuse thy name;
Or, if thou will not, be but sworn my love,
And I'll no longer be a Capulet.
'Tis but thy name that is my enemy.
Thou art thyself, though not a Montague.
What's Montague? It is nor hand, nor foot,
Nor arm, nor face, nor any other part
Belonging to a man. O, be some other name!
What's in a name? That which we call a rose
By any other name would smell as sweet.
So Romeo would, were he not Romeo called,
Retain that dear perfection which he owes
Without that title, Romeo, doff thy name;
And for thy name, which is no part of thee,
Take all myself.

O Romeo, Romeo! wherefore art thou Romeo? Deny thy father and refuse thy name; or, if thou will not, be but sworn my love, and I'll no longer be a Capulet. 'Tis but thy name that is my enemy. Thou art thyself, though not a Montague. What's Montague? It is nor hand, nor foot, nor arm, nor face, nor any other part belonging to a man.

O, be some other name! What's in a name? That which we call a rose by any other name would smell as sweet. So Romeo would, were he not Romeo called, retain that dear perfection which he owes without that title, Romeo, doff thy name; and for thy name, which is no part of thee, take all myself.

Act 2 scene 3, lines 15–30

FRIAR LAURENCE:
Oh, great is the powerful goodness that exists
in plants, herbs, stones, and their essences;
there is nothing living on earth that is so vile
that it hasn't some special quality that can be put to good use;
nor nothing so good that, if misused,
can't transform its nature, and thus cause abuse.
Virtues can be turned to vices when they are used for ill,
And sometimes vices can be turned to good, by force of will.
Within the tender layers of this delicate flower
lurks both poison, and medicinal powers;
for if it is smelled, it will deliver healing good;
but if tasted, it is lethal and will kill.
These two opposing forces exist
in men as well as in herbs — good and ill will;
and where the worse quality is predominant,
in no time that plant will die.

Act 2 scene 3, lines 15–30

FRIAR:

O, mickle is the powerful grace that lies
In plants, herbs, stones, and their true qualities;
For naught so vile that on the earth doth live
But to the earth some special good doth give;
Nor aught so good but, strained from that fair use,
Revolts from true birth, stumbling on abuse.
Virtue itself turns vice, being misapplied,
And vice sometime's by action dignified.
Within the infant rind of this weak flower
Poison hath residence, and medicine power;
For this, being smelt, with that part cheers each part;
Being tasted, slays all senses with the heart.
Two such opposèd kings encamp them still
In man as well as herbs — grace and rude will;
And where the worser is predominant,
Full soon the canker death eats up that plant.

O, mickle is the powerful grace that lies in plants, herbs, stones, and their true qualities; for naught so vile that on the earth doth live but to the earth some special good doth give; nor aught so good but, strained from that fair use, revolts from true birth, stumbling on abuse. Virtue itself turns vice, being misapplied, and vice sometime's by action dignified.

Within the infant rind of this weak flower poison hath residence, and medicine power; for this, being smelt, with that part cheers each part; being tasted, slays all senses with the heart. Two such opposèd kings encamp them still in man as well as herbs — grace and rude will; and where the worser is predominant, full soon the canker death eats up that plant.

Act 2 scene 5, lines 1–18

JULIET:
It was nine o'clock when I sent the nurse;
she promised to return in half an hour.
Perhaps she couldn't find him. That's not it.
Oh, she is lame! Love's messengers should be telepathic,
so they could travel ten times faster than the sun's beams
when they are chasing shadows off cloud-covered hills.
This is why Cupid employs swift-winged doves to transport him,
and it's also why the speedy Cupid has wings.
The sun is now marking high noon
in its daily journey, and from nine to twelve
is three long hours; yet she hasn't returned.
If she were in love, and could feel youthful passions,
she would move with the speed of a ball;
she would quickly toss my message to my sweet love,
and his back to me.
But old folks, often looking like they were dead —
are sluggish, slow, plodding and dull as lead.
Oh God, here she comes!

Act 2 scene 5, lines 1–18

JULIET:
The clock struck nine when I did send the nurse;
In half an hour she promised to return.
Perchance she cannot meet him. That's not so.
O, she is lame! Love's heralds should be thoughts,
Which ten times faster glide than the sun's beams
Driving back shadows over low'ring hills.
Therefore do nimble-pinioned doves draw Love,
And therefore hath the wind-swift Cupid wings.
Now is the sun upon the highmost hill
Of this day's journey, and from nine till twelve
Is three long hours; yet she is not come.
Had she affections and warm youthful blood,
She would be as swift in motion as a ball;
My words would bandy her to my sweet love,
And his to me.
But old folks, many feign as they were dead —
Unwieldy, slow, heavy and pale as lead.
O God, she comes!

The clock struck nine when I did send the nurse; in half an hour she promised to return. Perchance she cannot meet him. That's not so. O, she is lame! Love's heralds should be thoughts, which ten times faster glide than the sun's beams driving back shadows over low'ring hills. Therefore do nimble-pinioned doves draw Love, and therefore hath the wind-swift Cupid wings.

Now is the sun upon the highmost hill of this day's journey, and from nine till twelve is three long hours; yet she is not come. Had she affections and warm youthful blood, she would be as swift in motion as a ball; my words would bandy her to my sweet love, and his to me. But old folks, many feign as they were dead — unwieldy, slow, heavy and pale as lead.

O God, she comes!

Act 3 scene 1, lines 5–29

MERCUTIO:

You're like one of those guys that, when he walks into a bar, throws his sword on the table and says 'Dear God, don't let me have any need of this!' and by the time he's had his second drink, he attacks the bartender, when there was no need to at all. Come on now, you're as hot-headed as any guy in Italy; always ready to take offense, and always willing to be offensive. Come on, if there were two like you, there would soon be none, cause they would both kill each other. You! Why, you would pick a fight with a man for being hairier — or less hairy than you. You will quarrel with a man for cracking nuts because you've got *hazel* eyes. What eye but one like yours would look for such a quarrel? Your head is as full of quarrels as an egg is full of yolk; and yet your head has been as beaten as any egg-yolk for quarreling. You've quarreled with a man for coughing in the street because he woke up your dog that was sleeping in the sun. Didn't you fight with a tailor for wearing his new jacket before Easter? And with another guy for tying his new shoes with old laces? And you have the nerve to warn me not to quarrel?

Act 3 scene 1, lines 5–29

MERCUTIO:
Thou art like one of these fellows that, when he enters the confines of a
tavern, claps me his sword upon the table and says 'God send me no need
of thee!' and by the operation of the second cup, draws him on the drawer,
when indeed there is no need. Come, come, thou art as hot a Jack in thy
mood as any in Italy; and as soon moved to be moody, and as soon moody
to be moved. Nay, an there were two such, we should have none shortly, for
one would kill the other. Thou! why, thou wilt quarrel with a man that
hath a hair more or a hair less in his beard than thou hast. Thou wilt quarrel with a man for cracking nuts, having no other reason but because thou
hast hazel eyes. What eye but such an eye would spy out such a quarrel?
Thy head is as full of quarrels as an egg is full of meat; and yet thy head
hath been beaten as addle as an egg for quarrelling. Thou hast quarrelled
with a man for coughing in the street, because he hath wakened thy dog
that hath lain asleep in the sun. Didst thou not fall out with a tailor for
wearing his new doublet before Easter? With another for tying his new
shoes with old riband? And yet thou wilt tutor me from quarrelling!

Act 3 scene 1, lines 107–128 (combined)

ROMEO:
This gentleman, a close relative of the Prince,
and my dearest friend, has received this fatal blow
for my sake — my reputation's been ruined
by Tybalt's slander — Tybalt, who's
been my cousin for only an hour now. Oh sweet Juliet,
your beauty has made me a coward
and softened my manly temperament!
[Here comes furious Tybalt back again.]
He's alive and triumphant, and Mercutio's dead?
I send off to heaven my respectful meekness,
and will let fire-eyed fury guide me now!
Now, Tybalt, take back that 'villain' that
you called me; because now Mercutio's soul
is hovering just above our heads,
waiting for yours to keep him company.
Either you or I, or both, must go with him.

Act 3 scene 1, lines 107–128 (combined)

ROMEO:
This gentleman, the Prince's near ally,
My very friend, hath got this mortal hurt
In my behalf — my reputation stained
With Tybalt's slander — Tybalt, that an hour
Hath been my cousin. O sweet Juliet,
Thy beauty hath made me effeminate
And in my temper softened valor's steel!
[Here comes the furious Tybalt back again.]
Alive in triumph, and Mercutio slain?
Away to heaven respective lenity,
And fire-eyed fury be my conduct now!
Now, Tybalt, take the 'villain' back again
That late thou gavest me; for Mercutio's soul
Is but a little way above our heads,
Staying for thine to keep him company.
Either thou or I, or both, must go with him.

This gentleman, the Prince's near ally, my very friend, hath got this mortal hurt in my behalf — my reputation stained with Tybalt's slander — Tybalt, that an hour hath been my cousin.
O sweet Juliet, thy beauty hath made me effeminate and in my temper softened valor's steel!
[Here comes the furious Tybalt back again.] Alive in triumph, and Mercutio slain? Away
to heaven respective lenity, and fire-eyed fury be my conduct now! Now, Tybalt, take the 'villain'
back again that late thou gavest me; for Mercutio's soul is but a little way above our heads, staying for thine to keep him company. Either thou or I, or both, must go with him.

Act 3 scene 1, lines 149–173

BENVOLIO:

[Who began this bloody fray?]
Tybalt, who's dead, who Romeo killed.
Romeo, tried to reason with him, and asked him to consider
how petty the quarrel was, and pointed out how
displeased you would be. All this — he spoke
with gentle words, with calm demeanor, on bended knee —
but could not forge a truce with the hot-headed
Tybalt, who wouldn't hear of peace, but instead points
his piercing sword at brave Mercutio's breast;
who, equally enraged, draws his sword too,
and, like a true warrior, with one hand parries
Tybalt's sword and with the other thrusts his own
at Tybalt, whose skill
fights it back again. Romeo shouts out,
'Stop, friends! friends, part!' and as he speaks this,
his quick sword separates their fatal blades,
and he steps between them; but from under his arm
a spiteful thrust from Tybalt took the life
of bold Mercutio, and then Tybalt fled;
but by and by comes back to Romeo,
who only then was considering revenge,
and they go at it like lightning; and, before I
could draw my sword to part them, stubborn Tybalt was slain;
and, as he fell, Romeo turned and ran.
This is the truth, I swear it on my life.

Act 3 scene 1, lines 149–173

BENVOLIO:
[Who began this bloody fray?]
Tybalt, here slain, whom Romeo's hand did slay.
Romeo, that spoke him fair, bid him bethink
How nice the quarrel was, and urged withal
Your high displeasure. All this, utterèd
With gentle breath, calm look, knees humbly bowed,
Could not take truce with the unruly spleen
Of Tybalt deaf to peace, but that he tilts
With piercing steel at bold Mercutio's breast;
Who, all as hot, turns deadly point to point,
And, with a martial scorn, with one hand beats
Cold death aside and with the other sends
It back to Tybalt, whose dexterity
Retorts it. Romeo, he cries aloud,
'Hold, friends! friends, part!' and swifter than his tongue,
His agile arm beats down their fatal points,
And 'twixt them rushes; underneath whose arm
An envious thrust from Tybalt hit the life
Of stout Mercutio, and then Tybalt fled;
But by and by comes back to Romeo,
Who had but newly entertained revenge,
And to 't they go like lightning; for, ere I
Could draw to part them, was stout Tybalt slain;
And, as he fell, did Romeo turn and fly.
This is the truth, or let Benvolio die.

[Who began this bloody fray?] Tybalt, here slain, whom Romeo's hand did slay. Romeo, that spoke him fair, bid him bethink how nice the quarrel was, and urged withal your high displeasure. All this, utterèd with gentle breath, calm look, knees humbly bowed, could not take truce with the unruly spleen of Tybalt deaf to peace, but that he tilts with piercing steel at bold Mercutio's breast; who, all as hot, turns deadly point to point, and, with a martial scorn, with one hand beats cold death aside and with the other sends it back to Tybalt, whose dexterity retorts it.

Romeo, he cries aloud, 'Hold, friends! friends, part!' and swifter than his tongue, his agile arm beats down their fatal points, and 'twixt them rushes; underneath whose arm an envious thrust from Tybalt hit the life of stout Mercutio, and then Tybalt fled; but by and by comes back to Romeo, who had but newly entertained revenge, and to 't they go like lightning; for, ere I could draw to part them, was stout Tybalt slain; and, as he fell, did Romeo turn and fly. This is the truth, or let Benvolio die.

Act 3 scene 2, lines 93–126 (cut)

JULIET:
Oh, what a beast I was to speak against him!
Ah, my poor lord, who shall uphold your honor
when I, your wife of three hours, have questioned it?
But, why, you wretch, did you kill my cousin?
That wretched cousin would have killed my husband.
My husband is alive, who Tybalt would have slain;
and Tybalt's dead, who would have slain my husband.
This should cheer me; why am I weeping then?
Something else was said, far worse than Tybalt's death,
that's torturing me. I would rather forget it
but oh, how it forces itself into my consciousness
like horrendous deeds do into guilty sinners' minds!
'Tybalt is dead, and Romeo, banished.'
That 'banished,' that one word 'banished,'
is as bad as if ten thousand Tybalts had been killed. Tybalt's death
was bad enough, if that had been all she'd said;
but following immediately upon Tybalt's death,
'Romeo is banished.' To speak that word
is as though my father, mother, Tybalt, Romeo, Juliet —
all had been slain, all dead. 'Romeo is banished.'
There is no end, no limit, no measuring, or boundaries,
in that word's finality, — there are no words that can express
        such pain.

Act 3 scene 2, lines 93–126 (cut)

JULIET:
O, what a beast was I to chide at him!
Ah, poor my lord, what tongue shall smooth thy name
When I, thy three-hours wife, have mangled it?
But wherefore, villain, didst thou kill my cousin?
That villain cousin would have killed my husband.
My husband lives, that Tybalt would have slain;
And Tybalt's dead, that would have slain my husband.
All this is comfort; wherefore weep I then?
Some word there was, worser than Tybalt's death,
That murdered me. I would forget it fain,
But, O, it presses to my memory
Like damnèd guilty deeds to sinners' minds!
'Tybalt is dead, and Romeo, banishèd.'
That 'banishèd,' that one word 'banishèd,'
Hath slain ten thousand Tybalts. Tybalt's death
Was woe enough, if it had ended there;
But with a rearward following Tybalt's death,
'Romeo is banishèd.' To speak that word
Is father, mother, Tybalt, Romeo, Juliet,
All slain, all dead. 'Romeo is banishèd.'
There is no end, no limit, measure, bound,
In that word's death; no words can that woe sound.

O, what a beast was I to chide at him! Ah, poor my lord, what tongue shall smooth thy
name when I, thy three-hours wife, have mangled it? But wherefore, villain, didst thou kill my
cousin?
That villain cousin would have killed my husband. My husband lives, that Tybalt would
have slain; and Tybalt's dead, that would have slain my husband. All this is comfort; wherefore
weep I then? Some word there was, worser than Tybalt's death, that murdered me. I would forget it fain, but, O, it presses to my memory like damnèd guilty deeds to sinners' minds!
'Tybalt is dead, and Romeo, banishèd.' That 'banishèd,' that one word 'banishèd,' hath
slain ten thousand Tybalts. Tybalt's death was woe enough, if it had ended there; but with a rearward following Tybalt's death, 'Romeo is banishèd.' To speak that word is father, mother, Tybalt,
Romeo, Juliet, all slain, all dead. 'Romeo is banishèd.' There is no end, no limit, measure,
bound, in that word's death; no words can that woe sound.

Act 3 scene 3, lines 12–51 (cut and combined)

ROMEO:
Ah, banishment? Have mercy, say 'death';
for exile is a far more terrible sentence,
much worse than death. Do not say 'banishment.'
The world doesn't exist outside Verona's boundaries,
beyond is only purgatory, torture, hell itself.
Therefore banished from here is banished from the world,
and exile from the world equals death. Then 'banished,'
is just another word for death. Heaven is here,
where Juliet lives; and every cat and dog
and little mouse, every unworthy thing,
may live here in heaven and may see her;
but Romeo may not. There's more value,
more nobility, more graciousness
in nasty flies than in Romeo. They may alight
on dear Juliet's delicate white hand
and steal a tender moment upon her lips,
but Romeo may not, he is banished.
        How have you the heart,
being a priest, a holy father,
an absolver of sins, and my sworn friend,
to torture me with that word 'banished'?

Act 3 scene 3, lines 12–50 (cut and combined)

ROMEO:
Ha, banishment? Be merciful, say 'death';
For exile hath more terror in his look,
Much more than death. Do not say 'banishment.'
There is no world without Verona walls,
But purgatory, torture, hell itself.
Hence banishèd is banished from the world,
And world's exile is death. Then 'banishèd'
Is death mistermed. Heaven is here,
Where Juliet lives; and every cat and dog
And little mouse, every unworthy thing,
Live here in heaven and may look on her;
But Romeo may not. More validity,
More honorable state, more courtship lives
In carrion flies than Romeo. They may seize
On the white wonder of dear Juliet's hand
And steal immortal blessing from her lips,
But Romeo may not, he is banishèd.
        How hast thou the heart,
Being a divine, a ghostly confessor,
A sin-absolver, and my friend professed,
To mangle me with that word 'banishèd'?

Ha, banishment? Be merciful, say 'death'; for exile hath more terror in his look, much more than death. Do not say 'banishment.' There is no world without Verona walls, but purgatory, torture, hell itself. Hence banishèd is banished from the world, and world's exile is death. Then 'banishèd' is death mistermed.

Heaven is here, where Juliet lives; and every cat and dog and little mouse, every unworthy thing, live here in heaven and may look on her; but Romeo may not. More validity, more honorable state, more courtship lives in carrion flies than Romeo. They may seize on the white wonder of dear Juliet's hand and steal immortal blessing from her lips, but Romeo may not, he is banishèd.

How hast thou the heart, being a divine, a ghostly confessor, a sin-absolver, and my friend professed, to mangle me with that word 'banishèd'?

Act 4 scene 1, lines 50–67

JULIET:

[I should marry this count?]
Don't tell me, friar, that this is what you've heard,
unless you can tell me how I may prevent it.
If with all your wisdom you can't help me,
just assure me that my judgment is sound
and, with this knife, I'll kill myself.
God joined my heart and Romeo's, you joined our hands;
and before this hand, sealed in matrimony by you to Romeo's,
shall be handed over to another in marriage —
or my sincere heart should treacherously revolt
to love someone else — with this, I'll kill them both.
Therefore, use all your worldly knowledge,
to give me immediate advice; or, watch,
as, to resolve this dilemma, this bloody knife
shall play the umpire and find a solution for that dilemma
which all your years and wisdom
could find no honorable remedy for.
Don't take too long to answer. I long to die
if you cannot come up with a remedy.

Act 4 scene 1, 50–67

JULIET:

            [Be married to this County?]
Tell me not, friar, that thou hearest of this,
Unless thou tell me how I may prevent it.
If in thy wisdom thou canst give no help,
Do thou but call my resolution wise
And with this knife I'll help it presently.
God joined my heart and Romeo's, thou our hands;
And ere this hand, by thee to Romeo's sealed,
Shall be the label to another deed,
Or my true heart with treacherous revolt
Turn to another, this shall slay them both.
Therefore, out of thy long-experienced time,
Give me some present counsel; or, behold,
'Twixt my extremes and me this bloody knife
Shall play the umpire, arbitrating that
Which the commission of thy years and art
Could to no issue of true honor bring.
Be not so long to speak. I long to die
If what thou speak'st speak not of remedy.

[Be married to this County?] Tell me not, friar, that thou hearest of this, unless thou tell me how I may prevent it. If in thy wisdom thou canst give no help, do thou but call my resolution wise and with this knife I'll help it presently. God joined my heart and Romeo's, thou our hands; and ere this hand, by thee to Romeo's sealed, shall be the label to another deed, or my true heart with treacherous revolt turn to another, this shall slay them both.

Therefore, out of thy long-experienced time, give me some present counsel; or, behold, 'twixt my extremes and me this bloody knife shall play the umpire, arbitrating that which the commission of thy years and art could to no issue of true honor bring. Be not so long to speak. I long to die if what thou speak'st speak not of remedy.

Act 1 scene 1, lines 1–23 (cut)

LUCENTIO:
Tranio, since I had such a great desire
to see lovely Padua, nursery of the arts,
I have arrived in fertile Lombardy,
the productive center of great Italy,
and thanks to my father's love and approval, I come armed
with his good will and your good company.
My trusty servant, well accomplished in everything,
let us live here and perhaps begin
a course of learning and intellectual study.
And therefore, Tranio, for now I will study
virtue and that part of philosophy
I'll apply myself to that deals with happiness.
Tell me what you think, for I have left Pisa
and have come to Padua, like one who's left
a small pond to dive into the ocean.

Act 1 scene 1, lines 1–23 (cut)

LUCENTIO:
Tranio, since for the great desire I had
To see fair Padua, nursery of arts,
I am arrived for fruitful Lombardy,
The pleasant garden of great Italy,
And by my father's love and leave am armed
With his good will and thy good company.
My trusty servant, well approved in all,
Here let us breathe and haply institute
A course of learning and ingenious studies.
And therefore, Tranio, for the time I study
Virtue and that part of philosophy
Will I apply that treats of happiness.
Tell me thy mind, for I have Pisa left
And am to Padua come, as he that leaves
A shallow plash to plunge him in the deep.

Tranio, since for the great desire I had to see fair Padua, nursery of arts, I am arrived for fruitful Lombardy, the pleasant garden of great Italy, and by my father's love and leave am armed with his good will and thy good company. My trusty servant, well approved in all, here let us breathe and haply institute a course of learning and ingenious studies. And therefore, Tranio, for the time I study virtue and that part of philosophy will I apply that treats of happiness. Tell me thy mind, for I have Pisa left and am to Padua come, as he that leaves a shallow plash to plunge him in the deep.

Act 2 scene 1, lines 177–199 (cut and combined)

PETRUCHIO:
Now, by the world, this is a spirited gal!
I love her ten times more than I did before.
Oh, how I long to talk with her!
                    I will wait for her here
and woo her with spirit when she comes.
Suppose that she rants, why then I'll simply say that
she sings as sweetly as a nightingale;
say that she sulks, I'll say she looks as cheerful
as morning roses newly washed with dew;
say she clams up and will not speak a word,
then I'll commend her command of language,
and tell her she speaks with piercing eloquence.
If she tells me to get lost, I'll thank her
as though she'd asked me to stay with her a week;
if she denies to wed, I'll ask her to name the day
when I shall announce our engagement, and when be married.
But here she comes; and now, Petruchio, speak.

Act 2 scene 1, lines 177–199 (cut and combined)

PETRUCHIO:
Now, by the world, it is a lusty wench!
I love her ten times more than e'er I did:
O, how I long to have some chat with her!
                 I will attend her here
And woo her with some spirit when she comes.
Say that she rail, why then I'll tell her plain
She sings as sweetly as a nightingale;
Say that she frown, I'll say she looks as clear
As morning roses newly washed with dew;
Say she be mute and will not speak a word,
Then I'll commend her volubility,
And say she uttereth piercing eloquence.
If she do bid me pack, I'll give her thanks
As though she bid me stay by her a week;
If she deny to wed, I'll crave the day
When I shall ask the banes, and when be married.
But here she comes; and now, Petruchio, speak.

     Now, by the world, it is a lusty wench! I love her ten times more than e'er I did: O, how I long to have some chat with her!
     I will attend her here and woo her with some spirit when she comes. Say that she rail, why then I'll tell her plain she sings as sweetly as a nightingale; say that she frown, I'll say she looks as clear as morning roses newly washed with dew; say she be mute and will not speak a word, then I'll commend her volubility, and say she uttereth piercing eloquence. If she do bid me pack, I'll give her thanks as though she bid me stay by her a week; if she deny to wed, I'll crave the day when I shall ask the banes, and when be married. But here she comes; and now, Petruchio, speak.

Act 4 scene 1, lines 186–210

PETRUCHIO:
Thus have I shrewdly begun to exercise my rule,
and I hope to have a successful conclusion.
My falcon is now on guard and very hungry,
but till she submits she must not be allowed to eat,
because if she does she'll never learn to depend on me.
Another way I have to tame my wild bird,
to make her obey and know who is the boss;
is to, deprive her of sleep as we keep awake a hawk
who flutters and beats its wings and will not be obedient.
She ate nothing today, and nothing shall she eat;
last night she didn't sleep, and tonight she shall not:
as I did with the meat, I'll find some
imaginary flaw about how the bed was made,
and I'll fling the pillow over here, the bolster, there,
the coverlet this way, another way the sheets.
Yes, and tell her amid this frenzy, I intend
that everything I do is humbly offered in loving care of her,
and, to conclude, she shall stay awake all night;
and if she happens to drop off, I'll rail and brawl
and make such a racket that I will keep her awake.
This is the way to kill a wife with kindness,
and this is how I'll temper her angry, headstrong nature.
If anyone knows a better way to tame a shrew,
tell me now; it would be a blessing to know.

Act 4 scene 1, lines 186–210

PETRUCHIO:
Thus have I politicly begun my reign,
And 'tis my hope to end successfully.
My falcon now is sharp and passing empty,
And till she stoop she must not be full gorged,
For then she never looks upon her lure.
Another way I have to man my haggard,
To make her come and know her keeper's call;
That is, to watch her as we watch these kites
That bate and beat and will not be obedient.
She eat no meat today, nor none shall eat;
Last night she slept not, nor tonight she shall not:
As with the meat, some undeservèd fault
I'll find about the making of the bed,
And here I'll fling the pillow, there the bolster,
This way the coverlet, another way the sheets.
Ay, and amid this hurly I intend
That all is done in reverend care of her,
And in conclusion she shall watch all night;
And if she chance to nod I'll rail and brawl
And with the clamor keep her still awake.
This is a way to kill a wife with kindness,
And thus I'll curb her mad and headstrong humor.
He that knows better how to tame a shrew,
Now let him speak: 'Tis charity to show.

Thus have I politicly begun my reign, and 'tis my hope to end successfully. My falcon now is sharp and passing empty, and till she stoop she must not be full gorged, for then she never looks upon her lure.

Another way I have to man my haggard, to make her come and know her keeper's call; that is, to watch her as we watch these kites that bate and beat and will not be obedient.

She eat no meat today, nor none shall eat; last night she slept not, nor tonight she shall not: as with the meat, some undeservèd fault I'll find about the making of the bed, and here I'll fling the pillow, there the bolster, this way the coverlet, another way the sheets. Ay, and amid this hurly I intend that all is done in reverend care of her, and in conclusion she shall watch all night; and if she chance to nod I'll rail and brawl and with the clamor keep her still awake.

This is a way to kill a wife with kindness, and thus I'll curb her mad and headstrong humor. He that knows better how to tame a shrew, now let him speak: 'Tis charity to show.

Act 4 scene 3, lines 4–17

KATE:
The more my suffering, the more spiteful he appears.
What, did he marry me just to starve me?
Beggars, that knock at my father's door,
receive charity just for the asking;
and if not, they get it at the next house.
But I, who never learned to ask for things,
nor never had to ask for anything,
am being starved for food, I'm dizzy from lack of sleep,
with swearing I'm kept awake and with brawling, I'm fed.
And what vexes me more than any of this,
he does it all in the name of love —
as though if I were to sleep or eat
it would make me deadly sick or instantly kill me.
I beg you, go and get me something to eat;
I don't care what, as long as it's edible.

Act 4 scene 3, lines 4–17

KATE:
The more my wrong, the more his spite appears.
What, did he marry me to famish me?
Beggars, that come unto my father's door,
Upon entreaty have a present alms;
If not, elsewhere they meet with charity.
But I, who never knew how to entreat,
Nor never needed that I should entreat,
Am starved for meat, giddy for lack of sleep,
With oaths kept waking and with brawling fed.
And that which spites me more than all these wants,
He does it under name of perfect love,
As who should say, if I should sleep or eat
'Twere deadly sickness or else present death.
I prithee go and get me some repast;
I care not what, so it be wholesome food.

The more my wrong, the more his spite appears. What, did he marry me to famish me? Beggars, that come unto my father's door, upon entreaty have a present alms; if not, elsewhere they meet with charity. But I, who never knew how to entreat, nor never needed that I should entreat, am starved for meat, giddy for lack of sleep, with oaths kept waking and with brawling fed.

And that which spites me more than all these wants, he does it under name of perfect love, as who should say, if I should sleep or eat 'twere deadly sickness or else present death. I prithee go and get me some repast; I care not what, so it be wholesome food.

Act 1 scene 2, lines 225–254 (cut and combined)

ARIEL:
I salute you, great master! Revered sir, I salute you! I come
to do your bidding; whether it is to fly,
to swim, to dive into fire, to ride
upon the swirling clouds. As for the task you commanded
me to perform, Ariel, with all his powers [has
created the exact tempest that you asked for.]
I boarded the King's ship. First I'm on the prow,
then in the hold, then the deck, and in every cabin,
I appeared like a flame to the amazement of all. Sometimes I would
      divide myself
and burn in several places all at once; on the topmast,
the timbers, on the bowsprit — I flamed on each simultaneously,
then joined to create a giant flame. Each one of them
felt as if he were going mad and committed acts
of desperation. All except the sailors
jumped into the churning ocean and abandoned the ship
which I'd made to appear on fire. The King's son Ferdinand,
with his hair standing on end (making it look like reeds, not hair),
was the first man to jump, crying, 'Hell is empty,
and all the devils are here!'

Act 1 scene 2, lines 225–254 (cut and combined)

ARIEL:
All hail, great master! Grave sir, hail! I come
To answer thy best pleasure; be't to fly,
To swim, to dive into the fire, to ride
On the curled clouds. To thy strong bidding task
Ariel and all his quality [has
Performed to point the tempest that you bade me.]
I boarded the King's ship. Now on the beak,
Now in the waist, the deck, in every cabin,
I flamed amazement. Sometime I'ld divide
And burn in many places; on the topmast,
The yards, and bowsprit would I flame distinctly,
Then meet and join. Not a soul
But felt a fever of the mad and played
Some tricks of desperation. All but mariners
Plunged in the foaming brine and quit the vessel,
Then all afire with me. The King's son Ferdinand,
With hair upstaring (then like reeds, not hair),
Was the first man that leapt; cried, 'Hell is empty,
And all the devils are here!'

All hail, great master! Grave sir, hail! I come to answer thy best pleasure; be't to fly, to swim, to dive into the fire, to ride on the curled clouds. To thy strong bidding task Ariel and all his quality [has performed to point the tempest that you bade me.] I boarded the King's ship. Now on the beak, now in the waist, the deck, in every cabin, I flamed amazement. Sometime I'ld divide and burn in many places; on the topmast, the yards, and bowsprit would I flame distinctly, then meet and join. Not a soul but felt a fever of the mad and played some tricks of desperation. All but mariners plunged in the foaming brine and quit the vessel, then all afire with me. The King's son Ferdinand, with hair upstaring (then like reeds, not hair), was the first man that leapt; cried, 'Hell is empty, and all the devils are here!'

Act 3 scene 1, lines 37–90 (cut and combined)

FERDINAND:
                    Admirable Miranda!
Indeed most wonderful, on a par with all
that's best in the world! I've seen many ladies
who I've thought attractive, and often my
susceptible ear has become entranced by their
agreeable words. For various virtues
I have liked various women; but never one
so completely that some flaw in her
did not overshadow her graces,
thereby killing off my affection. But you, oh you,
so perfect and so incomparable, encompassing
all that's best! Hear my soul speak!
The very instant that I saw you, my
heart became yours, and yours it remains,
I am your servant.
Oh heaven, oh earth, be witnesses to what I say,
and reward my protestations with blessings
if what I'm saying is true! If I'm insincere, turn
all my good fortune to bad! I,
more than anything else in this world,
do love, prize, and honor you. Here's my hand.

Act 3 scene 1, lines 37–90 (cut and combined)

FERDINAND:

Admired Miranda!
Indeed the top of admiration, worth
What's dearest to the world! Full many a lady
I have eyed with best regard, and many a time
The harmony of their tongues hath into bondage
Brought my too diligent ear. For several virtues
Have I liked several women; never any
With so full soul but some defect in her
Did quarrel with the noblest grace she owed,
And put it to the foil. But you, O you,
So perfect and so peerless, are created
Of every creature's best! Hear my soul speak!
The very instant that I saw you, did
My heart fly to your service, there resides,
To make me slave to it.
O heaven, O earth, bear witness to this sound,
And crown what I profess with kind event
If I speak true! If hollowly, invert
What best is boded me to mischief! I,
Beyond all limit of what else i' the world,
Do love, prize, honor you. Here's my hand.

Admired Miranda! Indeed the top of admiration, worth what's dearest to the world! Full many a lady I have eyed with best regard, and many a time the harmony of their tongues hath into bondage brought my too diligent ear. For several virtues have I liked several women; never any with so full soul but some defect in her did quarrel with the noblest grace she owed, and put it to the foil. But you, O you, so perfect and so peerless, are created of every creature's best! Hear my soul speak!

The very instant that I saw you, did my heart fly to your service, there resides, to make me slave to it. O heaven, O earth, bear witness to this sound, and crown what I profess with kind event if I speak true! If hollowly, invert what best is boded me to mischief! I, beyond all limit of what else i' the world, do love, prize, honor you. Here's my hand.

Act 3 scene 1, lines 49–86 (cut and combined)

MIRANDA:
              I do not know
anyone of my sex; I cannot remember any woman's face,
only, from my mirror, my own; nor have I seen
any other man but you, my good friend,
and my dear father. How others in the world look
I don't know; but, I swear by my virginity
(my most precious possession), I would not wish
for any companion in the world except for you;
nor can I imagine there is anyone else,
except you, that I could like. But I'm rambling
somewhat wildly, and thereby am forgetting
my father's teachings. Away with bashful coyness!
I will be your wife, if you will marry me;
if not, I'll die your servant. You may not wish me
to be your mate; but I'll serve you forever,
whether you want me or not.

Act 3 scene 1, lines 49–86 (cut and combined)

MIRANDA:
                        I do not know
One of my sex; no woman's face remember,
Save, from my glass, mine own; nor have I seen
More that I may call men than you, good friend,
And my dear father. How features are abroad
I am skill-less of; but, by my modesty
(The jewel in my dower), I would not wish
Any companion in the world but you;
Nor can imagination form a shape,
Besides yourself, to like of. But I prattle
Something too wildly, and my father's precepts
I therein do forget. Hence, bashful cunning!
I am your wife, if you will marry me;
If not, I'll die your maid. To be your fellow
You may deny me; but I'll be your servant,
Whether you will or no.

I do not know one of my sex; no woman's face remember, save, from my glass, mine own; nor have I seen more that I may call men than you, good friend, and my dear father. How features are abroad I am skill-less of; but, by my modesty (the jewel in my dower), I would not wish any companion in the world but you; nor can imagination form a shape, besides yourself, to like of.

But I prattle something too wildly, and my father's precepts I therein do forget. Hence, bashful cunning! I am your wife, if you will marry me; if not, I'll die your maid. To be your fellow you may deny me; but I'll be your servant, whether you will or no.

Act 2 scene 2, lines 17–41

VIOLA:
I didn't leave a ring with her? What does this lady mean?
God forbid that she's been entranced by my looks.
She certainly looked me over thoroughly; indeed, so much so
that I was sure — from staring so hard — she'd forgotten how to
    speak,
for she spoke in fits and starts making no sense.
I'm certain she loves me; I see her love through this sly attempt
to summons me using this rude messenger.
None of my lord's ring? Why he never sent her one.
I am the man. If this is so, as it looks like it is,
poor lady, she'd be better off falling in loving with a mirage.
Disguise, I see you are a wicked thing
through which the devil works.
How easy it is for a pretty but deceitful face
to make an impression on a vulnerable woman!
Oh dear, our weak nature is at fault, not ourselves,
for since we were created like that, that's how we have to be.
How will this turn out? My master loves her dearly;
and I (poor monstrous thing) am in love with him;
and she (mistaking what I am) seems to be stuck on me.
What is going to happen? As long as I'm a man,
my situation makes it hopeless to get my master's love.
As I am really a woman (I remember those days fondly!),
won't poor Olivia's sighs all be useless?
Oh, Father Time, you're going to have to untangle this mess, not I;
this is too hard a knot for me to untie.

Act 2 scene 2, lines 17–41

VIOLA:
I left no ring with her. What means this lady?
Fortune forbid my outside have not charmed her.
She made good view of me; indeed, so much
That sure methought her eyes had lost her tongue,
For she did speak in starts distractedly.
She loves me sure; the cunning of her passion
Invites me in this churlish messenger.
None of my lord's ring? Why, he sent her none.
I am the man. If it be so, as 'tis,
Poor lady, she were better love a dream.
Disguise, I see thou art a wickedness
Wherein the pregnant enemy does much.
How easy is it for the proper false
In women's waxen hearts to set their forms!
Alas, our frailty is the cause, not we,
For such as we are made of, such we be.
How will this fadge? My master loves her dearly;
And I (poor monster) fond as much on him;
And she (mistaken) seems to dote on me.
What will become of this? As I am man,
My state is desperate for my master's love.
As I am woman (now alas the day!),
What thriftless sighs shall poor Olivia breathe?
O Time, thou must untangle this, not I;
It is too hard a knot for me t'untie.

I left no ring with her. What means this lady? Fortune forbid my outside have not charmed her. She made good view of me; indeed, so much that sure methought her eyes had lost her tongue, for she did speak in starts distractedly. She loves me sure; the cunning of her passion invites me in this churlish messenger.

None of my lord's ring? Why, he sent her none. I am the man. If it be so, as 'tis, poor lady, she were better love a dream. Disguise, I see thou art a wickedness wherein the pregnant enemy does much. How easy is it for the proper false in women's waxen hearts to set their forms! Alas, our frailty is the cause, not we, for such as we are made of, such we be.

How will this fadge? My master loves her dearly; and I (poor monster) fond as much on him; and she (mistaken) seems to dote on me. What will become of this? As I am man, my state is desperate for my master's love. As I am woman (now alas the day!), what thriftless sighs shall poor Olivia breathe? O Time, thou must untangle this, not I; it is too hard a knot for me t'untie.

Act 4 scene 3, lines 1–21

SEBASTIAN:
This is the air; that is the glorious sun;
this is the pearl that she gave me, I can feel it and see it;
and although I'm in a state of wonderment,
I don't think I'm mad. But where's Antonio?
I could not find him at the Elephant Inn;
yet he had been there, and I was led to believe
that he was roaming through the town in search of me.
His advice might be invaluable to me now;
for although my innermost feelings agree with my perceptions
that something is out of whack here (but not madness),
still these incidents and this flood of good fortune
is so far out of the ordinary, so unexplainable,
that I'm about ready to distrust everything I see
and dispute with my senses that try to persuade me
to any other conclusion except that I am mad —
or else the lady's mad. Yet, if that were the case,
she could not run her house, command her servants,
take care of and delegate business matters
with such ease and discretion and composure
as I perceive she does. There's something in all this
that is mysterious.

Act 4 scene 3, lines 1–21

SEBASTIAN:
This is the air; that is the glorious sun;
This pearl she gave me, I do feel't and see't;
And though 'tis wonder that enwraps me thus,
Yet 'tis not madness. Where's Antonio then?
I could not find him at the Elephant;
Yet there he was, and there I found this credit,
That he did range the town to seek me out.
His counsel now might do me golden service.
For though my soul disputes well with my sense
That this may be some error, but no madness,
Yet doth this accident and flood of fortune
So far exceed all instance, all discourse,
That I am ready to distrust mine eyes
And wrangle with my reason that persuades me
To any other trust but that I am mad,
Or else the lady's mad. Yet, if 'twere so,
She could not sway her house, command her followers,
Take and give back affairs and their dispatch
With such a smooth, discreet, and stable bearing
As I perceive she does. There's something in't
That is deceivable.

This is the air; that is the glorious sun; this pearl she gave me, I do feel't and see't; and though 'tis wonder that enwraps me thus, yet 'tis not madness. Where's Antonio then? I could not find him at the Elephant; yet there he was, and there I found this credit, that he did range the town to seek me out. His counsel now might do me golden service. For though my soul disputes well with my sense that this may be some error, — but no madness — yet doth this accident and flood of fortune so far exceed all instance, all discourse, that I am ready to distrust mine eyes and wrangle with my reason that persuades me to any other trust but that I am mad — or else the lady's mad. Yet, if 'twere so, she could not sway her house, command her followers, take and give back affairs and their dispatch with such a smooth, discreet, and stable bearing as I perceive she does. There's something in't that is deceivable.

Act 1 scene 2, lines 50–65

JULIA:
And yet I wish I'd looked at the letter.
It would be a shame to call her back again,
and ask her to forgive me for having reprimanded her.
What a fool she is — knowing I'm just a girl —
not to force me to read the letter!
Since girls, to appear modest, must say 'no' to things
which they would wish the asker to interpret as 'yes.'
Oh lord, how willful love is —
like a temperamental child — it will throw a fit,
then, next moment, turn round, and be sweet as sugar!
How rudely I ran Lucetta off,
when I would so much rather she were here!
How angrily I forced my face to frown,
when inside my heart was all smiles!
My punishment is to call Lucetta back
and ask forgiveness for my faults.
You there? Lucetta!

Act 1 scene 2, lines 50–65

JULIA:
And yet I would I had o'erlooked the letter.
It were a shame to call her back again,
And pray her to a fault for which I chid her.
What fool is she, that knows I am a maid,
And would not force the letter to my view!
Since maids, in modesty, say 'no' to that
Which they would have the profferer construe 'ay.'
Fie, fie, how wayward is this foolish love,
That, like a testy babe, will scratch the nurse,
And presently, all humbled, kiss the rod!
How churlishly I chid Lucetta hence,
When willingly I would have had her here!
How angerly I taught my brow to frown,
When inward joy enforced my heart to smile!
My penance is to call Lucetta back
And ask remission for my folly past.
What, ho! Lucetta!

And yet I would I had o'erlooked the letter. It were a shame to call her back again, and pray her to a fault for which I chid her. What fool is she, that knows I am a maid, and would not force the letter to my view!

Since maids, in modesty, say 'no' to that which they would have the profferer construe 'ay.'

Fie, fie, how wayward is this foolish love, that, like a testy babe, will scratch the nurse, and presently, all humbled, kiss the rod! How churlishly I chid Lucetta hence, when willingly I would have had her here! How angerly I taught my brow to frown, when inward joy enforced my heart to smile! My penance is to call Lucetta back and ask remission for my folly past. What, ho! Lucetta!

Act 2 scene 1, lines 16–31

SPEED:
[So, how can I tell you're in love?] Why, by these distinctive clues:
first, you've learned, like Sir Proteus, to fold your arms, like one
who's miserable; to adore love songs, like a robin redbreast; to keep
to yourself, like someone who's got the plague; to sigh, like a school-
boy who's lost his homework; to weep like a young girl whose
grandma's died; to fast, like someone on a diet; to keep your eyes
peeled, like someone who thinks he's going to be robbed; to whine,
like a kid asking for candy on Halloween. It used to be, when you
laughed, you sounded like a cock crowing; when you walked, you
strode like a lion; when you fasted, it was only right after dinner;
when you looked sad, it was 'cause you were out of cash. And now
you've been so changed because of a girlfriend, that, when I look at
you, I can hardly believe you're my same master.

Act 2 scene 1, lines 16–31

SPEED:
[Why, how know I that you are in love?] Marry, by these special marks:
first, you have learned, like Sir Proteus, to wreathe your arms, like a mal-
content; to relish a love song, like a robin redbreast; to walk alone, like one
that had the pestilence; to sigh, like a schoolboy that had lost his A B C; to
weep like a young wench that had buried her grandam; to fast, like one
that takes diet; to watch, like one that fears robbing; to speak puling, like a
beggar at Hallowmas. You were wont, when you laughed, to crow like a
cock; when you walked, to walk like one of the lions; when you fasted, it
was presently after dinner; when you looked sadly, it was for want of
money. And now you are metamorphized with a mistress, that, when I look
on you, I can hardly think you my master.

Act 2 scene 4, lines 122–135

VALENTINE:
I've paid the price for having condemned love,
whose lofty tyrannical judgments have made me suffer
with painful fasting, with groans of repentance,
with tearful nights, and heart-sore days;
for, to get revenge on me for having condemned love,
love has kept me up all night,
to keep my full attention on my breaking heart.
Oh, dear friend, love is a harsh taskmaster,
and has made me feel so humble, that I confess
there's nothing worse than the suffering one experiences for love,
nor nothing more joyous on earth than being in love.
So that now, there's nothing I'd rather talk of than love;
now all I wish to do is breakfast, lunch, sup, and sleep
on nothing else but love.

Act 2 scene 4, lines 122–135

VALENTINE:
I have done penance for contemning Love,
Whose high imperious thoughts have punished me
With bitter fasts, with penitential groans,
With nightly tears, and daily heart-sore sighs;
For, in revenge of my contempt of love,
Love hath chased sleep from my enthrallèd eyes,
And made them watchers of mine own heart's sorrow.
O gentle Proteus, Love's a mighty lord,
And hath so humbled me, as I confess
There is no woe to his correction,
Nor to his service no such joy on earth.
Now no discourse, except it be of love;
Now can I break my fast, dine, sup, and sleep
Upon the very naked name of love.

I have done penance for contemning Love, whose high imperious thoughts have punished
me with bitter fasts, with penitential groans, with nightly tears, and daily heart-sore sighs; for,
in revenge of my contempt of love, Love hath chased sleep from my enthrallèd eyes, and made
them watchers of mine own heart's sorrow.

O gentle Proteus, Love's a mighty lord, and hath so humbled me, as I confess there is no
woe to his correction, nor to his service no such joy on earth. Now no discourse, except it be of
love; now can I break my fast, dine, sup, and sleep upon the very naked name of love.

Act 2 scene 4, lines 185–207

PROTEUS:
Just as one fire is sometimes used to put another fire out,
or as one nail is used to drive out another,
so all thoughts of my former love
have been forgotten because of a new love.
Is it my eyes, or Valentine's praise,
her own perfection, or because this is deceitful,
that I'm so unable to be reasonable?
She is attractive; but so is Julia, whom I love —
whom I *did* love, for now my love has melted away,
just as a thing made of wax, when put into a fire,
looks nothing like what it once was.
I think my friendship toward Valentine has cooled,
and that I no longer love him as I used to.
Oh, but I love his girlfriend much too much!
And that's the reason I no longer love him.
How shall I show my love more reasonably,
when, for no reason at all, I've started to love her!
It's only her picture that I have seen so far,
and that has so totally dazzled my rational self;
but when I see how perfect she looks,
how could I not be dazzled by her?
If I can keep my eye from wandering, I will;
if not, to get her, I'll use all my skill.

Act 2 scene 4, lines 185–207

PROTEUS:
Even as one heat another heat expels,
Or as one nail by strength drives out another,
So the remembrance of my former love
Is by a newer object quite forgotten.
Is it mine eye, or Valentine's praise,
Her true perfection, or my false transgression,
That makes me reasonless to reason thus?
She is fair; and so is Julia, that I love —
That I did love, for now my love is thawed,
Which, like a waxen image 'gainst a fire,
Bears no impression of the thing it was.
Methinks my zeal to Valentine is cold,
And that I love him not as I was wont.
O, but I love his lady too too much!
And that's the reason I love him so little.
How shall I dote on her with more advice,
That thus without advice begin to love her!
'Tis but her picture I have yet beheld,
And that hath dazzled my reason's light;
But when I look on her perfections,
There is no reason but I shall be blind.
If I can check my erring love, I will;
If not, to compass her I'll use my skill.

Even as one heat another heat expels, or as one nail by strength drives out another, so the remembrance of my former love is by a newer object quite forgotten. Is it mine eye, or Valentine's praise, her true perfection, or my false transgression, that makes me reasonless to reason thus? She is fair; and so is Julia, that I love — that I did love, for now my love is thawed, which, like a waxen image 'gainst a fire, bears no impression of the thing it was.

Methinks my zeal to Valentine is cold, and that I love him not as I was wont. O, but I love his lady too too much! And that's the reason I love him so little. How shall I dote on her with more advice, that thus without advice begin to love her! 'Tis but her picture I have yet beheld, and that hath dazzled my reason's light; but when I look on her perfections, there is no reason but I shall be blind. If I can check my erring love, I will; if not, to compass her I'll use my skill.

Act 2 scene 7, lines 1–38 (cut and combined)

JULIA:
Advise me, Lucetta; dear girl, help me;
coach me, and find me some good way,
how, without losing my reputation, I can take
a journey to see my darling Proteus.
Oh, don't you understand — the mere sight of him feeds
   my very soul?
Take pity on the hunger I've suffered
having been starved of him for so long now.
If only you felt what it was like to love,
you would sooner attempt to start a fire using snow
as try to suppress the fire of love with mere words.
The more you try to stop it, the more it burns.
You know that a stream flowing along gently,
will, when impeded, form a torrent;
but when it is allowed to flow unimpeded,
it babbles over the glistening stones,
gently lapping against each reed
that it encounters on its path.
And, so along its circuitous route, it winds its way,
with contented pleasure, towards the raging seas.
Therefore let me go, and don't stand in my way.
I'll be as patient as that gentle stream,
and take pleasure in each step along the way,
till the last step brings me to my love;
and there I'll rest, just as, after all its struggles,
a blessed soul does when it reaches heaven.

Act 2 scene 7, lines 1–38 (cut and combined)

JULIA:
Counsel, Lucetta; gentle girl, assist me;
To lesson me, and tell me some good mean,
How, with my honor, I may undertake
A journey to my loving Proteus.
O, know'st thou not his looks are my soul's food?
Pity the dearth that I have pinèd in
By longing for that food so long a time.
Didst thou but know the inly touch of love,
Thou wouldst as soon go kindle fire with snow
As seek to quench the fire of love with words.
The more thou damm'st it up, the more it burns.
The current that with gentle murmur glides,
Thou know'st, being stopped, impatiently doth rage;
But when his fair course is not hinderèd,
He makes sweet music with th'enameled stones,
Giving a gentle kiss to every sedge
He overtaketh in his pilgrimage.
And so by many winding nooks he strays,
With willing sport, to the wild ocean.
Then let me go, and hinder not my course.
I'll be as patient as a gentle stream,
And make a pastime of each weary step,
Till the last step have brought me to my love;
And there I'll rest, as after much turmoil
A blessèd soul doth in Elysium.

Counsel, Lucetta; gentle girl, assist me; to lesson me, and tell me some good mean, how, with my honor, I may undertake a journey to my loving Proteus. O, know'st thou not his looks are my soul's food? Pity the dearth that I have pinèd in by longing for that food so long a time.

Didst thou but know the inly touch of love, thou wouldst as soon go kindle fire with snow as seek to quench the fire of love with words. The more thou damm'st it up, the more it burns. The current that with gentle murmur glides, thou know'st, being stopped, impatiently doth rage; but when his fair course is not hinderèd, he makes sweet music with th'enameled stones, giving a gentle kiss to every sedge he overtaketh in his pilgrimage. And so by many winding nooks he strays, with willing sport, to the wild ocean.

Then let me go, and hinder not my course. I'll be as patient as a gentle stream, and make a pastime of each weary step, till the last step have brought me to my love; and there I'll rest, as after much turmoil a blessèd soul doth in Elysium.

Act 4 scene 3, lines 12–37 (cut)

SILVIA:
Oh, Eglamour, you are a gentleman —
don't think I'm just flattering you, for I swear I'm not —
who is valiant, wise, compassionate, accomplished.
You're not unaware of the feelings
I have for Valentine — who's been exiled,
nor of the fact that my father wants to force me to marry
that foolish Thurio, whom I hate with all my soul.
You've been in love, and I have heard you say
that you never suffered such grief
as when your lady — your true love — died,
upon whose grave you vowed to remain forever chaste.
Sir Eglamour, I want to go to Valentine,
to Mantua, where I hear he lives;
and, since the roads are dangerous,
I want you to accompany me,
because I have such trust in your good faith and honor.
Don't even mention my father's anger, Eglamour,
just think of my grief, a lady's grief,
and how right it is for me to run away
rather than be forced into this horrible marriage.
I beg you, with all my heart,
which is as full of pain as the sea is of sands,
to be my companion, and to go with me.
If not, to keep what I have said a secret,
so that I may venture forth alone.

Act 4 scene 3, lines 12–37 (cut)

SILVIA:
O Eglamour, thou art a gentleman —
Think not I flatter, for I swear I do not —
Valiant, wise, remorseful, well accomplished.
Thou are not ignorant what dear good will
I bear unto the banished Valentine,
Nor how my father would enforce me marry
Vain Thurio, whom my very soul abhors.
Thyself hast loved, and I have heard thee say
No grief did ever come so near thy heart
As when thy lady and thy true love died,
Upon whose grave thou vow'dst pure chastity.
Sir Eglamour, I would to Valentine,
To Mantua, where I hear he makes abode;
And, for the ways are dangerous to pass,
I do desire thy worthy company,
Upon whose faith and honor I repose.
Urge not my father's anger, Eglamour,
But think upon my grief, a lady's grief,
And on the justice of my flying hence
To keep me from a most unholy match,
Which heaven and fortune still rewards with plagues.
I do desire thee, even from a heart
As full of sorrows as the sea of sands,
To bear me company, and go with me.
If not, to hide what I have said to thee,
That I may venture to depart alone.

O Eglamour, thou art a gentleman — think not I flatter, for I swear I do not — valiant, wise, remorseful, well accomplished. Thou are not ignorant what dear good will I bear unto the banished Valentine, nor how my father would enforce me marry vain Thurio, whom my very soul abhors. Thyself hast loved, and I have heard thee say no grief did ever come so near thy heart as when thy lady and thy true love died, upon whose grave thou vow'dst pure chastity.

Sir Eglamour, I would to Valentine, to Mantua, where I hear he makes abode; and, for the ways are dangerous to pass, I do desire thy worthy company, upon whose faith and honor I repose. Urge not my father's anger, Eglamour, but think upon my grief, a lady's grief, and on the justice of my flying hence to keep me from a most unholy match, which heaven and fortune still rewards with plagues. I do desire thee, even from a heart as full of sorrows as the sea of sands, to bear me company, and go with me. If not, to hide what I have said to thee, that I may venture to depart alone.

Act 5 scene 4, lines 31–53 (cut and combined)

SILVIA:
Your coming here makes me very unhappy.
Had I been attacked by a lion,
I would rather have been breakfast to the beast
than be rescued by fickle Proteus.
Oh, heaven knows how much I love Valentine
whose life is as precious to me as my soul!
And, as much as that is (for it couldn't be more),
I detest the lying, deceitful Proteus.
Therefore leave; ask nothing more of me.
Look into Julia's heart, your first and best love,
for whose dear sake you once swore
a thousand separate vows of love; and all those vows
are reduced into one big lie by loving me.
Your word is worthless now, you're just a two-timer,
and that's awful; it's better to not love at all
than to be a two-timer, that's one love too many.
You traitor to your true love!

Act 5 scene 4, lines 31–53 (cut and combined)

SILVIA:
By thy approach thou mak'st me most unhappy.
Had I been seizèd by a hungry lion,
I would have been a breakfast to the beast
Rather than have false Proteus rescue me.
O, Heaven be judge how I love Valentine
Whose life's as tender to me as my soul!
And full as much, for more there cannot be,
I do detest false perjured Proteus.
Therefore be gone; solicit me no more.
Read over Julia's heart, thy first, best love,
For whose dear sake thou didst then rend thy faith
Into a thousand oaths; and all those oaths
Descended into perjury, to love me.
Thou hast no faith left now, unless thou'dst two,
And that's far worse than none; better have none
Than plural faith, which is too much by one.
Thou counterfeit to thy true friend!

By thy approach thou mak'st me most unhappy. Had I been seizèd by a hungry lion, I would have been a breakfast to the beast rather than have false Proteus rescue me. O, Heaven be judge how I love Valentine whose life's as tender to me as my soul! And full as much, for more there cannot be, I do detest false perjured Proteus. Therefore be gone; solicit me no more.

Read over Julia's heart, thy first, best love, for whose dear sake thou didst then rend thy faith into a thousand oaths; and all those oaths descended into perjury, to love me. Thou hast no faith left now, unless thou'dst two, and that's far worse than none; better have none than plural faith, which is too much by one.

Thou counterfeit to thy true friend!

Act 2 scene 4, lines 1–33 (cut)

JAILER'S DAUGHTER:
Why should I love this gentleman? Chances are
he'll never love me. I'm a nobody,
my father is merely the keeper of this prison,
and he is a prince. To marry him is hopeless,
to be his whore would be stupid. Oh, darn it,
what extremes are we gals driven to
when we hit the age of fifteen? First, I saw him;
and seeing him, I thought he was quite a man;
he has as much as would please a woman
(if he chose to bestow it on her) as I've
ever laid eyes on. Next, I pitied him,
as would any young gal, of like mind,
that ever fantasized. Then, I loved him,
extremely loved him, infinitely loved him! —
           Once he kissed me —
I loved my lips for the next ten days.
I wish he would do that every day!
What should I do to make him realize I love him?
For I want him. Say I attempted
to set him free? What would the law say about that? To hell
with the law and my kinfolk! I will do it —
tonight; and before tomorrow's out he will love me.

Act 2 scene 4, lines 1–33 (cut)

JAILER'S DAUGHTER:
Why should I love this gentleman? 'Tis odds
He never will affect me. I am base,
My father the mean keeper of his prison,
And he a prince. To marry him is hopeless,
To be his whore is witless. Out upon't,
What pushes are we wenches driven to
When fifteen once has found us? First, I saw him;
I, seeing, thought he was a goodly man;
He has as much to please a woman in him —
If he please to bestow it so — as ever
These eyes yet looked on. Next, I pitied him,
And so would any young wench, o'my conscience,
That ever dreamed. Then, I loved him,
Extremely loved him, infinitely loved him! —
　　　　　Once he kissed me —
I loved my lips the better ten days after.
Would he would do so every day!
What should I do to make him know I love him?
For I would fain enjoy him. Say I ventured
To set him free? What says the law then? Thus much
For law or kindred! I will do it,
And this night; ere tomorrow he shall love me.

Why should I love this gentleman? 'Tis odds he never will affect me. I am base, my father the mean keeper of his prison, and he a prince. To marry him is hopeless, to be his whore is witless. Out upon't, what pushes are we wenches driven to when fifteen once has found us? First, I saw him; I, seeing, thought he was a goodly man; he has as much to please a woman in him — if he please to bestow it so — as ever these eyes yet looked on. Next, I pitied him, and so would any young wench, o'my conscience, that ever dreamed. Then, I loved him, extremely loved him, infinitely loved him! — Once he kissed me — I loved my lips the better ten days after. Would he would do so every day! What should I do to make him know I love him? For I would fain enjoy him. Say I ventured to set him free? What says the law then? Thus much for law or kindred! I will do it, and this night; ere tomorrow he shall love me.

ABOUT THE AUTHORS

Between them, Fredi Olster and Rick Hamilton have appeared in over sixty productions of Shakespeare's plays. They were Beatrice and Benedick in *Much Ado About Nothing,* Kate and Petruchio in *The Taming of the Shrew,* Lady Macbeth and Macbeth in *Macbeth,* Rosalind and Berowne in *Love's Labour's Lost,* and Helena and Demetrius in *A Midsummer Night's Dream;* Rick was Hotspur in *Henry IV, Part 1* and Marc Antony in *Julius Caesar;* Fredi was Gertrude in *Hamlet* and Portia in *Merchant of Venice* — among the many roles they have performed.

Their extensive work in regional repertory theater includes several seasons at the American Conservatory Theatre in San Francisco, where Fredi was Kate and Rick was Tranio in Bill Ball's widely acclaimed production of *The Taming of the Shrew,* which was televised for *Theatre in America* (PBS) and was recently re-released and is available at www.broadwayarchive.com. They have also spent several seasons with the Oregon Shakespearean Festival, the Milwaukee Repertory Theatre, the Utah Shakespeare Festival, the Alley Theatre, and the Dallas Shakespeare Festival, among others.

Rick has directed for the Commonweal Theatre Company in Minnesota, the California Theatre Center, Shakespeare in the Park in Fort Worth, the Pacific Repertory Theater, and the New Play Festival/OSFA.

Rick, who was in the original Broadway production of *Amadeus,* directed by Sir Peter Hall, has also appeared on television and in film. His work includes *The Principal, Babylon 5,* and the soon-to-be-released independent film *Dirt.* Fredi's television work includes appearances on *The Lou Grant Show, Cagney and Lacy, Babylon 5,* and a recurring role on *Walker, Texas Ranger.*

Rick and Fredi have coauthored a series of Shakespeare books for beginners, published by Smith and Kraus: *Discovering Shakespeare: Workbooks for Students and Teachers.* Books in the series include *A Midsummer Night's Dream, The Taming of the Shrew, Much Ado About Nothing, Romeo and Juliet,* and *Macbeth.*